The LEAKY
IRON BOAT

○WATERWAYS

HOLLAND
1. Ijsselmeer
2. van Harinxma Canal
3. Prinses Margriet Canal
4. Starkenborgh Canal
5. Hoofdvaart
6. Tjonger Canal
7. Mepplerdiep
8. Ijssel River
9. Neder Rijn
10. Lek River
11. Rhine River
12. Rhine-Herne Canal
(Germany)
13. Zuid Willemsvaart
14. Maas River
15. Waal River
16. Beneden Merwede
17. Bergse Maas
18. Nieuwe Merwede
19. Hollands Diep
20. Noord Canal
21. Ketelmeer
22. Hollandsche Ijssel
23. Vecht River
24. Amsterdam-Rhine Canal
25. Ringvaart
26. North Sea Canal
27. North Holland Canal
28. Volkerak
29. Krammer
30. Ooster Schelde
31. Wester Schelde
32. Wilhelmina Canal

BELGIUM
33. Albert Canal
34. Bocholt-Willemsvaart
Canal
35. Dessel-Schoten Canal
36. Beneden Nete Canal
37. Louvain Canal
38. Brussels-Charleroi Canal
39. Lower Schelde
40. Dendre River
41. Upper Schelde
42. Lys River and Canal
43. Terneuzen Canal
44. Ghent-Bruges Canal
45. Canal du Centre
46. Meuse River
47. Sambre River
48. Lower Schelde
49. Canal de Furnes

0   50   100 kr

0   30   60 mi

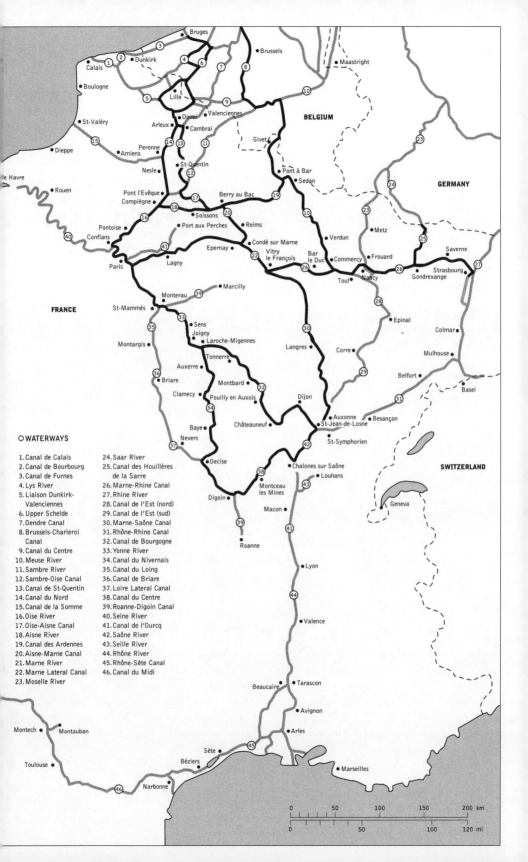

○ WATERWAYS

1. Canal de Calais
2. Canal de Bourbourg
3. Canal de Furnes
4. Lys River
5. Liaison Dunkirk-Valenciennes
6. Upper Schelde
7. Dendre Canal
8. Brussels-Charleroi Canal
9. Canal du Centre
10. Meuse River
11. Sambre River
12. Sambre-Oise Canal
13. Canal de St-Quentin
14. Canal du Nord
15. Canal de la Somme
16. Oise River
17. Oise-Aisne Canal
18. Aisne River
19. Canal des Ardennes
20. Aisne-Marne Canal
21. Marne River
22. Marne Lateral Canal
23. Moselle River
24. Saar River
25. Canal des Houillères de la Sarre
26. Marne-Rhine Canal
27. Rhine River
28. Canal de l'Est (nord)
29. Canal de l'Est (sud)
30. Marne-Saône Canal
31. Rhône-Rhine Canal
32. Canal de Bourgogne
33. Yonne River
34. Canal du Nivernais
35. Canal du Loing
36. Canal de Briare
37. Loire Lateral Canal
38. Canal du Centre
39. Roanne-Digoin Canal
40. Seine River
41. Canal de l'Ourcq
42. Saône River
43. Seille River
44. Rhône River
45. Rhône-Sète Canal
46. Canal du Midi

By the same author

Travels with 'Lionel'

Stephen Harris: *Designer/Craftsman*

Co-author

The Craftsman's Way

The LEAKY IRON BOAT

Nursing an Old Barge Through
Holland, Belgium and France

Hart Massey

Illustrations by Joe Weissmann

TORONTO • BUFFALO

Published in 1997 by
Stoddart Publishing Co. Limited

Distributed in Canada by
General Distribution Services Inc.
30 Lesmill Road
Toronto, Canada M3B 2T6
Tel. (416) 445-3333
Fax (416) 445-5967
e-mail Customer.Service@ccmailgw.genpub.com

Distributed in the United States by
General Distribution Services Inc.
85 River Rock Drive, Suite 202
Buffalo, New York 14207
Toll-free Tel. 1-800-805-1083
Toll-free Fax 1-800-481-6207
e-mail gdsinc@genpub.com

01   00   99   98   97   1   2   3   4   5

Cataloging in Publication Data
Massey, Hart, 1918–
      The leaky iron boat : nursing an old barge through
Holland, Belgium, and France

ISBN 0-7737-5870-4

1. Europe – Description and travel.   2. Boats and boating – Europe.
3. Canals – Europe – Recreational use.   4. Massey, Hart, 1918–   .
5. Massey, Melodie.   I. Title.

D967.M3 1997   914.04'558   97-930318-4

Printed and bound in Canada

for Melodie, Joss and Polly, my companions on the voyage

Contents

Preface

This is a book about a boat and the two people who were its crew. Neither of us had much to do with boats until well into our fifties. I was a cox while at university in England but steering a long, thin, fragile shell tells one little about the skills needed for a barge. During the war the Royal Canadian Air Force gave us both experience but none of it marine except for my brief sea passage in a tank landing craft to a Normandy beach in 1944. In post war years Melodie's holidays aboard her father's cabin cruiser on the St. Lawrence might have provided useful training had he not been so loath to let his daughter share in the running of his elegant craft.

Later came marriages and babies and taking life seriously. Melodie produced a daughter from a first marriage, and a son from her second to me, while I spent five years becoming an architect at the University of Toronto. I began my practice of architecture in Ottawa, and a few years later Melodie became a remedial teacher in a school for children with learning disabilities. She remained at the school until 1970 when I retired from architecture. By then the attractions of a long familiar old house deep in rural Ontario appeared so irresistible we moved there to begin what became an entirely different kind of life. It was a major decision, a happy and successful one, never once regretted.

The change greatly enriched our lives in many unsuspected ways. A new and tranquil existence supplanted the hard-working city life in Ottawa, providing a more leisurely pace to each day with time for long walks with dogs, for reading and for travel to distant places on a scale never possible before. Even in my sixties the occasional mad adventure, like learning to fly, didn't seem totally ridiculous. But it was the crafts each of us worked hard to master that formed the core of our days. Melodie's interest was the myriad and complex techniques of stitchery and she became a proficient practitioner with work recognized for its originality and quality. I had learnt to weld steel while in Ottawa and later taught myself the technique of casting bronze, silver and gold by the lost wax method. This allowed me to make small objects in precious metal, bigger pieces in bronze, and far larger work in steel, making use of wind movement and pivoting mirrors. I later became interested in writing and have spent several years engaged in that challenging pursuit.

Our time passed in this way pleasantly and fruitfully until one day in 1975 when we joined some friends for a cruise of an hour or so on the Trent Canal in Ontario. It was enough to open our eyes to the kind of life boats could offer. This revelation so enthralled us that we rented a boat that same year, and for ten days glided dreamily through the golden landscape of late autumn, seen from the water as if for the first time. Addicted and emboldened we soon ventured overseas to spend two weeks on the Canal du Midi in the south of France. In the following six years, the water steadily drew us back, mostly to France but also to a nostalgic trip on the Thames in England, mountain-ringed Lake Garda in northern Italy, and again to a canal and river voyage in Canada. These short annual holidays gave us much pleasure and essential experience, but by 1982, we had found that hire-boats were no longer enough. We wanted to spend more of our time on the water, and needed something a good deal larger to live on. The fateful decision was then made and we bought *Lionel*, a 1922 vintage sixty-foot Dutch barge. The story of its purchase, conversion, and first journeys is told in an earlier book, *Travels with 'Lionel.'* It was an unforgettable time: a testing, occasionally exciting, initiation into the world of European barges.

Hart Massey
Canton, Ontario, Canada

Trouble Your *Schip*!

In the spring of 1986 I left Melodie in Canada with plans to join me later, and flew to France alone. I picked up our car near Auxerre in Burgundy, then drove north through Paris and on to Friesland in northern Holland. It was a long way, over five hundred miles, and as the journey neared its end, the many hours on the road were beginning to tell on my body, trapped for mile after mile, tense and rigid behind the wheel. Aching arms and imprisoned legs made such insistent complaints that releasing them had become one of the most important things engaging my mind. Although somewhat dazed by the endlessly unfolding ribbon of road, pleasant boating memories danced around in my head during the final stretch across the damp green billiard table of Holland's Friesian lake district. Soon I would actually be aboard *Lionel*, our old barge, and there was enough pleasure in that prospect to keep me pushing on.

With expectations of cruising sunlit waters soon again I reached the outskirts of Sneek (pronounced "snake") and headed for the boatyard. Parking the car, I wearily climbed out, luxuriated in a slow-motion stretch of blessed relief and started picking my way through the rotting old boats, banks of winches, trees, tethered goats, and general boatyard clutter that crowded about the workshop buildings. Around the corner of one I almost ran into the tall, lean figure of Johannes, the boss of the old family-run yard. For a man with much charm and a ready smile Johannes looked unduly glum. I expected a warm welcome for we had parted on the best of terms only six months before when I had left our boat in his yard. Perhaps there had been a boatyard crisis or serious illness in the family. Could he just not be feeling well? I couldn't figure it out. He was a taciturn man at the best of times but conversation between us wasn't eased by the slim grasp each had of the other's mother tongue. And then it came: "Trouble your *schip*." What did Johannes mean by "trouble"? My mind quickly raced through the likely problems as we walked slowly towards *Lionel*. An electrical problem? A burst pipe? A broken pump? But Johannes was not a man to bandy words about loosely in any language. Trouble undoubtedly meant exactly that, and I felt the first cold tingling of apprehension.

We crossed the grass to *Lionel*, which I was relieved to see still looked much the same. At least, it hadn't burnt to the waterline or sunk out of sight. Without much reason I began to feel better. Then we went inside and down the stairs into the saloon. The trouble became plain enough. The saloon contained a particularly repulsive lake. About twelve inches of water covered the floor, joined in unholy matrimony with shiny black islands of oil from the engine-room bilge, floating sinuously about in large blobs and casually making indelible imprints on *Lionel*'s finer cabinet work. The unpleasant flood had not only stained the woodwork but had ruined the carpet, now resting ashore in a two-tone crumpled heap, having been ripped from the floor in a vain attempt to save it. The water had also done as yet unknown damage to costly power tools, walkie-talkies, radios, electronic odds and ends, hardware, spare cushions, bedding, flags, and other valuable but nameless things, all stored below flood level in cupboards under the seats.

It was a dismal scene but perhaps more depressing still was the news that the cause of it all was a leak in the hull. The boat was in fact sinking, slowly yet surely, headed for the bottom. But for the watchfulness of Johannes and his son, our beloved boat might have been sitting in the mud of the canal. My faith in the old Dutch barge was badly shaken and I felt then that *Lionel* would have to work overtime to regain my lost confidence. Having sprung a leak, it now seemed to me different, like a trusted friend who lets you down. It wasn't, after all, for lack of loving care. In the previous year we had sailed it to Holland from the south of France, mainly for the voyage but also to have its hull cleaned, examined, repaired and tarred by an experienced Dutch boatyard. All this had been done in August, and in the following spring, just before my arrival, the boatyard had taken *Lionel* out of the water again for a further two coats of tar. After all that I foolishly felt protected against leaks but, I suppose, one can never be sure about boats.

The cause of the leak was then unknown but there was no time to dwell on what lay behind *Lionel*'s sudden and dramatic decision to stop floating. Immediate action was required. Much of the water was pumped out, the boat poled into position over underwater trestles, and for the third time in this boatyard, winched out of the water sideways up sloping railway tracks. Once high enough, it was wedged in place and sat there like a huge leaky eavestrough, water running in a steady stream from the hole in its bottom.

Although I wanted to, I couldn't stay to see the hole patched. The remaining members of *Lionel*'s crew, my wife, Melodie, and our Dalmatian bitch, Joss, were about to arrive at Amsterdam's Schiphol airport the next day so I took to the road again. Joss, as usual, was still groggy from her sedative, but Melodie was surprisingly chipper after the long flight from Toronto. We immediately drove north to Sneek, arriving there as the boat was being returned to the water. I greatly hoped that *Lionel* would once again take the business of being a boat seriously.

Water problems of a different kind, however, continued to plague us. Before I left for Amsterdam an inordinate number of leaks in the plumbing and heating pipes had spread water across the floor of the boat in areas hitherto dry as desert sand. I managed to control some of these by turning off every tap and valve I could find, but stupidly neglected the shower, which of course then splashily added its own little bit to the all-pervading wetness. Having done as much as I could, I had then gone to meet Melodie. I didn't mention any plumbing troubles to her.

The day after we returned to Sneek, yet more trouble appeared. In spite of having been filled recently, I found one of the water tanks almost dry. This struck me as odd. While Melodie was out shopping I filled it again. The results were disastrous. By the time she returned, water was pouring out under the WC, running down the corridor and invading both cabins. Once the tank was again completely empty the water had sluiced through the only dry place in the boat and had gathered in the bilge. Johannes came to view the latest disaster and confirmed my suspicion that a hidden pipe was broken. Professional help was called for.

While waiting for the plumber I cleaned the engine room and, in so doing, managed to drop the heavy removable steel companionway on my foot. This hurt. I continued to work, limping about the boat, and then got the throbbing foot stuck in a bucket of water at the bottom of the same ruddy stairs. The plumber finally arrived, quickly overcame one problem and we all thought that would be the end of it. It wasn't. When the tank was filled, water again poured out from under the WC and coursed down the corridor. The plumber promised to return two days later to sort this out. We still did not know the cause of the trouble but by then had guessed where it was. As one grows to expect on a boat, it was in a remote corner behind cabinetwork and very nearly, but not quite, inaccessible.

The spring weather was dreadful in Holland that weekend, reverting once again to its North Sea mood. Gone were the sun and those rare soft breezes. Low clouds hurried east, blotting out the blue sky and, impelled by a fiercely cold wind, released spasmodic, stinging showers of driving rain. It really *was* like living on a small island in the North Sea. Melodie had a cold and went to bed. I cooked dinner and afterwards did a mammoth washing up, bringing the whole business to a dramatic, and perhaps appropriate, climax by spilling all the dirty dishwater over the kitchen floor, adding yet another species of wayward liquid to the already water-logged boat.

The plumber duly returned, fixed the last leaking pipe and departed. I filled the water tank, with no calamitous results, and considered that *Lionel* was, for the moment, at any rate, watertight both in its outer skin and its several arteries. My mind then turned to insurance. Surely, I thought, it is the very kind of thing I have been paying all those premiums for. My agent, hundreds of miles away at the other end of the line, wasn't so sure: "Your policy doesn't cover burst pipes, the amount of money involved is small, and you will lose your 'no claims' bonus." I was unprepared for this rebuff. The costs didn't seem "small" to me, but he was probably right. I made no claim, grumbled about it, paid the bills, and idly wondered about the whereabouts of St Nicholas, the alleged patron saint of mariners.

The Navigator

For anyone going by boat from Sneek to Amsterdam, Holland's large inland lake, the Ijsselmeer, gets in the way. If you dislike large bits of open water the problem can only be avoided by taking the long way around, by canal and river. The year before we had gone north this way. The most direct and daring route is almost due south on the Ijsselmeer from a jumping-off point at Stavoren on the east coast. The third route is a compromise involving a shorter journey on open water and then south on the North Holland Canal. I favoured the last as offering some experience of the Ijsselmeer as well as a chance to see an unfamiliar part of Holland. Melodie, however, had never shown marked enthusiasm for adventures on large bodies of water and only agreed to this route reluctantly.

The Ijsselmeer is roughly forty-eight miles from north to south and thirteen miles wide. It is now a freshwater lake and much changed from the days before the 1920s when it was the Zuiderzee, a rambunctious inlet of the salty North Sea, which played havoc with the coastal dykes and caused extensive flooding. For centuries the Dutch have battled with this ever-present threat in the heart of their small country, expending untold effort to control it, and indeed, to make their waterlogged land possible at all. The final taming of the Zuiderzee between the wars was, up to that time, the biggest project of its kind ever undertaken in Holland.

At the end of the last century the hydraulics engineer, Cornelius Lely, proposed to solve the problems of the Zuiderzee by building a long dyke at the northern end to close its link to the sea. Other dykes would be built on the eastern side of the Zuiderzee to form large polders of reclaimed land. Water would be pumped from behind these secondary dykes, the land de-salted, and over 500,000 new farming acres created. The smaller Ijsselmeer, thus formed, would also be de-salted, creating a huge reservoir of fresh water for agricultural and domestic use. The whole ambitious plan has now been in place and working for more than fifty years, the new town of Lelystad on the largest polder honouring the man responsible.

Although the Ijsselmeer is considerably smaller in area than its troublesome predecessor, it is still not a body of water to be taken lightly by mariners. The crossing distance of thirteen miles on our route was no shorter than it had always been, the water was still very shallow, varying between ten and a rare twenty feet, and the wind still swept over it, sometimes in sudden gusts and squalls that created dangerous seas in a matter of minutes.

The reality of this was dramatically brought home to us in the boat-yard at Sneek. In the middle of the plumbing crisis aboard *Lionel*, Johannes had quietly mentioned that they too had a problem. In his stumbling English the story gradually came out. His boatyard was famous in Holland for building a particular type of traditional wooden sailing boat. They had recently chartered a large one to four men and a woman, all experienced sailors. A few days before, it had been struck by a sudden squall in the Ijsselmeer, had capsized and sunk in fifteen feet of water. The four men had clung to the mast still sticking out of the water but the woman was trapped below and drowned. In the days before we left Sneek, the sunken boat had been raised and returned to the boatyard to be dried out before going out on a new charter. It was a grim warning that added considerably to Melodie's apprehension.

In the middle of May we finally disengaged ourselves from the boat-yard with much paying of bills and many goodbyes to all the members of Johannes's family, far more than I knew existed. For the first time since we had returned to Holland, the weather was warm and mellow, the sky blue and the breezes light. With the superb Dutch waterway charts in front of me at the wheel, we headed confidently for Stavoren, on the Ijsselmeer coast, our place of departure for the crossing.

As we cruised south on the ruler straight canal, the placid Friesian landscape slipped silently away on all sides to an ever present flat horizon. Narrow drainage channels put sparkling knife cuts through the lush green meadows where the region's black and white cows munched away in matey groups. The utter flatness of it all was relieved now and then by the spire of a village church, the red-tiled roof of a giant Friesian barn or the ghostly presence of a lonely rust-coloured sail floating across the fields on some distant canal. The terrain was ideally suited to the sky, a vast encompassing dome of space from horizon to horizon. In Holland, more often than not, clouds chase each other across the country from west to east in loosely grouped squadrons or in rain-laden dense grey masses. In Friesland, particularly, the days were rare when something wasn't going on up there.

Finding one's way through Holland with the Dutch charts promised childishly simple navigation but the euphoria of the day—the sun, being on the move again, the glittering water all around us—made me less watchful than I should have been. In the confusion of canals and lakes south of Sneek I lost count of the turnings to right or left and soon realized I was lost. I bumbled on hoping for a sign or at least someone to ask, but there weren't any of either, nor did anything outside the boat resemble anything on the chart I was examining so carefully. Melodie, soon guessing we were lost, inevitably asked: "Where are we?" She not only saw through my fudged answer but seemed quite upset that I had allowed my navigation to get so ridiculously out of hand.

In failing light and the absence of any navigational revelations, we tied up for the night under trees at an attractive island mooring. It seemed like a peaceful place but I was surprised by how much the boat was rocked during the night, causing great distress to Joss. But then I realized the waves were coming from large barges hurrying past on the nearby Prinses Margriet Canal, a main thoroughfare running south from Sneek. Having discovered this, it was simple enough to backtrack next day and regain our intended route to Stavoren.

Our crossing of the Ijsselmeer was planned from Stavoren to Medemblik, on a roughly southwesterly course. The distance was only thirteen miles as the crow flies, taking just over an hour and a half at moderate cruising speed. I would have to steer by compass most of the way since land would be out of sight in flat, featureless northern Holland, and there would be few, if any, prominent visual landmarks.

The compass arrangements on *Lionel* were primitive if not laughable. I had asked experienced friends for their advice and later made enquiries in Holland about buying a proper marine compass. However, such a thing required expert installation, and careful adjustment to compensate for the presence of steel near it. It all seemed very time-consuming, difficult and expensive so I settled instead for a silly little dinghy compass bought some time before at a ship chandler in England. I mounted this minuscule device on the ceiling of the wheelhouse as far as was reasonably possible from steel and the motor of the windshield wiper. This arrangement was undoubtedly idiotic but the compass was still more or less visible, and it would have to do.

The weather on the day of the crossing seemed to bode well. The sun burnt its way through a thin morning haze and the winds were surprisingly light for Holland. At Stavoren, boats were waiting at a lock to enter the Ijsselmeer and during the half-hour before our turn came, we both anxiously scanned the open water ahead. Because of the breakwater and other boats, it was not easy to be sure, but it seemed all right, so we went through the lock and joined the milling throng of yachts near the shore. Once around the end of the breakwater, I was faced with sailing boats in every direction. Several minutes of evasive jockeying were needed before I could even think about setting a course for our planned landfall at Medemblik.

Advancing farther into the Ijsselmeer, the other boats soon fell away behind us and we immediately realized that the relatively calm water along the shore was not going to accompany us all the way across. Farther out, a vigorous breeze from the southeast pushed closely spaced ranks of four- to five-foot waves across our path, their lines exactly parallel to our course. It had become a sea for sailors out for a challenge rather than the millpond we thought more suitable for a sixty-year-old canal barge and its even more aged crew.

It was a rough, uncomfortable ride. Flat-bottomed *Lionel* rolled excessively in the waves and, at first, I thought, dangerously so. We were quite unprepared for this kind of thing. Poor Joss was very scared and curled up miserably on the wheelhouse floor. Things started to fall off shelves, glasses broke, pictures came off walls and everything loose ended up on the floor. At one point a large vase of flowers on the shelf in front of the wheel went over, spilling water onto everything, including charts, books and binoculars. Not content with that the water ran down in little cataracts over the VHF radio, a walkie-talkie, the instrument panel, reference

books, more charts and shelves holding the boat's stationery. In my haste to clear the whole mess out of the way quickly, I gathered it all up in my hands and threw it on the floor, managing at the same time to lob our French dictionary neatly into Joss's water bowl.

It was a demanding trip on another score. In order to read the small numbers on the face of the silly little two-inch compass mounted on the ceiling above my head, I had to steer my way across the Ijsselmeer with neck arched and head bent back. This arrangement was an uncomfortable one, and not at all recommended for aspiring navigators.

The chart was helpful but should have been more so. Perhaps the fault was mine but it is an old story with me. Many of the buoys shown weren't present in the water, and many that weren't shown at all kept popping up in front of *Lionel*. What were they telling me? Did they mark shallow water? Sunken wrecks? Or perhaps just fishing nets? I found it confusing and decided to give all doubtful buoys a wide berth. Added to these confusions was another. I had planned on using the high radio tower at one end of the great northern dike as a check on my navigation. Someone had said: "Oh it sticks up into the air so far you can see it from miles away." Well, it may to some eagle eyed souls but after careful and repeated scanning with binoculars we never once caught even a faint glimpse of this outstanding navigational beacon.

Despite everything, however, we got to the other side, more or less where we should have been. Landfall was made on the long, straight dike just north of Medemblik after we had skirted a frenzied flutter of small, fast sailing boats busily chasing each other around a regatta course. I knew where we were but Melodie was not convinced. The experience south of Sneek doubtless had something to do with this and she decided, embarrassingly, to verify the navigation herself. As we entered the harbour she shouted to a happy crowd sitting in the sun on the breakwater, "Is this Medemblik?" There was a loud answering yell of "YES!" and a ripple of laughter along the wall. Humiliating as this was, I could only hope that Melodie's failing confidence in my navigation might, thereby, get a much needed boost.

North Holland Canal

Like so many towns along the shores of the Ijsselmeer, Medemblik is now a yachtsman's harbour. Sailing boats, running the full gamut in size, type, age and cost crowded the small space, rafting out four or five deep from the quays. Two 150-foot sailing palaces showed off their majestic white hulls on one side of the harbour, in haughty seclusion from the common herd clustered in cosy togetherness on the other. In the outer harbour, fast, high-tech racing craft littered the shore and skittered about in preparation for the next round of endless races on the wind-roughened Ijsselmeer. We felt like interlopers among the yachts packed tightly around us like herrings in a can—the only barge in a forest of metal masts, their myriad ropes all slapping and clanging in the wind.

Medemblik is no longer a place for barges or even fishing boats. It had once been home to something earthy and purposeful, and the magnificent old houses around the port spoke of wealth derived from the sea. In the past, the ports along these shores had supported a large fishing fleet of stout wooden boats plying their trade in the Zuiderzee and on the North Sea. These same ports had also supplied many of the crews for little Holland's far flung adventures around the world. The port of Hoorn, ten miles down the coast, provided a noted navigator, Willem Schouten who on a voyage to South America used his home town to name the feared Cape Horn. Abel Tasman almost certainly started his long voyage to the South Pacific from the same area, resulting in the circumnavigation of Australia and the discovery of Tasmania, the large island off its south coast. There are still men fishing the waters of the Ijsselmeer but the fishing industry is too small to have much impact on most of the ports, and the few barges now using the Ijsselmeer are transients bound for inland destinations. The yachts have largely taken over.

On a bright sunny morning we left the yachts of Medemblik and went through the first lock of our southerly journey to Amsterdam. We knew it was a holiday but after going through one lock assumed the rest would also be operating. Only half a mile down the canal the next lock was closed. When a long wait produced no result I went to investigate in *Lionel*'s dinghy, a convenient but flighty little craft. I found a bathing-suited lock-keeper and his plump, pink wife sitting in comfortable garden chairs quietly enjoying the sun on what he informed me was a holiday. This seemed odd but the man was quite convinced that he, at least, was on holiday and we were forced to moor till the following day.

Where we were tied up had some undesirable features, particularly for Joss who was separated from the shore by ten feet of water and two moored boats. So we decided to move *Lionel* to the opposite shore where more congenial conditions prevailed. This meant backing the boat about two hundred feet before I could turn it into the far bank, never an easy manoeuvre with a barge. Control in reverse is limited, if not erratic, and an alarming hazard faced us immediately astern where a boatyard was putting the finishing touches to a huge and immaculate white schooner to be taken over shortly by its new owner. It was the kind of obstacle you have no wish to brush against with a grubby iron barge, but I began to back up anyway. All seemed to be going remarkably well when a wind, slight until then, gusted strongly, pushing *Lionel* slowly but decisively towards the great white yacht. This prompted instant action aboard both boats. The one man working on the yacht rushed headlong to the rail. I immediately brought *Lionel*'s rearward motion to a halt and then Melodie and I also dashed to our rail. As three human beings strained desperately to prevent the imminent, fateful kiss, the wind and *Lionel*'s momentum seemed easy winners, but at the last critical moment, with no more than an inch of air separating the boats, the barge's determined sideways drift was thankfully halted.

There was then a general and very firm consensus that any repetition of the incident should be avoided at all costs and, appreciating our predicament, the man on the yacht offered his help. He and a colleague carried our ropes across the canal in a rowboat. Once secured on the far side we pulled *Lionel* across. Thanking our helpers profusely, they declined our offered bottle of wine, feeling perhaps it was thanks enough to have the black threat to their pristine handiwork safely out of harm's way.

In windy but otherwise passable conditions our journey to Amsterdam continued the next day. Its only diversion was a cranky railway bridge near Alkmaar. Too low to pass under when in train mode, it made occasional concessions to boats by raising itself lethargically when aware of their presence. But how did one let it know? No bridge-keeper was in sight and when we arrived on the scene several boats were waiting impatiently for a red light to turn green. After a train rumbled across it finally did. The bridge went up and the waiting boats surged forward.

Lionel followed closely behind. Then the light went red again. As the bridge came down just in front of our bow, I jammed the propeller in reverse, bringing the boat to a juddering halt in a cloud of blue diesel exhaust. Clearly we needed to learn the secret of the bridge. An intricate exchange of hand signals between Melodie and a man on the far bank resulted in the discovery of a neatly concealed push-button on the shore so awkwardly placed that groping with a long wooden boat-hook held like a lance seemed the only way to prod it into action. But finally the fickle light went green again and the bridge began to rise. Never has a barge shot out of a mooring faster. *Lionel* raced down the canal, accelerating rapidly to pass under the unpredictable bridge before it changed its mind again, and crushed *Lionel* under its massive steel trusses.

As we neared Amsterdam, flowers played a brief but vivid role in the landscape close by the canal. In the natural course of things one wouldn't normally think that a small northern country like Holland could be the world's greatest exporter of flowers. Climate alone argues against it. Tulips come to mind, of course, and their brilliant slashes of colour in the fields form an indelible image that all approaching Amsterdam by air in April or May are unlikely to forget. On our way to the city from the north we had seen these brilliant stripes of colour from a different angle as field workers removed the blooms, leaving them in pink, yellow, red, white and purple conical piles beside the canal, sacrificing the flowers to strengthen the bulb, the bigger side of the tulip business. Although Holland markets more than 9 million bulbs a year, it grows millions of other flowers, all but 10 percent raised in heated greenhouses. Over 80 percent of them fly to countries all over the world after auctions in mammoth buildings such as that at Aalsmeer, south of Amsterdam, usually reaching their destinations no later than the following day. I was not greatly surprised when, some months later, I was told by a local florist in Ontario that he could buy Dutch roses cheaper than those from a greenhouse a mere seventy miles away.

City of Boats

Amsterdam is certainly a city of boats, but that doesn't mean mooring one there is easy. The great harbour has its own forbidding commercial imperatives that discourage, even intimidate, the small private barge. The part of the harbour near the main railway station offers moorings of a kind, but they are not tempting. Barges are lived on there, jammed together in a scruffy huddle three to four deep, but joining them implies questionable security and poor shore access.

By far the nicest place to moor a boat in Amsterdam would be on one of the quiet small canals that add so much to the core of the lovely old city. Boats of all kinds use them: private barges, small, large, smart and shabby, cabin cruisers, old wooden sailing barges, rowboats, workboats, tour boats and yachts. The visitor, however, is not really encouraged to park in the heart of Amsterdam, and, anyway, access to many of the small canals was denied *Lionel* by their low bridges. On the basis of an earlier reconnaissance we decided to forego the obvious attractions of central Amsterdam and look elsewhere.

Just before the North Holland Canal enters the main harbour, it passes Flora Park, a pleasant and peaceful spot with large trees, grass and most that one might need close by, including a bus for the ten minute ride into the city, and a pool where the sensible Dutch allowed naked swimming on certain days. Shopping for food was hardly convenient but wasn't a problem once I'd retrieved the car from Sneek. We shared this idyllic mooring with a few Dutch boats and an old sailing barge, or *tjalk*, being made ready for a freighter voyage to New York where it would take part in the celebrations marking the restoration of the Statue of Liberty. Joss thoroughly approved of Flora Park.

For centuries water and boats have been vital elements in the life of Amsterdam. They made possible not only its simple beginnings as a small fishing settlement but also Amsterdam's eventual growth into a thriving commercial centre. Dykes were built to keep out the sea, and behind these defences the city grew. Men went to sea to fish, and later ventured further afield in great voyages of discovery, from which a vast world trade resulted. The Dutch continue to love boats, and Amsterdam is home to craft of every kind from the smallest dinghies, private motor cruisers and sailing yachts to commercial barges for European waterways, and the great ships for long sea voyages. As one would expect in a city where boats are so important, Amsterdam is a rich resource for mariners, unlike any other place I know. Here you can buy anything for a boat, find the skills for even the most exotic repairs, and discover experts in all the arcane branches of marine design. The few things I needed for *Lionel* were basic, but I knew they were unlikely to be stocked by the fancier suppliers catering to yachts. The barge ship-chandlers were certainly there but often so hidden away and hard to find that one could easily pass them by. But once I found the unobtrusive doorway, and walked through uncertainly, a dimly lit cave opened out before me, a room crowded to its lofty ceiling with a vast and varied treasure of boat stuff in every size, type and metal I could possibly yearn for. Having been so frustrated in France, where it always seemed so difficult or impossible to obtain what one wanted, the marine suppliers of Amsterdam were a delight. Here the answer to an enquiry was not, as it was so often in France, "We don't carry it," "It doesn't exist," "It will take six months to get," but rather, "Yes, it's available in several sizes and types. Just tell me what you want."

Ship-chandlers are a vice with me. Taking advantage of this rare opportunity, I launched myself on a buying spree akin to a kind of madness only a boat owner could understand. I bought more of the beautiful but expensive official charts to help us find our way south through the tortuous Dutch waterways. I coveted sophisticated, brassy compasses, but cost helped me stand firm in the face of their siren appeal. I haunted the down-to-earth barge ship-chandlers for ropes, chains, wood bumpers and all the heavy gear barges need. I bought rope, paint and enough cans of varnish to last for years. I found a vast warehouse tucked away in a remote corner of the harbour with high shelves piled to the ceiling with a mother-lode of neoprene in all its shapes and complexities. I found exactly what I had come for and took back to the boat a vast resource for *Lionel* to draw on into the foreseeable future. When would I ever find so much of this stuff again?

My favourite haunt of all the ship-chandlers in Amsterdam was a dark, high-ceilinged old store called Granaat on Oude Schans. Its special line was hardware of the kind used for boats and buildings, basic stuff in steel, aluminum, bronze and, most of all, brass. Old-time stores of this kind are rare, now found only in ancient port cities like Amsterdam where they have carried on their trade for generations. Granaat's high walls were covered with shelves holding a marvellous jumble of objects, and drawers plastered with samples of what each contained. The peculiar smell and faint yellow glow of brass permeated the entire place. Light from the few bare bulbs hanging high above reflected off bits of brighter metal here and there, making them sparkle like crystal in the gloom. For anyone addicted to such things, Granaat was an unexpected bonanza, a special kind of treasure house, a place I could have explored for hours, delving into the room's dark corners and hidden secrets. I coveted much in that old store but it was a dangerous trap for the brass junkie. I only bought an excessive number of brass screws, and sadly dragged myself away, leaving behind so much that I sorely yearned to own, but knew deep down that I really didn't need.

Up to the time of our arrival in Amsterdam, *Lionel*'s main anchor was an insubstantial piece of steel that I was sure would not hold our forty-ton boat if its engine died on one of the great fast running rivers lying to the south. On the more dangerous waters I endured an ever present anxiety featuring *Lionel*, with engine dead, being swept downstream out of control, its light anchor scraping ineffectually along the bottom. It was something that had to be corrected if only for my peace of mind but surprisingly, a heavy second hand replacement could not be found in Amsterdam. A "reliable source," however, had reported seeing a yard "overflowing with used anchors" in Dordrecht, a famous barge town forty miles south of the city. It sounded just the place.

The hunt for an anchor in and around Dordrecht was not a success.

After driving for miles along a high windswept dyke searching for the alleged used anchor yard it was found at last, a deserted and derelict weed patch, with no anchors in sight. Disappointed, we paused at a small restaurant advertising a "snack lunch." It was a formidable offering from the lower reaches of basic Dutch cooking—three fried eggs in flaccid, greasy repose on a thick slice of overcooked beef, sitting masterfully on a mammoth chunk of buttered white bread, surrounded by assorted vegetal companions. After this depressing gastronomic overkill a helpful soul told us of yet another yard where he'd seen "lots of anchors." We dashed off with renewed enthusiasm only to find what seemed to be part of a naval dock-yard— giant anchors lying about here and there—immense things that wouldn't have disgraced a battleship, but might well have taken *Lionel* to the bottom with them. Further searches only showed that Dordrecht was no more fruitful in anchors than Amsterdam and I returned to *Lionel* wondering about this strange gap in the country's otherwise bountiful supply of boating gear. The heavier anchor I wanted was found much later when it was almost no longer needed.

Simple Pleasures

I have always been fond of Amsterdam but it's not to everyone's taste, and Melodie is one of those with reservations. Parts of the city make her feel nervous and insecure, a hint of something threatening, created perhaps by its reputation for drugs and the free-wheeling youth attracted to it in large numbers. But every city has young people and drugs, and Amsterdam is much the same as the rest though perhaps more tolerant than most. In other ways, however, particularly its physical presence, it is unique. Like much of the country itself, Amsterdam defies nature's obstacles; its builders not only succeeded in making Amsterdam work in spite of them, they left a glorious city core, an old brick watery heart, threaded with canals and furnished with the warm, human evidence of those who built such a beautiful background for Amsterdam's orderly and vital urban life.

For me its pleasures have always been found in simple things. I enjoy long walks beside its beautiful little canals, the dark water throwing back wavy images of gabled houses, boats, arched bridges, brickwork and cast-iron railings. At every turn there is something to surprise and please the eye: the ornamental steps to high front doors, lofty old rooms behind broad, uncurtained windows, the tops of church spires, a black tangle of parked bicycles, the spare white elegance of a church nave glimpsed through open doors, flowers, the patterned brick paving and water, always water. In my walks I kept away from the trams and noise of rackety, jostling Damrak and Rokin, both busy commercial streets, preferring the quieter places along the small parallel canals that define the old city. Often I strolled the edges of the harbour to examine the boats there and once wandered through the old red light district where near naked ladies sat motionless in picture windows waiting hopefully for trade, one aspect of the city's refreshingly open approach to much of what other places drive underground.

Museums abound in Amsterdam, and I was familiar with many, but apart from a flying visit to renew old acquaintance with the Vermeers at the Rijksmuseum and the van Goghs nearby, I restricted myself to only one other, the great Museum of National Maritime History in the old Admiralty Dockyard. It is a fine museum, but as I walked from room to room I found myself constantly drawn to the windows and the working reality in the water below. It is not the museum's fault; it has done its job well. The fault is more in the nature of museums and the nature of boats, perhaps also in me. Boats in a museum are simply artefacts drained of life and purpose. Beautiful, but artefacts nevertheless. I prefer the living, working, floating boats and, given a choice, would opt for them any day over their great-grandmothers sitting silent, still and lifeless in a museum display. Amsterdam, after all, is a museum in its own right, but a living one in which the working boats play an important role. Walking its streets and quays was always more a pleasure for me than wandering with creeping fatigue from room to room, even in such a museum.

When it came to food, it is not elegant restaurant meals that come back vividly to mind but the informal eating and drinking the city offered: the good, plainly cooked fish to be found in small, boisterous restaurants, the intriguing delights of an Indonesian *rijstafel* with twenty or more little dishes of spicy surprises on the table in front of one, the street vendors' snacks with hot sauces and fried potatoes offered in the Dutch way, with mayonnaise, and the summer delicacy of lightly cured herring fresh from the fishing boats, held by the tail and fed into one's mouth, head thrown back.

More than anything it was the bars of the city that commanded my affection, although the word "bar" doesn't properly describe what they are. While they certainly do sell every kind of alcohol from basic beer to stronger and more exotic stuff, the atmosphere of the Amsterdam bar is uniquely Dutch. Some venerable institutions have sawdust on the floor, and nearly all, old or new, are furnished more like Dutch living rooms than bars, with comfortable wooden chairs and tables, the latter often covered with intricately patterned carpeting. Several regulars can often be found sitting around large dining room tables talking or playing cards.

Our first experience of an Amsterdam bar was on a frigid late October day some years before when, shivering with the cold, we withdrew into its sheltering warmth for revival. On that occasion, smoked eel and ice cold *genever* did the trick, the strong, almost tasteless Dutch gin brought to our table in the traditional way, the small glasses so brimful, the gin was above their rims. Since then, I have drunk coffee in these bars, quenched my thirst on hot summer days with excellent Dutch beer and eaten light lunches— no kin to the Dordrecht experience. In them you can find soup, the basic *broodje*, a Dutch form of sandwich or stuffed roll, in all its different varieties, and hot dishes such as a favourite of mine, *saté ayam*, chicken barbecued on bamboo skewers, in the Indonesian way with a hot peanut sauce.

I am very fond of these warm, friendly bars, their club-like feeling, their Dutchness, their happy atmosphere, their relaxed informality, their tolerance of dogs, and the gentle camaraderie to be found in them.

Force 8 on Hollands Diep

Early in June the fresh spring greenery of Flora Park was left behind as we dropped through the last lock on the North Holland Canal and entered Amsterdam harbour with some trepidation. Melodie fears such places because of their enormous scale and the threatening leviathans that customarily inhabit them. Although the large expanse of water seemed calm enough and not as busy as it often was, the overlying veil of fog made a confusion of channel-markers and landmarks in my groping navigation to what I hoped would be the correct exit.

The fuzzy images of reality around the boat belied the clarity of the chart in front of me. Only by making some astute guesses did we gain the relative security of the Amsterdam-Rhine Canal, leaving it shortly to turn off for Muiden on the south shore of the Ijsselmeer and go upstream on the Vecht River. Flowing north from Utrecht, the Vecht is an unambitious but mostly beautiful meandering waterway. Its natural attractions and its light traffic have, alas, made the northern reaches particularly popular with houseboat dwellers, whose unlovely and unboat-like craft huddle together bow to stern along each bank. This dense occupancy greatly dims the northern Vecht's reported allure and makes tying up for the night difficult. In these situations, however, there is often a bit of shallow water no

one else wants, and with the help of grapnels, we managed a mooring of sorts, but naturally went aground in the process.

The usefulness of grapnels for mooring was a late discovery in our life aboard *Lionel*. I had welded two out of steel, each with four hooks and a shaft attached to ropes. When thrown onto the bank they would usually catch in the growth there and allow us to pull the boat close enough for one of us to get ashore. They didn't always catch, of course, and on occasion had to be thrown several times before they did. And, always, they had to be thrown with care. Too much abandon might cause them to fall uselessly in the water or fly about in uncontrolled arcs, as Melodie's sometimes did, putting the boat, the crew, or both in some hazard. Then there were the occasions when a tenacious grapnel refused to be tugged free, forcing someone to go ashore and release it. But, regardless of such minor eccentricities the grapnels were godsends for the aging crew of a large iron boat.

The arrangements at the mooring were far from ideal for old Joss, then fourteen years old with dreadfully weak back legs. She immediately fell into the water as she went down the ramp. Our Dalmatian has always done her best to avoid anything more than dipping her toes in water. She dislikes it intensely, and must have loathed the total immersion she endured on that occasion. It was only a brief dip, however, and I soon yanked her out by the collar. Not at all grateful, she looked at me as if I was to blame for the whole thing, shook off the water, collected herself and trotted away down the river bank for her essential evening walk.

The next day, the unlovely houseboats disappeared behind us, the river narrowed as we went upstream, and began at last to live up to its reputation. Bright green fields stretched away on either side, dotted here and there with sheep, pure-white newborn lambs giving life to an otherwise static scene with little white bursts of movement as they bounded about, wiggling rubbery tails. Trees now played a larger part in the landscape, especially great chestnuts, then in full bloom with tier upon tier of white or pink candles mounting to their crowns. Near Maarssen, the river acquired yet another dimension as dignified old brick mansions appeared with greater frequency. Squatting on wide green lawns under guardian trees, they were large, noble, but comfortable looking houses, a few with playful little gazebos at the water's edge.

At Maarssen, a charming old brick waterway town, we left the Vecht to rejoin the busy Amsterdam-Rhine Canal, leading to the Lek. This river, with its companion, the Waal, form the two main branches of the Rhine running west across southern Holland. They are both big, active rivers, alive with barges, as are their several even wider tributaries to the west, all churned up by increasingly frenzied comings and goings as the great port of Rotterdam is approached.

Because the Lek and the Waal run in a more or less east to west direction, they must be crossed by any boat going south in Holland, except those on the Maas (Meuse) close to the eastern border of the country. The Lek, carrying light traffic at the time of our crossing, caused no concern and we continued south on the attractive, tree-lined Merwede Canal, whose insouciant lock-keepers seem not to care whether their traffic lights show green, red/green or even red and think it odd that one should pay any attention to them at all. This canal took us as far as Gorinchem, on the Waal, struggling all day with a strong crosswind.

On approaching Gorinchem, a bridge-keeper told me to turn left onto a branch canal. This advice didn't agree with the chart, and I decided not to take it. I later found that the canal he'd recommended was blocked at the river end. His bad advice could have caused dreadful trouble. To have gone down the canal, found it a dead end, and then in the confined spaces of a small Dutch town, had to turn our sixty-foot boat, or even worse, had to back all the way out, would have been like a scenario for a captain's ghastly nightmare.

There were a lot of boats tied up at Gorinchem and little place left to moor except near the lock leading into the Waal. I saw a difficult but possible mooring there if we could manage to tie the front of the boat to a few feet of grassy bank and the other end to a steel mooring post in the water some distance away. It was not going to be easy, and as we approached the task, there was that air of tension aboard *Lionel* that usually accompanies difficult manoeuvres. Melodie stood in the bow with a rope in her hand, poised to give it her best shot. I was at the wheel trying

to be cool but, Melodie insists, tightly clenching my teeth. We need not have worried. In that country of boat-loving people, help is never very far away. An old man, seeing our predicament, came running to take our ropes. He could not help with the mooring post in the water at the stern, but I managed that from the boat and we were soon secured for the night.

Barge crews naturally deal with all such tricky situations as part of a normal day's work and with a casual skill that shames the amateur. Gorinchem was packed with barges, leaving little room for late arrivals like the unloaded barge that shortly approached from the stern. All that remained for it were the widely spaced barge mooring posts in the water, inexplicably called *Ducs d'Albe* in France. There was a brisk offshore breeze and, as the barge approached, the wind started to blow its high bow away from the mooring post. The man at the bow of the barge, needing to act quickly, threw the heavy barge rope twenty feet across the water. It snaked out, and when almost at full stretch, looped neatly over the mooring post. That is skill. It is also skill to get a similar rope off a bollard you can't see ten feet above your head in a lock. To do these things with any rope is difficult enough, but to do them routinely with the heavy, almost unmanageable two-inch-thick barge ropes commands respect.

We planned to leave Gorinchem, when conditions were right, for an all-day run down the Waal and then into the wide Hollands Diep, both carrying the Rhine's potent currents, its pollution, and much of its heavy traffic towards the sea. But the next morning was unpleasantly cold. A strong westerly made the day restless with showers and blustery winds that delayed departure, and cut short our exploration of the old town. The long walk back on the high, exposed river dyke built on top of the town's defensive ramparts was turned into an arduous and unpleasant experience by the miserable weather. It was no day for boating.

We had no wish for such a wind on the wide rivers that lay ahead, and hoping to sneak by before it gathered strength, we rose at five the next morning to get through the last lock before the river. It was an old brick construction that seemed forgotten by the efficient Dutch waterway system. In spite of the lock's great size, its massive gates could only be worked slowly by hand. Even with this tedious delay, *Lionel* still emerged at 6:15 in the company of a 1,000 ton barge, and we picked our way carefully through a clutch of loaded barges waiting to enter the lock from the opposite direction.

A friend, entering the Waal at this same point with his newly acquired barge, reports being daunted by the prospect facing him. He found few large gaps in the heavy streams of traffic going in both directions. The novice captain was gripped by indecision. No ideal moment seemed to present itself but he couldn't hang around all day. Finally, he acted. Screwing up his courage, he scuttled across between the menacing barges. Relieved at reaching the other side unscathed, he nervously proceeded upstream, carefully minding his own business. It wasn't long, however, before he saw a cluster of large boats just ahead, taking up much of the river, and ominously festooned with red flags and flashing lights. Huddled about the hull of an overturned ship, they were engaged in a full scale salvage operation. This was bad enough but an impressively large yellow salvage boat headed his way, also flashing lights. It was time, he thought, to take every possible precaution. He therefore hoisted what he assumed was a radar target to the masthead. Feeling a little comforted by that, he hesitantly continued upstream. Suddenly, out of the corner of his eye, he became aware of a grey shape sidling up alongside. It was a police boat. This puzzled and worried him, but he heard a calm voice say in English: "Is everything all right, sir? Are you in any trouble?" "No! No trouble at all. I'm fine thanks," he quickly replied. "Well sir, in that case," the policeman politely pointed out, "you'd better take that ball down. It's a distress signal, meaning you've lost your engine or rudder or both."

On leaving the lock, we too were immediately in the midst of heavy traffic on the Waal, but turning downstream, avoided the problem of crossing it. An hour or two later we entered Hollands Diep, a part of the river that starts a modest mile in width but later swells to almost two. It is a broad, characterless stretch of water, giving the navigator no feeling of contact with either of its flat and featureless shores. Apart from boats, the flatness of both land and river seemed undisturbed by anything except periodic bridges crossing over in ponderous, stilted strides. The Hollands Diep, exposed to every wind that blows, flows west into the teeth of the prevailing one. As *Lionel* entered the eastern end of Hollands Diep, the westerly, upstream wind was already vigorous and picked up rapidly as we advanced into it. It was clearly not the best kind of day to travel on these waters.

As the wind increased the waves did too, breaking repeatedly in frothy white tumbles. It is not a deep body of water, so the waves tend to be close together and steep, soon six to seven feet high, but luckily striking us from dead ahead. In the past *Lionel* had been modified as a bunker boat, or small tanker, to carry diesel fuel to barges working such rivers and seemed quite prepared for what was happening on Hollands Diep. With powerful engine and high sharp bow, it plunged and lurched through the oncoming seas, seeming more confident than its crew. It was more like being on the open sea than on a river, but there was no turning back. Both boat and crew simply had to ride it out.

As *Lionel* met each wave, the bow rose alarmingly, and the entire heavy iron boat then came crashing down with a shuddering whack as it hit solid water below. The whole hull forward of the wheelhouse shivered and shook as it never had before. Waves broke over the bow, sometimes in dense brown masses, like thick beef broth, quite different from the solid jade-green ocean sailors know. On the outside everything was streaming water, not only from the spray but also now from a driving rain. The combination completely overpowered the windshield wipers.

Lionel was totally drenched. Water sought out the weak points around windows and skylights, causing little leaks in a normally watertight boat. At least with the experience of the Ijsselmeer behind us we had taken precautions to prevent the wild ride causing chaos below, and fearing the river might be salty as it neared the sea, Melodie had protected the deck geraniums by moving them all down to the saloon, where in its subdued light, they bobbed back and forth together in a sort of loose limbed rock and roll.

Surprisingly, there seemed to be no more than the usual amount of alarm on board. Joss doesn't care much for a world that's moving around a lot, but accepts the trials of life pretty much as they are thrown at her. She curled up resignedly in a corner of the wheelhouse as close as she could to us. Melodie, having seen how well the boat was riding the waves, had also adjusted to the rough weather but navigational concerns (once again) began to gnaw at her as visibility worsened, the wind increased, and our intended landfall approached.

Our problem now really boiled down to visibility. Both boat and crew seemed to be in good shape but we could see very little around us. The odd channel marker bounced by in a maelstrom of water and through the rain I could see the faint line of the shore on either side. When it came to other barges, however, I was concentrating so hard on the critical zone immediately ahead of the boat, which was fuzzy enough, that I was only vaguely aware of them as large, wet, ghostly shapes sliding by to right and left.

Our destination was Volkerak lock, a sort of giant's gateway leading south to the port of Antwerp. It is an enormous complex of locks designed for heavy traffic, comprising three of the largest commercial locks in Holland, each over 1,000 feet long by 80 feet wide, and a smaller lock 450 feet by 50 feet, the whole ensemble covering roughly two square miles. One's first encounter with the immensely long approach quays, the high towers supporting the mammoth guillotine gates, and the giant lock's aura of remote and omnipotent mechanical indifference, is an awesome, even intimidating experience. On closer acquaintance it did not improve.

When you are tossing about on Hollands Diep, however, your only thought is of a sheltered mooring, intimidating or not. Having been told that smaller barges were not welcome at the large commercial locks, the problem was to discover which of the faint shapes on the shore was the right one for *Lionel*. The tall towers were obvious enough even in the rain, but it was only after rounding the almost mile-long quay of the commercial locks that the partly hidden entrance to the smaller lock became visible. With the wind roaring and the rain sheeting down, we moored at last with immense relief, Melodie surpassing herself in speed and efficiency at a difficult mooring on the lee side of the quay, the only secure and relatively still thing we had been near for several storm-tossed hours.

In our anxiety to reach security as fast as possible, we had tied to the long floating quay's extreme end. Once moored, I walked the quarter mile up to the lock to look around, but found no one in sight. It was a most unpleasant place. The lock structure and a multi-lane highway above it

formed a giant tunnel through which a frigid wind whipped at high speed. On my way back I chatted to some of the other boat owners along the quay, who told me two things: the first of these was that the wind was blowing Force 8 on the Beaufort scale (gale force with winds 39–46 MPH), and the second was that we probably would have to change our mooring since that side of the quay was reserved for boats waiting to go through the lock, which we decidedly were not on that dreadful day.

The first of these I hardly needed to be told and the second I decided to ignore until Authority presented itself. This I thought unlikely considering the weather and the hundreds of yards Authority would have to walk to reach our boat. Having disposed of the problem so neatly, I was relaxing on board when a loud voice suddenly boomed over a loudspeaker just outside. It was like God fingering a lowly sinner. I could make nothing out of Authority's stream of righteous Dutch but I distinctly heard the word "Lionel" and I knew what Authority meant. Reluctantly we put on rain gear again, undid all the carefully tied ropes, and moved the boat to the other side of the quay.

The unrelenting west wind and a constant pulsing rain kept us pinned to the Volkerak quay for several days. It was bitterly cold for June. Several layers of sweaters and the wheelhouse gas heater were needed most of the time. In her own way Joss suffered from Volkerak too. Grass was an impossible distance away down the long wooden-slatted quay. Even if she had been able to manage the slats there were further traps at the end of the quay in the shape of stairs made of steel "egg crate" gratings. The slats alone were bad enough, spaced far enough apart for her feet to fall through. This, combined with the weak back legs of an old dog, made the necessary daily walks something to be feared. She had to walk very carefully but was never quite sure where those two wobbly legs might land. On several occasions one of them went through. She was then painfully trapped, sitting quite motionless and hurting until one of us pulled her out. We were all glad to leave Volkerak, a place remembered as a welcome refuge in a storm, for its impressive scale, for its dreadful weather, but certainly not for its amenities.

La Douane

There are three main water routes leading south from Holland. We'd taken the fast-flowing Rhine into Holland from the east the previous year in an unforgettably swift, hectic, and at times thrilling downstream run, but the great river was not a route I could ever persuade Melodie to travel again aboard *Lionel*, so it was not even considered for our journey south. A little farther west the Maas River, later to become the Meuse, can be travelled south from Nijmegen, through Belgium and into France almost to Nancy. This route is much used by barges, popular with pleasure boats and may well be the easiest of the available waterways.

The last way out of Holland and into Belgium consists of two not dissimilar alternatives farther west again. One goes across Walcheren, and the open water of the Western Schelde, to make landfall at Terneuzen where a canal leads to Ghent. The Western Schelde, however, is a very exposed body of water, travelled by all the deep water ships using the great port of Antwerp—two excellent reasons for ruling it out. The last remaining route is the one we took: south on the Volkerak, then along well-marked channels or canals into Belgium and through the port of Antwerp.

Melodie and I don't always see eye to eye on the most desirable way of getting from A to B. All sorts of factors come into play, but the major cause of difference lies in our two natures. Melodie cherishes security and stability, the tranquillity of small canals, the quiet enjoyment of country-side and town, the comfort of the known as opposed to the excitement of the new. I am less insistent on security, enjoy a constantly changing scene, wish to experience all I can, welcome the challenge and freshness of new adventures. The two points of view, I think, have much to do with the basic differences between the sexes and experience suggests they are typical of many couples who share boats.

In planning our trip south we had discussed with some care where we would go. Melodie had endured the crossing of the Ijsselmeer, not at all her favoured kind of boating, and we both assumed that calm would reign for the rest of the journey. Then came the storm on Hollands Diep and we now faced the Port of Antwerp, which Melodie, unknown to me, contemplated with foreboding.

With the promise of better weather, we rose very early one morning, passed through the huge Volkerak lock and set off down the Volkerak itself, leaving it shortly to enter the Schelde-Rhine Canal, which runs through flat land and shallow sea inlets, but has Kreekrak lock to add some spice to an otherwise bland voyage. This lock, another memorable giant, has two chambers side by side, each of vast dimensions, and when we passed through, was crowded with 1,500 ton barges, several of their smaller brethren and two tugs.

At the border, Dutch customs seemed quite disinterested but the Belgian *douane* was to be another matter. On this route into their country, Belgium concentrates its customs operations in the port of Antwerp and I had been told to visit a customs office at its northern entrance. We had a rough idea where to find it, and cruised very slowly along the quays studying the buildings carefully through binoculars. We saw no signs saying *douane* or even anything that looked remotely like a customs office. Mystified and frustrated at not being able to comply with the rules, we finally abandoned the search.

Under an azure sky dappled with little puffs of cloud we moved tentatively into the great port, feeling small and vulnerable in that world of giants. The port, about thirty-five miles from the open sea, is one of the two largest in Europe. The approach canal alone is a quarter mile wide and, in the working port, only slightly narrower fingers of water stretched for one to two miles towards the cluttered horizon. The fifty-five miles of quays in the port were lined with large boats, most of them ocean-going

freighters, their bright paint work standing out against a background of spidery cranes, cooling towers, oil storage tanks and warehouses.

On that lovely, almost windless day, slipping quietly by the ships, I gazed in wonder at the immensity of it all, trying to conjure up some notion of the massive flow of goods going through it. I enjoyed the thrill of simply being present in such a place, but at the same time Melodie was feeling something close to fear, perhaps from the imagined threat posed by all our giant-sized neighbours during *Lionel*'s cruise through the port. She did not tell me about it at the time nor did I sense what she was going through. Perhaps, even now, she would not be able to explain it adequately to herself except as a kind of irrational fear. Unknown to me, poor Melodie had endured similar sensations at other times aboard *Lionel* but had borne them with a remarkable silent stoicism.

Having felt our way carefully through the immense port, we went under a lift bridge at its eastern end and entered the Albert Canal. There was some funny and inexplicable business at this bridge. The bridge-keeper lowered a wooden shoe to Melodie standing in the bow. She thought he wanted money and climbed up to his cabin to tell him we had no Belgian francs. All he wanted, however, was to give us an enigmatic numbered card. Some of the mystery surrounding the card was removed later, but first we moored to make enquiries about the whereabouts of the elusive *douane*.

In Act One of the comedy that followed, I set off in a taxi, sketchy directions in hand, expecting to return shortly. Judging from the final taxi bill I must have explored most of the great port. I called at no fewer than four widely separated offices before the taxi driver found the right one, exactly where it was supposed to be, housed in a small, shabby wooden hut with DOUANE on a sign no larger than a desk nameplate over the door. It was so cunningly concealed that I am not surprised we had missed it, even with the help of binoculars. When I presented our passports and boat's papers to a fat, tough-looking character in his paper strewn office, he sniffed through his moustache and handed them back saying: "Où est votre bateau?" When I told him where the barge was moored he confirmed my worst fears: "Je dois regarder le bateau." I didn't look forward to a return journey of almost eight miles through the port but was fortunately saved from that by his suggestion that we take *Lionel* the following day to another customs office close to our mooring.

We spent an uncomfortable night on a narrow section of the Albert Canal in Antwerp's industrial zone, a road on one side, an elevated autoroute on the other, both filling the night hours with restless rushing noise. It was not a good introduction to Belgium, but the next day was even worse, its only pleasant features being warmth and a blue sky.

In Act Two, the mysterious numbered card was partly explained by a pleasant English-speaking woman wearing a navy blue uniform who told me to take the card to two buildings a quarter of a mile away. I duly pedalled off on the boat's bicycle, and paid 35 francs for God knows what in one of the buildings, and considerably more in the other, to obtain the magic green form needed to pass through Belgium.

Back once more through the lift bridge for the beginning of Act Three. Around the corner we searched for another customs office which we hoped would finally deal with *Lionel*. After making enquiries I found a drab little brick building also cleverly camouflaged behind moored barges, cranes, trucks, warehouses and heaps of miscellaneous goods on the quay. The customs officer showed little interest in *Lionel*, Melodie, Joss or me but seemed obsessed by the eight or so opened and unopened bottles of wine and spirits we had on board. It appeared to be *une grande problème*.

We started off in French, one of the two official Belgian languages, but

at his request soon switched to English, his surprising preference. Apparently, the difficulty with the bottles was that some were not sealed during our passage through the port. Because of this we had infringed regulations that make the port of Antwerp a sort of gigantic bonded warehouse. *Le douanier* was unsure how to deal with this unusual problem, and I waited while bureaucratic indecision forced him to make long phone calls to superiors. At last, he came back to the boat, looked at the bottles and, with me at his heels, trooped back to the office where he filled out a form, consulted a tattered old rule-book, decided the form wasn't needed and announced: "You're free to go." What a waffler that *douanier* turned out to be!

Back yet again we went through the lift bridge and down the Albert Canal, a busy waterway linking Antwerp and Maastricht to the east, but we soon turned off onto a canal encircling Antwerp to the south. Before that, however, we faced our first Belgian lock. That was to be Act Four of a troublesome few hours.

The lock was a large double in heavy use, one of the locks filling with barges on our approach. We waited patiently hoping to squeeze in at the back of the pack but the gates closed on the first lock and, expecting the other to open in a few minutes, I rashly left the only available mooring, to hover hopefully outside the lock. I soon realized this had been a mistake. There was nothing whatsoever to tie to and my job at the wheel became a constant jockeying of the boat this way and that to keep it more or less in one place in spite of wind, the lock sluices and an especially troubling current coming at *Lionel*'s port beam.

The canal below the lock was generous enough but a bridge under construction had reduced its width by two thirds. The remaining channel soon filled with barges in line abreast, constantly pressing forward, as Belgian barges are prone to do. This soon created a barge traffic jam, and since barges don't like being bumped, even slightly, it became imperative to prevent *Lionel* drifting sideways into them. It was an unpleasant predicament. I called the lock-keeper on the radio to ask him in French, if having waited so long, we could enter the lock first. The lock-keeper replied with a string of guttural grunts, which I could only assume was Flemish, Belgium's other language.

The only other "amateur" in this rapidly assembling herd of working giants was a dainty little motor cruiser that came dancing by to moor where only such a small boat could, at the lock retaining wall. After talking to the lock-keeper, one of its crew reported that the two pleasure boats were to enter the lock last. Under trying conditions we had already waited over half an hour for this lock and I wasn't sure I'd abide by that instruction. I soon wished I had.

When the gates opened and the chamber was empty of barges, even Melodie, whose actions are more tempered by caution than mine, agreed that there was little point hanging around any more. I pushed the throttle forward, entered the lock with despatch and determination, taking up a position out of the way right at the upstream end. I felt sure that nobody could object since we were going into the lock anyway and would occupy no more space at the front than the back. I was dreadfully wrong. Lock-keepers are not flexible thinkers, which may partly explain, I suppose, why they are lock-keepers. That lock, at any rate, revealed no pliancy in its rigid governing body of two, an older and a younger. On seeing *Lionel*'s bold invasion of his lock, the latter promptly and decisively signalled me to back out.

It was humiliating. I felt like a schoolboy being sent to a corner. Yet, like it or not, lock-keepers are dictators on their own turf and must be obeyed. I set about trying to meet his wishes. Backing up a boat in ideal conditions is difficult enough; doing it in that lock at that time was impossible. A 350 ton barge was alongside *Lionel*, larger barges were pushing in to fill the remaining space behind and for reasons that I will never understand the young lock-keeper had persuaded Melodie to give him a stern rope which he tied to a bollard, thereby eliminating any control whatsoever I might have had over events.

The rope and the entering barges soon stopped any progress backwards. *Lionel* found itself at an angle in the lock, the wild currents in the chamber bouncing the stern off one wall and the bow off the other. At the wheel I was quite helpless. The older lock-keeper shouted at the younger, the younger shouted at us, and a sour-faced woman on a barge joined the chorus with a few shrill comments of her own. I watched with alarm as probably even angrier *mariniers* tried to push their barges into the lock. The enormous Rhine anchors and massive bow of a 1,500 tonner flexed our deck railing as it nudged us gently but firmly out of the way. It was like being kissed by a whale.

We were stuck, but in a kind of compromise between the lock-keepers' demands and what was possible we got *Lionel* straightened out; bow and stern ropes on bollards above but every other rope on the boat in a muddle on the deck. At this moment Joss casually sauntered out of the wheelhouse to see what was going on and became entangled in the ropes. It was a truly dreadful incident. One thing piled on another until a ridiculous, bad tempered total shambles was achieved, which, but for the wooden-headed lock-keepers, need never have happened at all.

When it was over at last and the upper gates opened on what I truly hoped would be a brighter world, we advanced down the canal licking our wounds, feeling angry and humiliated. "At least," Melodie observed, "that will give them all something to talk about."

Strictly Business

From Antwerp two direct routes led south to Brussels. One was the busy Schelde, the haunt of unfamiliar tidal currents, ocean freighters and large "European standard" barges. That route must certainly be avoided. If the stationary monsters in the port of Antwerp had slightly freaked the only other member of *Lionel*'s small crew I didn't want to contemplate what the lower Schelde might do. We chose the other option, the Nete Canal.

At Lier I bought some sketchy Belgian waterway maps, both inadequate and expensive but better than none at all. At least they gave minimal information about locks and their VHF channels, but the absence of good maps was only one sign of many that the pleasure boater in Belgium is a second class citizen. This is constantly driven home, in the shortage of pleasure boat facilities, and in the attitude of barge captains and lock-keepers. Perhaps it is not surprising. Belgium doesn't invite holiday cruising because much of it is scenically bland if not bleakly industrial. This was certainly true of the route south to Brussels and beyond, the canal passing through what felt like the intestinal tract of the country. With sloping stone banks to resist the wash of many barges, the wide canal was lined on either side for most of its length with quays, warehouses and factories, the last announcing their noxious presence with foul fumes and weirdly coloured effluents. The Brussels-Charleroi was a workaday, no nonsense canal meant strictly for business.

It was a sombre cruise through this jumbled industrial backyard, spotted with decrepit relics of better days. Grimy structures with glassless windows and crumbling vine-covered walls were grim with old age and the dirt of their own operations. The scenery sprouted with cranes, high brick chimneys and enigmatic outcroppings of rusty steel. The only signs of life were plumes of smoke, jets of steam, occasional strange yellow vapours, and sometimes the glow of molten metal from the depths of dark foundry caverns. Even the working factories on this canal looked old and tired. It was a depressing trip past barely surviving remnants of a long-gone industrial age, a desolate man-made landscape, relieved only by the occasional brilliant yellow patches of sedum growing on the canal walls.

The canal itself was one of the dirtiest I can remember. Melodie and I are not squeamish about swimming in canals and have done so often, but

nothing could have persuaded me to dip even a toe into the filthy water of that one. The locks did little to improve matters, being high, lacking convenient mooring devices and usually packed with barges. They each had an office in a glazed cabin on the top where minor bureaucratic matters were transacted and where I had to go every time to present the boat's transit papers, pay a small charge and perhaps get ticked off for exceeding the speed limit of 6 kilometres per hour, which the vindictive lock-keeper had discovered by timing *Lionel* between locks.

Those journeys to the lock office meant scrambling over other barges or tankers, whose decks were littered with countless obstacles to trip over or inflict painful wounds, before climbing a high, oil covered ladder. If we were against the lock wall I had to face the same slimy ladder with a rope looped over each arm and the important documents gripped between my teeth. Added to these unpleasant features, a thick tarry residue of diesel fuel so layered the locks that ropes and deck became coated, requiring frequent and tedious clean-ups. We often thought longingly of Belgium's neighbours to north and south.

Although Brussels has a marina of sorts on its outskirts, the only mooring for a barge within easy reach of the city's centre was the special barge basin at the usual back end of a large industrial zone thick with warehouses, coal piles and oil storage tanks. The last time I had arrived in Brussels it had all been so different, one of the high moments for me in the Second World War. I was an intelligence officer with a Canadian Typhoon squadron operating in close support of the army, oddly not Canadian but British. After the break-out from Normandy we had rushed north on the heels of the Guards Armoured Division, hopping from airfield to airfield, arriving in Brussels just as it was liberated. I recall driving through the streets of the city in a jeep, with crowds of delirious citizens lining our route, shouting and throwing flowers, the first time since the Normandy beachhead anyone had seemed genuinely glad to see us. It was a marvellous time; the jubilation didn't stop for days nor the generosity of the *Bruxellois*.

The Belgians are experienced at being occupied, and were remarkably prepared for their liberation. From cellars, attics and thousands of hiding places came bottles and jealously hoarded food to celebrate the long awaited day. The happy, outgoing people took us into their homes, sat us around their dining-room tables, gave unstintingly of whatever they had to eat and toasted us with those special bottles of Burgundy and long-cherished

Armagnac, brought out for the first time in five or more years. Brussels then was a far cry from the depressed, shortage plagued city I had expected. Nightclubs and bars were crowded, restaurants thrived, ample food was available, and there were things to buy in many stores. Almost overnight Brussels seemed to have become its old self again.

The "conquering hero," however, often sees a city in a special, rose-tinted way that can never be the same again, and so it was for me. With that vivid memory still alive, Brussels seemed, many years later, quite ordinary and a little drab. Melodie and I drove into the centre with a Belgian friend, walked the streets, revisited the Grand Place, and had an indifferent lunch of *frites* and a steak tasting suspiciously like horse. The beer, however, was excellent and the café, at least, was a pleasant old-fashioned place, its ornate interior remaining much as it must have been when built at the turn of the century.

Brussels is a tempting town for the shopper. Its elegant food stores in particular held a magnetic attraction for *Lionel*'s superb cook, who, at some expense, stocked the boat's larder with *spécialités Bruxelloises*. And I did some shopping of my own. Belgium is one of the great beer countries of Europe, producing the stuff in enormous quantity, much of high quality, for export and their own substantial thirst. But what intrigued me most was the incredible variety of beers available: dark beers, light beers, strong beers, weak beers, bitter beers, sweet beers, spiced beers, herbed beers, beers of indefinable strangeness and on it went in endless flavours and combinations, with odd ingredients added, created for a market that must like funny things done to its beer. I decided to try some of them and bought six or eight of the more exotic ones, which I tested over the following days. They were certainly different, a few quite weird and two downright unpleasant. After it was over, a bitter taste still lingering in the back of my mouth, I was glad to return to simpler brews.

An imminent rendezvous at Ronquières with our son took us away from Brussels, and on a lovely summer day we set off down the Brussels-Charleroi Canal, going through six difficult locks, along with a small motor yacht from Ostend and a 1,350 ton barge. As the yacht and *Lionel* occupied the front of each one, we eyed the threatening bow of the big bruiser coming closer and closer as it edged into the lock. Even large barges, however, can be handled with unusual delicacy and we had nothing to fear from it. By the middle of the afternoon we'd passed through the last of the high, troublesome locks (one with a forty-five-foot lift) and tied up at the foot of the great inclined plane of Ronquières.

It was partly this canal oddity that determined our route through Belgium. We, or more accurately I, wished to have the experience of riding the world's largest inclined plane, an engineering wonder of the European waterways. Until the 1950s this canal was only used by 300 ton barges. It was then improved to the 1,350 ton European standard, the inclined plane and ten new locks replacing thirty-eight old ones. The travelling time on this stretch of the canal was thus reduced by twenty hours.

When first seen, the inclined plane is impressive. The basic facts speak for themselves—a vertical lift of 223 feet, a slope from bottom to top almost a mile long, and a 410-foot observation tower at its upper end. The slope is laid with double sets of tracks to carry the two water-filled tanks in which boats ride. Each tank can carry one 1,350 tonner or four 300 ton barges and rolls on 236 steel wheels, like a gigantic mechanical millipede.

During our transit only one of the tanks was operating. The other sat motionless near the bottom of the slope, having come to a stop there five years before, trapping a barge within its steel prison for eight days before being released. For whatever reason, that tank had not worked since, all traffic being laboriously carried up and down by only one tank, with consequent delays, and drastically reducing some advantages of the whole expensive contraption, although the one available lift was still a marked improvement over the staircase of locks it replaced. A barge captain's casual dismissal of the lift at Ronquières as being more for tourists than working barges seems to me quite unfair.

At the bottom of the ramp *Lionel* was behind several barges in a line that stretched down the long quay; 300 tonners loaded with grain, timber and steel wire, larger ones mostly unloaded and one with coke piled so high it blocked the view ahead from its wheelhouse. This would not be possible on earlier boats steered only with a wheel but is no problem on the modern barge equipped with remote control power steering that the captain can use from the deck. *Lionel* lay behind the unloaded 1,350 tonner, *Marinus*, a large barge about 220 feet long, run by a jolly and unusually talkative Belgian couple in their late thirties. The amply built captain had lost a leg and now stomped unconcernedly about the deck with an artificial limb. Their normal pattern of work, as on many barges, was to share time at the wheel except while mooring or locking, when the *marinière* usually steered the boat and the captain handled the ropes, bad leg or not. Because the *Marinus* was unloaded, making it unwieldy in a

wind, it had been ballasted with a foot or two of water, turning the hold into a shallow, murky but refreshing swimming pool.

When we first met them on a roasting hot June day, the bikini-clad *marinière*, her two small children and the boat's dog were all playing in the water at the bottom of the cavernous hold. The captain remained above at the top of an aluminum ladder leading below. As we talked to him, he called the dog who promptly, bravely and a little unsteadily climbed up the ladder, not at all an easy thing to do with only a paw at the end of each leg.

Finally reaching the head of the line, we moved forward into the tank and squeezed in behind *Marinus* by placing our boat at an angle across its stern. It was a long, leisurely ascent up the inclined plane, the half-hour trip accompanied by a background noise of subdued whines and rumbles. The higher we went, the better the view and the more dramatic the great tracked ramp became, dropping away alarmingly below the slowly rising tank, its great weight held only by thin cables.

As the couple on the *Marinus* stood on the stern of their boat and we on the bow of ours, they talked about their lives, their long, hard-working days, the loads they carry, the education of their children in special boarding schools for barge people, the waterways they had travelled, other barges and their stories. It was a brief but rewarding time for Melodie and me, for we had seldom found barge people so willing to talk and so full of the lore of their demanding trade. On parting, we gave a small Canadian flag to the children, and a jar of maple syrup to their parents, who were delighted to find it was free.

After Ronquières, one of the rare green moorings on the Brussels-Charleroi Canal can be found near the top of the old staircase of locks. At the summit the water was clean and the day so gloriously hot we swam in the canal and barbecued lamb chops beside the boat. Next day, such green pleasantness was nowhere to be seen as we cruised down the drab, uninteresting canal, enlivened only by a passing barge with ten dogs running about its deck, all barking and jumping with excitement. Never before had we seen the deck of a serious working barge so alive with noise and wagging tails. We burst into laughter as it passed but the drab canal soon took over. Ragged industry, much of it derelict, continued to blight what landscape there was beyond the sloping canal walls. Even the dour little towns looked dirty and unkempt. There was no relief from this grim Belgian scenery, even past Charleroi on the Sambre River. Substantial improvement would only come after Namur, reached in the third week of June.

Namur and the Belgian Meuse

Nine days slogging through a filthy canal against a backdrop of broken-down factories and the unsightly detritus of their operations had been quite enough. To moor at last on the stone quay in Namur under crisply trimmed lindens was a refreshing delight. Near the heart of the city, we tied up on the Sambre just before it joins the Meuse. Namur possesses a pleasant urban quality, but like so many of its neighbours in the east of Belgium, the city was much buffeted by war. Yet in spite of that, Namur retains its own special atmosphere and commands a magnificent river site, boasting a citadel high on a rocky hill, and at its doorstep to the east, the Ardennes, the most beautiful countryside in Belgium.

As it goes through Namur, the Sambre is both narrow and swift. It also carries many barges, and every day they came charging past in their impetuous Belgian way, sometimes so close that, in the resulting turbulence, *Lionel* struggled wildly against its mooring lines, banging its hull noisily against the quay. The Belgians hardly ever slowed down when passing moored boats, as their Dutch and French brothers usually did, and clearly paid little heed to the waterway speed limit. These short, turbulent meetings with the barges, however, had an oddly intimate quality. In their roaring passages close to *Lionel* the warm weather allowed us to peer through open doors into their wheelhouses without embarrassment. Most were surprisingly small, providing room for hardly more than someone standing at the wheel, the necessary controls and a radio. Others were little daytime living rooms, with a table, two chairs and sometimes a refrigerator packed into the tiny space. More often than not, decorations filled what was left of the wheelhouse: flags and decals gathered on travels, good luck charms, plants burgeoning from fifteen or more little pots and the window heads dressed with the customary lacy fringes favoured by the Dutch and Flemish. The living quarters on most of them were also minimal and one could easily conjure up an impression of what it was like for a family with young children to live through the winter in the cramped little rooms below.

Ever since the fifteenth century, Namur has been celebrated for its stilt walkers, originating perhaps in the frequent flooding of the Sambre and the Meuse. Even jousts were held by unsteady contestants on stilts, and this is still an annual event during the *Fêtes de Wallonie* each September. Stilts were, at one time, also used by soldiers during floods; in the seventeenth century, the Governor of Namur sent a company of soldiers to Archduke Albert, then governing the territory, telling him they would not come walking or riding. This may have slightly puzzled the Archduke and when they arrived on stilts he was so tickled by the feeble little jest that he granted Namur perpetual exemption from a tax on beer.

As is so often the case when we are not on the move, much of my time is spent tackling a technical problem on *Lionel*, which far too frequently is well beyond my competence to solve. In Namur it was the hot water heater, verifiably kaput, and after several attempts by the on-board handyman to fix it, it clearly needed an expert. I finally found a plumber who promised to come to the boat. That was only the first move in a now familiar game that dragged out for our entire stay in Namur.

Every boat owner knows the way it goes. You find a plumber, he promises to come next day. You wait around for him to arrive. He doesn't. Your whole day is wasted. You try to make contact again. If you are moored in Namur without a telephone, you walk to his place of work (seven times). You find it locked. You then abandon all hope of getting the plumber and return, annoyed, to the boat. A day later while having drinks with friends in the wheelhouse, who should arrive but the plumber (with his daughter). He examines the hot water heater, tells you all you need is a new thermocouple, which you can easily install yourself. You buy one, find you can't install it and return unhappily again to square one.

On the longest day of the year, we left Namur, slipped down the last few yards of the Sambre and turned upstream on the Meuse. For the first part of the southerly journey upstream the river flowed in wide sweeping bends through the forested hills of the Ardennes. Oak, beech, chestnut and pine mingled on the slopes where imagination placed deer and wild boar certain to be there among the trees. It was a lovely stretch of river, and much enjoyed by the Belgians who flocked there in the summer.

It is also a working river with its usual quota of hustling barges, but there are tour boats too, and along the river banks, attractive old-fashioned white holiday hotels, the occasional casino, and summer houses. Tiny cottages are interspersed with the houses of the more affluent, which sport odd architectural features. One owner's beloved idiosyncracy: a waterside swimming pool designed to look like a boat. Once in a while these summery frivolities are put in their place by a matronly old château of stone and brick, with a slate roof alive with chimneys, elaborate dormers and weather vanes on decorative finials. One of these was a small but exquisite domed stone pavilion sitting on a rolling lawn as smooth as green velvet. It was set back from the river against a forested hill with a geometrically precise plantation of square clipped linden screening the pavilion except for a wide approach avenue on the axis of the house. Though far from grand in scale, that little formal composition, in the context of its wild surroundings, had a remarkable presence, almost a classical perfection that put to shame many of man's wilder architectural expressions along the wooded shore.

Approaching Dinant, the ever-present memories of war returned once again. At the end of 1944, in a last desperate offensive, the Germans attacked in the Ardennes. The German Luftwaffe, then on its last legs, mustered what aircraft it could to attack our forward airfields. I was then stationed at the Eindhoven airfield in southern Holland, and on the morning of January 1, 1945, I was suffering from the previous night's party. Not long after dawn I heard an awful racket outside my hut and walked out to see about seventy Messerschmidt 109s and Focke Wulf 190s swarming over our heads, trying their hardest and nearly succeeding in wiping out the entire airfield, aircraft and all. I watched this destructive spectacle for a few moments but soon was aware of an FW 190 coming fast and low across the field in my direction. The muzzle flashes of its twenty-millimetre cannon were clear enough, and true or not, I decided the pilot had a personal interest in me. In a futile evasive manoeuvre I flung myself face first into the dust. It probably made only the slightest difference to the final outcome. A split second later Flight Lieutenant Massey's war came to a sudden bloody halt.

Dinant is a town squeezed into a narrow two-and-a-half-mile strip between the river and a high cliff. Supposedly, one of the most picturesque spots on the river, it was overrun with tourists and suffering in the usual ways from their presence. But a beautiful mooring appeared just above the town. It had everything: marvellous views, tranquillity, water, and most of the services boats require. I had hoped for shore power as well but out of our huge collection of electrical devices purchased in France and England, not one mated with the outlets of Dinant. As I was putting away my electrical gear, I thought for a moment about Europe's Common Market and wondered what it all meant if the countries involved couldn't even cooperate on standardizing something as simple as electrical plugs.

The pleasures of that mooring held us for two days, with much reading, eating and dozing, interspersed with enjoyment of the spectacular river scenery where late one afternoon we watched a storm gathering in the valley. During its most violent phase Melodie commented on the number of fish jumping in the river. It seemed a strange time for them to be doing that and the "fish," we soon realized, were golf-ball-sized hailstones. They came plummeting down from the roiling heavens like little bombs, speckling the river with their splashes and bouncing off *Lionel*'s steel upperworks with loud metallic boings.

The following morning, in the haze and heat of a late June day, *Lionel* passed through the last three Belgian locks and arrived at the border with France. The Belgian *douane* seemed much concerned by the absence of an apparently important document, possibly the one the bottle-obsessed *douanier* in Antwerp had decided not to give me. In the office there was a good deal of shoving papers back and forth, digging into loaded filing trays, consultations with colleagues, and much bureaucratic frustration. In the end, however, pressure of other work forced them to let me go. Next was the French *douane*, which I had expected to be more troublesome. Because of this I had done a careful count of our small cellar, wine and spirits, bottles open and full. Surprisingly, all was sweetness and French *insouciance*. The only man on duty during the sacred lunch hour was in an unusually amiable mood. He cared not a whit about the bottles, the boat, Joss or even our passports, waving me on into France with a smile and a friendly remark.

Beautiful War Zone

In the shade of a Stella Artois beer umbrella we lunched at a waterside café before cruising up the Meuse into France. The French, for some Gallic reason, call their part of the river the Canal de l'Est (Branche Nord), and it is quite different in character from the Belgian Meuse. The locks are smaller, generally less efficient but a lot pleasanter, reverting in most cases to the traditional hand-operated gates and paddles. Gone are the tour boats, the hotels, the casinos and the summer houses. The French Meuse is a pastoral river, with few vacationers and only light commercial traffic. The countryside is otherwise much the same as in Belgium, the river's eddying currents still follow the twisting valley through the hills and forests of the Ardennes. After Revin comes the most spectacular scenery of the French Meuse. The river doubles back and forth in tight hairpin turns to find its way through a valley, sharply defined by steep hills, mostly wooded but with outcrops of rock where even the most tenacious trees couldn't take hold.

Les Dames de Meuse follow soon after, the spectacular high cliffs so named to perpetuate the legend of three unfaithful women turned to stone by a wrathful God for deceiving their knightly husbands. Farther on, dark veins of slate begin to appear, snaking up and down along the sides of hills, explaining the local industry based on slate and the prevalence of slate roofs in the region. Soon the hills withdraw from the river as the valley broadens and fields gradually push the forests back. In this lovely, benign countryside we moored each night by willow edged pastures sweeping smoothly up from the lapping water to the forest above and sometimes a village, hidden but for its church spire poking above the trees. There was perfect isolation, the silence broken only by the clomping about of curious cows, the faint rustling of birds and fish jumping in the river.

The small French locks, though slower than the hard-working Belgian ones, were a pleasant change, like meeting familiar old friends again. Although they normally meant much more work for Melodie, she didn't mind. Once we were helped by an incredibly willing lock-keeper, who presented us with an acrobatic performance. In a trade that must be one of the most lethargic of them all, lock-keepers are hardly ever frantic with activity, but this particular lock-keeper did the whole thing himself—at speed. The paddles are simple enough and the lock-keeper's usual responsibility, but the gates are another matter. That man closed or opened all four gates, mostly from one side of the lock, by pushing or pulling with a boat hook, shoving with his legs and making chancy leaps across the gaps between the half closed gates. It was a sparkling act brimming with brio and pride, at the end of which he asked Melodie for one geranium out of the sixty or so on *Lionel*'s deck. He probably also deserved applause but, a fine geranium waited for this *éclusier extraordinaire* as we slowly left his lock.

In spite of the river's notoriety for rain and general bad weather, our southward journey continued in a string of eight flawless summer days. The Meuse was looking its best; a carpet of rolling fields spread from riverbank to forest, clothed in the green of new hay and pale ochre of ripening wheat. The sweet scent of hay and elderberry blossom drifted across the water as kingfishers darted from perch to perch, herons flapped ponderously away in front of the boat and cows stood knee deep in the shallows, lazily watching *Lionel* pass. In the canal cuts wild cherries could sometimes be picked from the boat, a little sour but good for making tarts, and there were always quiet country moorings where we could swim naked in the river and cook our evening meals on the bank.

As it meanders along, the beauty of the lovely river is often sadly burdened with the legacies of war. Going south, we passed the twin towns of Charleville-Mezières which great advancing armies bombarded six times between 1815 and 1944. War cemeteries were often seen from the river, row after regimented row of white crosses for the Allies, black ones for the Germans, but they marked the graves of only a mere fraction of the men killed along the Meuse; countless others lie elsewhere. This evidence of man's savagery couldn't help but cast a pall over the summer's bright countryside.

At Verdun, the old fortress town and one of the key points of French defence during the Great War, over 700,000 men, from both sides of the conflict, died here on the battleground. Those identified were buried in military cemeteries, but the bones of 100,000 unknown men are kept in a giant ossuary and, to this day, the fragments of yet more men still occasionally work their way to the surface of the farmlands over which they fought. In 1916 eight villages around Verdun were wiped off the map, never to rise again, and in the battleground there is not a tree now standing that grew before the war. Verdun was by far the most severe battle of that war but it would be hard to find any town, village or hamlet in this part of France that does not bear tragic memories and wounds from those dreadful times.

By Rouvrois the valley of the Meuse becomes flatter. The hills move far away from the river, now much narrower, resembling the Thames near Oxford. Increasingly it becomes unnavigable so more of our time was spent travelling on the lateral canal running beside it. The hay crop was being cut on the sloping fields to either side, leaving behind large cylindrical bales, which prompted the mischievous thought that the merest nudge would send them rolling into the water. Everywhere the wild flowers were in full summer dress: magenta and purple vetch, buttercups, wild roses, the blue and white of bottle gentians. Queen Anne's lace shared the crowded banks with purple fireweed, forget-me-nots, and at the water's edge proud flags held sway with their yellow blooms and slender, pointed leaves waving gently in the slight summer breeze. And everywhere I looked, myriad red poppies sprinkled the fields, sometimes so densely they looked like rich scarlet slashes on the land.

The quiet pleasures of water travel in France continued day after day. We cooked our meals outside, swam morning and evening, read a lot and slept soundly through the tranquil nights. Friesian cows ambled across the pastures to investigate us and Joss investigated them. She nosed towards them nervously but could not long stand their presence in a territory she had pre-empted as her own. Mustering a small reserve of courage, she would then leap forward in a determined barking charge to send them galumphing off across the field, udders swinging wildly.

Even the hard-working commercial barges seemed seduced by the warm weather, an easier time for them and one to be enjoyed while it lasted. They did not pursue new work diligently and lived a more relaxed life than in the colder months. Many had their children home from school for the summer and a holiday spirit pervaded their boats, with picnics beside the canal, the demounted wheelhouses often replaced with colourful umbrellas and the younger crews stripped down to beach wear. Fishermen were out in force, many with their wives quietly knitting or reading in the shade nearby, and in many of the locks lunch was eaten in the open air, a large happy gathering of family and friends sitting around a table laden with salad, bread, cheese and bottles of dark red wine.

Water travel was a leisurely affair through the sultry heat and green of summer but progress slowed to a crawl as *Lionel* found itself behind a loaded barge for most of the trip to Commercy. The barge moved at snail's pace between locks and once at a lock, took an unconscionable time going through, extended by chats and wine sipping with lock-keepers, and then made an incredibly slow exit. I wondered about this last phenomenon for some time before I realized that it was not a matter of choice. The loaded barge displaces most of the water in the lock, leaving only inches to spare on either side and not a lot below. When the barge leaves, water flows back into the lock along these constricted channels, a process that can't be rushed. Time is needed to fill the lock and it is small wonder that the loaded barge has such a struggle getting out. Even more time is needed when the barge is going downstream and the amount of water in the lock chamber below its keel is further reduced.

Commercy, the most southerly town of any size on the Canal de l'Est (Branche Nord) is perhaps best known for being the supposed home of the *madeleine*, the small sponge cake that Marcel Proust made widely known in his novel, *À la recherche du temps perdus*, whose hero embarks on an almost interminable train of memory after dipping a *madeleine* into his tea. Although one can buy these little cakes in other places, legend has it, at least, that they were first served to Stanislas, the ruler of Lorraine, who for a time occupied the château in Commercy. Choosing to believe that the town was their true home, I sent off a large package of *madeleines* to an old blind friend in England who at that time was patiently going through the "talking book" version of Proust's great work, volume by volume. I admired his perseverance and thought he should have some of the genuine stuff as nourishment along the way.

Lionel also needed nourishment, and before leaving Commercy, 500 litres of white gasoil was delivered by tank truck. Of the two types of diesel fuel used in France, the cheaper red is permitted for domestic heating and commercial boats, while pleasure boats must use the more expensive white on pain of heavy fines. Since the temptation to use red fuel is great, some boat owners take the chance and hope for the best. But *les douaniers* are vigilant. We had a friend who once took such a chance, filled his tank with red fuel but inserted a short closed-ended tube containing white gasoil in the top of the filler pipe to fool any nosy *douaniers*. His boat was inspected later in the day and luckily the ruse wasn't noticed. The inspectors, however, were to return the following morning for a more thorough look. In the meantime our friend got a bad case of cold feet and rapidly sold his red fuel to a nearby barge. He could then face *les douaniers* in all innocence on their next visit. It isn't really worth the gamble. *Lionel* has been inspected three times: at Aigues Mortes in Provence, and twice on the Canal de Bourgogne. The second visitation was made unusual by the

silver-festooned full-dress uniforms worn and the apparent embarrassment of the men who seemed apologetic about being on board. They were
pleasant enough, however, and even in full-dress uniform went about their
messy work in the engine room before joining us later for a glass of wine
in the wheelhouse.

Electronic Treadmill

The Canal Marne au Rhin is an important waterway. Running roughly east to west it is the vital link in a canal and river system that joins the Rhine at Strasbourg to the English Channel at le Havre via the Marne and the Seine. The full length of the canal proper is about 180 miles, including 152 locks, many of them automatic, an inclined plane and four tunnels. *Lionel* joined the canal roughly 120 miles from the Rhine, and so had only a third of its total distance to travel but more than half of the eighty-one locks and one long tunnel.

The first locks, all automatic, came in a bunch of twelve, less than a mile apart, each one alerted to the presence of a boat either by radar or, in the lock itself, by two-foot-long metal arms just above water level. The system is designed for commercial barges and it works well for them. Being only a few inches narrower than the lock chamber itself, they cannot help pushing the arm back on entering the lock and another on leaving, which activates the next lock when they are close together. It is a reasonably efficient system for commercial barges but also an electronic treadmill. Once started into a chain of locks, passage through one lock activates the next one, and there is little option but to keep going. If you stop to have lunch, or admire the view, the resentful system goes out of whack and help may have to be summoned by phone.

It should all have been a lot easier than it was. The problem was *Lionel*'s width, about two feet less than a commercial barge, requiring it to be steered into the lock precisely, only inches from the lock wall. This is not easy to do. If not close enough to the wall the arm was not pushed back far enough; an error the other way resulted in a shower of stone dust as the boat hit the lock wall with a painful bang. After several misses, minor collisions and too few successes we both decided that it was better to stay clear of the arms and push them back with a pole rather than the boat. As we approached the locks, Melodie held a long wooden boat hook to joust with the awkward little arms, only knowing she was the victor when the signal lights flashed the right colour. She got very hot and frazzled by these frequent bouts, eventually finding some cooling relief from the water sprayed over her face from a Windex bottle. Leaving the lock was a lot easier because I could usually slide the boat along the lock wall to push the other arm back, but it was critical that this be done properly. If it was botched the next lock would not be alerted and one could be trapped between the two locks until a canal employee came to sort things out.

The country was soon quite different from the upper Meuse; more open, poor farming land mostly, interspersed here and there with patches of forest. Nearing the summit the water became a beautiful dark turquoise, clearer and cooler than any canal we had ever seen. At the end of a hot summer day it was irresistible, so whenever possible we took off our clothes and swam, Melodie stepping carefully down a ladder while I dived off the deck, eyes and mouth tightly closed against whatever unhealthy stuff might be lurking below. At the summit, moored in the canal cut leading to the mouth of the Mauvages Tunnel, Melodie discovered a mother-lode of wild strawberries ripening on the bank. We ate and drank them as they floated around in our glasses of Blanquette de Limoux, a favourite *vin mousseux*.

The Mauvages Tunnel is the longest of the four tunnels on the canal, a shade under three miles, but generous in width and height, with a tow-path down one side. Commercial barges are normally towed through by a tug (*toueur*), powered by electricity from overhead wires, and slowly dragging itself along by means of a chain on the canal bottom. Because smaller boats tend to weave from side to side when towed they are allowed to go through under their own power, a hundred yards behind the mother hen *toueur.*

The *toueur* entered the tunnel the next morning with *Lionel* following, all searchlights on, and eyes focussed on the riding light of the old tug ahead. There were only a few feeble lights in the tunnel and every few minutes even these would go out as the tug tripped a switch that turned one section off and the next one on. When this first happened, the sudden unexpected removal of what little light there was plunged us briefly into the tunnel's wet blackness, sparking a scramble for flashlights to boost our boat's skimpy candle power.

Even with all the available lights of the boat, and those of the tunnel walls, I still had to stand up all the way to see the tow-path railing clearly—my best guide to where *Lionel* was at any time. The passage took nearly two hours at a speed so slow there was only the barest steerage way, forcing me to concentrate hard on steering to avoid hitting one wall or the other. The tedium was at least relieved by seeing the names of friends' barges scribbled on the walls and listening to a tape of Cézar Franck's *Symphony in D* as we went along. Finally, the faint grey light at the other end began to appear but it was not the bright sunny day we had left behind, instead we emerged under dark, angry, low hanging clouds, home to a roaring thunderstorm which pelted us with sheets of rain.

Through seventeen automatic locks the following day, *Lionel* descended towards the Marne, along the lovely, narrow valley of the Ornain. Trees dominated the landscape, only a few acres having been won for farming from the uncompromising terrain. The landscape, however, had a pleasant blend of scale, the dark green forest edged small planted fields and meadows where black and white cows cropped the grass. As elsewhere at this time of year, wild flowers were in their finest summer form. Examining a botanical guide carefully, Melodie picked out violet harebell, foxglove, pink rosebay, willow-herb, and red-berried elder with its bunched bright jewels and yarrow, carrying the generic name "Achilles" because the legendary hero supposedly used its leaves to cure his soldiers' wounds. Mature trees bordered the canal, thick grey stone-like trunks stippled with moss and lichen supported a shading crown of feathery leaves. It was nature on an intimate scale, with small hills, valleys, streams and villages, lacking the drama of the Meuse but with its own special charm.

Manual locks followed the automatic ones, using a system of *éclusiers volants*, or flying lock-keepers. A lock-keeper, usually on a scooter, goes with each boat through several locks, and much to Melodie's delight, preparing them before the boat's arrival. The system makes for a very swift passage, accelerated in these particular locks by a lever arrangement linking the two downstream gates so that both can be opened or closed from the same side.

We tied up for the night and again put our aluminum ladder over the side and had a swim. Later, a loaded barge came by, causing the usual maelstrom of swirling currents. As its wheelhouse came abreast of ours, we saw the captain's wife with a shocked look on her face, holding one hand over her mouth, and pointing to the water with the other. The passing of the barge, I soon realized, had silently lifted our ladder off its hooks and freed it to sink to the bottom. By fishing around with an ever handy grapnel I recovered the ladder but from then on tethered it firmly with a rope.

Red Currant Conserve

After the tunnel, the country flattened and spread out, the hills were lower, the forest sparser, and the fields bigger. Bar-le-Duc, the first town of any size, seemed far removed from the runny red currant jam that bears its name. My mother had made this special conserve when I was a boy and in our family we ate it with Bath Olivers and cream cheese. Melodie has also made Bar-le-Duc, which at one time we combined with cottage cheese to make the latter more palatable but probably cancelling any dietary benefit the cheese might have had.

Bar-le-Duc, the town, was an unpleasant shock. The only possible mooring was beside a canal work yard where a generator ran throughout the day to power the tools noisily grinding the rust off the resonant hull of a steel work boat. Added to those harsh, insistent decibels was the constant shunting of trains in the nearby rail yard, punctuated every few minutes by the brief but overwhelming presence of an express rocketing through the town. Bar-le-Duc is not a place that one can easily grow to love.

While Bar-le-Duc's history is hardly a fascinating one, it does claim some fame because it was such an important hub during the First World War for supplying the defenders of Verdun along what the French now call *la Voie Sacrée*. The town also boasts a rare and strange curiosity in the form

of what must be one of the oddest monuments ever commissioned by a
widow to the memory of her dead husband, a certain René de Châlon,
Prince of Orange, killed at the siege of St-Dizier in 1544. His widow,
Anne of Lorraine, gave the sculptor specific instructions to depict her
husband as he would appear three years after death. The final work, now
called *la Squelette*, is not a true skeleton but rather the image of a partly
decomposed René, an undersized shield hanging limply from his right arm
and the left raised in a gesture of feeble defiance. It is a bizarre, unpleasant, even macabre work, which one can only hope the client, at least,
found to her liking.

The famous conserve that bears the town's name is, of course, still
made there. I mounted a special bicycle expedition to buy some but had
to scour the town before locating the elusive stuff in a *patisserie* of the better kind and it is not hard to understand why. Bar-le-Duc comes in two
versions, made from red or white currants, both prepared entirely by
hand, using only *grosseilles épépinée*, or currants with the seeds removed.
There must be several ways of doing this but the French have opted for
the time honoured method which involves the painstaking seed removal
by young women using goose feathers. The result of all this labour is
delicious and worth seeking out but demands a high penalty from the connoisseur. I was determined to have some of *le vrai* Bar-le-Duc but was
stunned by the price. At a cost of eighty francs for two minuscule jars of
the viscous liquid, its consumption must be most carefully rationed and
only the proper accompaniment provided. God forbid that anyone could
contemplate smearing it on anything so humdrum as lowly breakfast toast.

After Bar-le-Duc, a flying lock-keeper hurried us through twenty
locks to Sermaize-les-Bains, where we tied up with difficulty among a
thick growth of lilac-flowered water mint, a nearby molasses refinery
perfuming the evening air. Strangely, we'd noticed wire haired dachshund
puppies patrolling several locks that day. These delightful little beasts had
waddled over to the lock, where we made friends as their whiskered
snouts sniffed at us over its edge. That canal had an unusually high dachshund population, and we came at last to a lock with a likely explanation.
There were dachshunds everywhere, mother dachshunds, father dachshunds, cousin, aunt and uncle dachshunds and yet more puppies chasing
each other madly around the lock-house, across the vegetable garden, in
and out of the house. With hair awry and a drawn, haggard face, the
woman of the place seemed quite dispirited and, I felt sure, with little

persuasion, would gladly have given the whole ruddy pack of them away.

As we travel the waterways of Europe, Melodie is the flower spotter, looking for new ones, enjoying them and checking their names in a book. On the canals, however, it is not so much the wild flowers that provide the real splashes of colour as the occasional lock where a keen gardener has been at work. We passed through such a lock in the day's run from Bar-le-Duc, the lock-house festooned with flowers in a brilliant jumble of colours, and more in the flower beds beside the lock. It was a bright change from the lock-houses we had seen that day, mostly unoccupied, shuttered and bare. Melodie was silent as I started taking photographs. Being more observant in flower matters than I, she quietly pointed out afterwards that all the flowers on the house were artificial, the kind the French use to decorate graves. Once told, it all became clear and far from lovely. I was shocked. These deceptive creations are bad enough on graves, but to dress an entire house in them was startling, if not creepy.

The important barge town, Vitry-le-François, came twelve locks later. At the junction of three important canals, Vitry is a busy place. Barges cram the narrow, dirty waterway in the industrial zone below the town and manoeuvre in it with difficulty. As we arrived in the midst of this strung-out huddle of barges, no mooring was in sight. A kind *marinier* offered his barge, but it is difficult getting Joss to shore and back over another boat, so we finally settled for the grain elevator quay hoping a barge on more pressing business wouldn't drive us away.

In Vitry, *mariniers* can have their barges repaired in its boatyards, load and unload cargo at its quays, take on fuel and supplies, and enjoy the camaraderie of a shifting barge community. Some barges are just passing through, others are laid up for months at a time, and some are permanently moored, their owners living a retired life on their boats. Vitry also has a *bourse*, an exchange, where barge captains are brought in touch with brokers arranging for the transport of goods.

The *bourse* is a vital part of a barge captain's life. It is there that he enters his name for work, chooses his load, its destination, meets the broker and his own friends, hears the news and leaves messages. Having finished one job, the *marinier* presents himself to the nearest *bourse* with his papers and takes his place amongst those waiting for new work. When the *bourse* opens, a blackboard shows each job, the place of loading and unloading, the kind of cargo, the tonnage and price per ton, the date cargo will be ready for loading and the name of the broker. Each *marinier* in his turn has a chance to select the work he wants. If everyone refuses a particular trip it is offered once more, and after the second refusal, the cargo is sent by road or rail.

Out of curiosity I went to the *bourse* on a hot summer day and stood in a corner of the room packed with *mariniers* and their families, abuzz with friendly chat. Business and work seemed the last thought in their heads. As each job was announced and written on the board, the captains in their turn had to make their decisions, saying either "prends" (I'll take it) or "passe" (not interested). Unlike the factory worker who has little choice, the barge captain thus decides whether he works or not. On that day all I heard was "passe." In those warm, lazy days I imagine the mere thought of slogging down a canal through countless locks from dawn to dusk had small appeal, and understandably so. After enduring the heavy costs and low returns of their trade, these normally hard-working people seldom scratch more than a meagre living from their efforts. And it was, after all, summer, a time to enjoy life a little.

Langres

From Vitry the Canal Marne à la Saône runs south, following the valley of the Marne to its source near Langres, then climbs up to the summit and finally drops steeply to the river. It is a nineteenth-century canal 135 miles long with two tunnels and 114 locks.

The first day's run to St-Dizier was through long, straight stretches, uninteresting enough in themselves, and made even more tiresome by the plodding pace of a loaded barge just ahead. At St-Dizier, our overnight stay was affected unpleasantly by the small herd of malodorous goats which had been provided lodging on the straw-covered lower floor of the nearby lock-house. There was, however, little we could do other than try very hard to think of the goats and their all-pervasive aroma as just a touch of harmless local colour.

A Spanish army besieged St-Dizier in 1544 and it was in that action that the man, now immortalized as *la Squelette* in Bar-le-Duc, was killed. Because the small group of brave defenders were able to delay the advance on Paris of a much larger Spanish army, the king of France, François I, was so pleased on hearing the news that he is believed to have said: "Allez braves gars," roughly meaning "Well done, stout fellows." The citizens of St-Dizier have clung ever since to the nickname, corrupting it over time to *bragards*, almost certainly the origin of the English word, braggart.

As I was dressing at seven the next morning a loaded barge rose slowly through the early mist in the lock just behind us. Not wishing to repeat the tortoise pace of the previous day, I shouted at Melodie to undo our mooring lines. Foregoing the usual engine warm up, I started it, and propelled *Lionel* away from the quay in what must have been the fastest take off ever seen on that canal, a barge version of a fire truck roaring off to fight a blaze. We then belted down the canal, climbing through thirteen locks towards the summit, in well forested hilly country, evergreens more and more in evidence.

When the canal closed for Bastille Day on July 14, we were stuck at Joinville, alongside a desolate quay behind the municipal maintenance yard. An unloaded Belgian barge joined us later with a young couple on board, newly mated but the honeymoon clearly over. The girl was young, attractive and apparently sweet-tempered, but the young captain was a sour fellow who shouted at us angrily as he passed for not telling the previous lock-keeper we were going to stop. Even my offer of help with his mooring lines was rejected with ill humour. The Alsatian puppy aboard was by far the most relaxed member of that crew.

Three hours after arriving at Joinville the loaded barge, last seen at St-Dizier, finally pounded past, providing ample justification for our panic start, and evidence of the priority loaded barges enjoy even on Bastille Day. During the next two days we did odd jobs, ate well, dozed, read, went for a walk along the Marne, drank in a café and observed our unsociable Belgian neighbours with more than casual interest. In our little neck of the woods nothing much happened on Bastille Day. The Belgian couple snapped at each other, she burst into tears, they went below, perhaps to mend hurt feelings, then reappeared some time later, having put on better clothes—a white dress for her, white shirt and dark pants for him. They got out their barbecue and cooked a string of sausages as the eager puppy bounced happily around but the puppy's was the only joy to be seen at the meagre holiday feast. The future didn't look bright for that partnership, so important on a working barge, and it seemed bound to founder unless the overbearing young captain turned himself around.

Setting off firecrackers is a year-round game for French boys, but the bombardment intensifies as Bastille Day approaches. The things they toss about with such abandon are not little spluttering squibs or the watered-down affairs one sees these days on suburban lawns. They are startlingly loud and frightening, the sort of thing that has been banned in my own country. Every little boy in Joinville had his supply of them. Their loud bangs always worried poor Joss, who shook with fright and ran for the small comfort of her bed below. At Joinville when the bangs got very close and very loud, I told the boys how frightened Joss was, gave each a franc and persuaded them to take their noises elsewhere. It worked, but only up to a point. When I went to bed early, Melodie remained in the wheelhouse to see what was only the upper third of the distant fireworks popping up silently behind the canal-side trees. It must have been a rather remote experience.

Climbing higher toward the summit, tall conifers lined the canal. Meadows and fields of wheat and corn undulated on the gentle hills of cleared land between large patches of pine and spruce. Because of the forested hilly terrain farming was on a small scale, meadows predominating, dotted here and there with sheep and dairy cows. It had an alpine feel, a sense of leaving the lowlands and entering a different landscape where the winters would be colder and snowier and the piles of wood beside the lock-houses badly needed.

Moorings were always pleasant on that part of the canal. The countryside was beautiful and isolated with many trees for securing the boat. Since the days were warm, we cooked meals in the open air and swam a lot. However, like many "country" moorings, they had their hazards, especially nettles, Melodie's particular foe. All nettles are unpleasant but the European version seems a particularly vicious relative of the milder Canadian one, its stings persisting, scratched or not, for up to twenty-four hours. Melodie suffered greatly from them and we began using an effective "de-stinging" ointment bought in England. Prevention, however, is better than cure, and Melodie, who must often jump onto the bank when mooring, armoured herself against nettles with thick slacks, a long sleeved top, rubber boots and industrial rubber gloves up to her elbows, looking very much like someone about to tackle a toxic chemical spill.

Two more days and twenty-five locks at last brought us to Langres, sitting on a hill far above the canal. The mooring itself was wretched: a sandy quay with little to tie to, occupied by piles of gravel, blocks of stone, and a rusty loading conveyor which hung over the boat like a giant praying mantis. High tension power lines swung across the canal overhead, and 200 yards away a main line railway track burst spasmodically into rackety, swooshing life. But Langres was a place to visit and we stayed for a few days at the miserable mooring, one rope fastened to a bit of bent iron sticking

out of the ground and the other wrapped around an enormous block of stone.

We had been helped through the last few locks by a flying lock-keeper who had rushed ahead in his little yellow van to prepare each one. Flying lock-keepers greatly speed progress but working the manually operated locks is hard labour, even shared with a crew member. As a small token of thanks we had been tipping the lock-keepers one franc per lock. The last lock-keeper of the day got ten francs and a glass of whiskey for all his help and kindness. He came aboard almost furtively, seeming much concerned that his *chef* might see him with the whiskey. Scanning the tow-path nervously, he gulped it down and sped away.

Langres, in the northeastern corner of Burgundy, occupies a commanding site on a 1,500-foot hill between the valleys of the Marne and Bonnelle. It was a strong point even in Roman times, and later a medieval fortress town with encircling ramparts, many of them now restored. It is also the birthplace of the philosopher and encyclopedist, Denis Diderot.

The two-mile trek from the canal to Langres should be done if for no other reason than to walk around the ramparts tightly hugging the old town. From there, one has spectacular views of the country below, and into the distance where the large reservoir for the canal sits placidly in the summer haze. But a visit to Langres offers more than this. Although it has no remarkable single buildings, (even the cathedral of St Mammés is a disappointment), the fabric of the town, packed tightly within its encircling walls, provides all one could wish for in such a place: a pleasant mix of old stone houses, narrow crooked streets, little gardens and squares.

In the little central square there is, of course, a statue of Diderot, the town's most famous son, but a newer statue as well, with fresh flowers at its base. It was erected to the memory of Jeanne Mance by former citizens of Langres now living in Montreal. This devout middle-class woman worked in a hospital caring for the sick and wounded at the time of the Thirty Years War (1618–1648), but was excited by the challenge of a pioneer existence in New France. In 1641, at the age of thirty-six, she sailed for Quebec in a two-ship expedition commanded by Paul de Maisonneuve who hoped to establish a post on the island of Montreal, then a rugged forest wilderness dominated by the fierce Iroquois. Jeanne Mance founded a small hospital there with money largely from her aptly named French benefactress, Madame de Bullion.

After 1651 the constant fighting with the Iroquois escalated and resulted in heavy losses for the embattled settlers who were in danger of being wiped out. The hospital was closed, and the few remaining settlers took refuge behind the high wooden walls of the stockade. With the little settlement in imminent danger of extinction, Jeanne Mance gave what money she had saved for the hospital to Maisonneuve who went to France for help. He returned with reinforcements and the settlement was saved. A fountain plays in the pleasant little tree-shaded square where her simple statue now stands in civilized urban surroundings as different as they could be from the wild and dangerous place where Jeanne Mance chose to spend her life.

There's Fog in the Tunnel!

Shortly after we arrived at Langres, we were joined on the scruffy quay by an American couple on their way north in a tiny sailboat. After weeks of little contact with such compatible people, it was a happy meeting for us. Soon we would be facing the three-mile summit tunnel at Balesmes. Suzette and Jim had been through it a few days earlier, and in doing so had experienced the very predicament that has been known to turn tunnel navigators' hair prematurely grey.

Passage through long tunnels is controlled either by lights or, more commonly, by designated hours for one-way passages. These are posted on signboards for each direction, but should be confirmed with a lock-keeper close to the tunnel entrance. If you take a chance, as our friends did, a dreadfully unpleasant surprise may await you inside. Suzette and Jim had arrived at the southern portal of the tunnel to find the traffic lights out of order, no passage times posted, and no one to ask. Not knowing what to do, they had simply gambled and entered the tunnel. After groping their way with two small flashlights through perhaps a mile of black space they saw a light ahead. Assuming it must be daylight from the tunnel's other end, they only grasped a little later what was truly happening. When the awful realization finally dawned, they knew it was not daylight at all but the powerful searchlight of a loaded barge ponderously but steadily approaching. Panic seized them. A cataclysmic collision seemed imminent—a collision in which their small boat would vanish in an explosion of wood splinters. Something had to be done—and done fast. Cool reason then slowly began to regain control. The two gathered up their passports, money, flashlights, a hand-held foghorn and took to the tow-path. They rushed toward the advancing barge, flashlights flashing and foghorn blowing until one of them suddenly remembered the airline tickets. The onward rush was halted. Hurrying back to their boat, the airline tickets were retrieved and they dashed off again down the muddy tow-path, running, flashing and blowing.

The barge captain at last got their frantic message and slowly brought his heavy boat to a halt. In French, English or both, there followed a confused and strained conversation, the words of the breathless runners and the predictably annoyed barge captain echoing back and forth in the dark space of the tunnel. Since the barge had clear priority, the yacht had no option but to back out. Although not an easy manoeuvre, they managed it with guidance from the resigned *marinier*, one of them walking along the tow-path with a rope to keep their boat straight.

There was no such drama in our journey through the long tunnel, but it wasn't exactly free of problems either. Down the narrow canal cut leading to the entrance we glided past the still trees and the sad sight of a drowned deer floating in the water. As we approached the tunnel mouth the searchlight was turned on, and the generator started to power the new floodlights mounted on *Lionel*'s bow. Having been through other tunnels whose gloomy insides were barely visible, I hoped the added candlepower would pierce the darkness enough to give me just a slight hint about where we were going.

As *Lionel*'s sharp bow poked its way into the tunnel, we left the warm summer day behind and were engulfed by the dimly lit stone vault arching over our heads. Advancing farther into the cold, damp tunnel, the blackness increased. At that moment I expected the new floodlights would show their worth, but soon realized their light was reflecting off something immediately ahead that looked like cotton wool. I could see nothing but reflected glare from the cloudy mass ahead. Melodie exclaimed: "There's fog in the tunnel!" Indeed there was or something very much like dense fog and we were soon immersed in it. I was almost steering blind until Melodie adjusted the searchlight to focus on the only thing we could see—

the tow-path railing a foot or so away from the boat. We blindly groped along in this way for 200 yards until the fog cleared.

The cooler air of the tunnel at last won the skirmish with its warmer opponent, the condensation vanished, and our passage continued in the normal dripping blackness one expects in poorly lit tunnels. It was a long, tedious and tiring journey, which couldn't come to an end too soon for me. Long tunnels like that, with their walls slowly sliding past, mesmerize me and affect my concentration. Even if I'm constantly alert and trying hard to steer a straight course, I become slightly dazed and wander off, perhaps bump a wall, over correct and start off on an erratic zigzag that usually takes some time to straighten out.

As the cox of several rowing eights many years ago, I remember that the most difficult course for me was not the wide Boat Race course from Putney to Mortlake or the narrow curving Thames where college races are held at Oxford, but the dead straight course at Henley, its two booms converging to their distant vanishing point near Henley Bridge. The effects of perspective could fool one into thinking that the boom was getting closer and closer when it really wasn't. The pilot has similar difficulties in a tunnel, which are compounded by its narrowness and its barely visible interior.

After the Balesmes Tunnel, the descent to the Saône was steep and rapid, many of the locks so close together that Melodie bicycled from one to the other. It was a smooth day's run of twenty-two locks as the canal leaves the alpine countryside behind to be taken over increasingly by farmland. The canal was secluded and well supplied with trees, making country moorings idyllic, with wheat and brilliant fields of sunflowers ripening beyond the banks. It was the first time I had seen sunflowers in such profusion and marvelled at these dense chrome-yellow masses in the landscape, every one of the countless flowering heads turned the same way on its tall stalk.

I thought then that they all finished each day facing the setting sun, and wondered what happened in the morning when the great burning ball poked its head above the eastern horizon to start a new day. Did they do a twist through 200 degrees or more? If so, it would be something that one might see happening and perhaps even hear. The farmers are up early enough to observe such things but they may not care. I care but never seem able to rouse myself at dawn. Although I considered deputizing early rising Melodie to make observations at the appropriate time, it now appears, from watching sunflowers in our own garden, that they don't turn at all but face east to the morning sun and remain that way all day. This was also confirmed by the American photographer, David Douglas Duncan, who travelled through France photographing sunflowers for a book and reported his surprise at this fact. It was a disappointing discovery for both of us. It was also disappointing to discover that a field of sunflowers isn't always the bright splash of yellow one expects. Heavy rain in late summer can turn them into quite different plants with yellowing leaves, flowers turning brown and finally black. In the final phase of its premature demise the sunflower is a depressing sight. It shows no will to continue life, the seeds rot, the heads flop over at the neck and the crop is lost.

The lock-houses of the Canal Marne à la Saône are grim colourless affairs, and the lock-keepers generally apathetic tenants who add little life or interest to their surroundings. In many cases, they are temporary help who sit out the long day in cars or small concrete block huts with only a radio to keep them company. With these lock-keepers, the house is no longer used, but sits vacant and abandoned. There are no gardens, no vegetables or eggs to buy, no dogs, no children, and no one to talk to apart from the frequently bored youth posted there to work the lock for the occasional boat, and he never has any interesting canal news.

The last four or five locks on the canal, however, were of an entirely different kind, clearly loved and looked after by their occupants. What a difference it made! Flowers were everywhere in abundance, real flowers: around the lock, in window boxes, in pots on millstones, on cartwheels, and even hanging from an antiquated mowing machine. At one lock, where an old *marinier* had retired, his garden was embellished with mementos of his trade, some probably from his own barge: a small stern anchor, ventilators and a row of old propellers bearing pots of flowers. And there was one sensational lock with exquisite flowers in a formal arrangement around the house and on either side of the lock, all conceived and cared for by an attractive woman in her forties. On leaving the lock I said: "C'est la plus jolie écluse sur le canal, Madame," and in a loud aside to Melodie, "et la plus jolie éclusière." It isn't always as easy to plant a smile on a lock-keeper's face.

At last on the wide, calm Saône we turned downstream into familiar territory. It is a lovely river where commercial barges sometimes moor to the bank in the summer for a kind of busman's holiday in the country with all the essential ingredients present: beautiful scenery, peace and quiet, good swimming and fishing. Just after entering the river, we passed such a barge with the captain pottering about on deck. Then, out of the wheelhouse came the *marinière*. She seemed to be wearing a light brown body stocking from her feet to her head of jet black hair. At that point, Melodie said: "I don't think that woman's wearing any clothes." I too then examined her more closely. Sure enough, she was wearing nothing but a superb, even tan from head to toe. In our travels we have often seen unclothed bodies of both sexes, and in France there is nothing unusual about that. Yet it is very rare to encounter nudity on a commercial barge. The men and women working such boats tend to be conventional, if not prudish, by nature, and I found it refreshing to discover at least one free spirit among them.

The stepped quay at Pontailler is one of the more agreeable stops on the river, with a little park nearby much enjoyed by Joss. The green Michelin guide for Burgundy, which goes out of its way to find something to say about almost everything, gives Pontailler only the briefest mention. Nevertheless we enjoy stopping there for its good mooring, its quiet village atmosphere and for les Marroniers, a surprisingly good restaurant for such a small place.

Like all French villages, Pontailler has its war memorial. As these things go it was quite an impressive one, with a symbolic bronze grenade at each corner and a tall marble obelisk surmounted by a triumphant cockerel, head held high. It bore many names, most from the slaughter of the Great War, from which even the smallest villages didn't escape; the war almost wiped out the entire male population of some. There was also a far shorter list of those who died in the Second World War, followed by one name

from the Indo-China war and two from the vicious Algerian battles of the 1960s. But the most moving of all were the names of three people, all from the same Jewish family, under the words: DÉPORTÉ. MORTS AU CAMP D'AUSCHWITZ. I have made a point of looking at war memorials wherever we go in France and am struck by how often they record similar tragedies.

After the confinement of the canal, it was marvellous to be on a river again, broad enough to relax at the wheel—an impossible luxury in narrow waterways. Moored to another stepped quay, we spent a weekend at Auxonne, an attractive old garrison town where a young Napoleon served briefly as second lieutenant at the time of the Revolution. His regiment of artillery had no problem with the oath of allegiance to the new regime as most of its officers were from *la petite noblesse*, not the true aristocracy, and their only role in the Revolution at that point was to suppress the local food riots. The few Napoleonic relics remaining in Auxonne are in the old fortified barracks where a little museum makes as much as it can out of his presence in the town and the slim material available.

Farther down the river the town of St-Jean-de-Losne sits at the southern gateway to the Canal de Bourgogne, at one time an important north-south link in the waterway system. The town itself remains a centre of barge activity because of its strategic location on or adjacent to other vital waterways much used by commercial traffic. St-Jean-de-Losne started as a tiny settlement beside the flood-prone Saône. Almost totally destroyed by brigandage in the Hundred Years War (1338–1453), it was finally fortified and supported a population of about 600, a number established in the rough-and-ready census of the day by counting the chimneys and assuming a family of five gathered around each hearth below. The flooding river could not have been an easy neighbour to live beside but at least once during the Thirty Years War (1618–1648) it flooded in the nick of time to save a handful of scared but stout-hearted men from attack by a large Austrian army.

After a night at Chalon sur Saône we left the river as it turned south, and headed north on the Canal du Centre through attractive open country with shallow hills, wide valleys and big fields filled with crops of corn. It was a twisty canal with many blind corners where it was always prudent to expect a loaded barge rounding the bend in the middle of the canal. Higher hills topped with forest and a patchwork of vineyards appeared beyond Chagny. The canal followed a rise of land that looked down on a valley of vineyards, dense willow and tall poplars. After mooring I noticed flashes of light reflecting from a little stream at the valley bottom, winding

its way like a well-kept secret through the dark enclosures formed by trees. It was a playful stream, twisting, turning, tumbling over rocks, and at one place the water fell over a small stone dam looking like quicksilver in the twilight. Unexpectedly deep, the stream was so tempting I took off my clothes, and went into the cool water. By then almost dark, I swam around in the pool below the dam and sat for a while with water playing on my shoulders before tearing myself away from this small watery Eden to walk back to the boat.

When *Lionel* last travelled this canal during the winter of 1983 there was heavy barge traffic mostly carrying coal, but in the late summer there were few barges. It has always had a good reputation with *mariniers* for its efficiency and speed. The locks are well run, and Melodie enjoyed chatting with their pleasant keepers as she helped work their locks. On one occasion, however, she reported having to bypass very carefully the corpse of a one-and-a-half-inch diameter brown and yellow snake whose four-foot length was looped over a rung of the ladder she was climbing. Melodie, fortunately, is not one of those likely to scream and jump off into the lock when faced with that kind of thing a few inches from her nose.

Between Digoin and Decize the canal changes its name to the Canal Latéral à la Loire and acquires some of the beautiful Loire countryside. The towns here play only a minor role, while the landscape in close contact with the boat on either side dominates this canal and its neighbour to the north. It is an unusual, at times almost private canal, narrow in width, with the country so close on either side it feels sometimes as if the water isn't there at all and the boat is moving through the landscape itself. And occasionally it offers quite special and unusual moorings rarely found elsewhere. One I remember had no towpath on either side and a dense shield of trees. This ensured no intruders, nothing but the infrequent boat. There was no distant view but in other ways the ambiance was ideal, trees for mooring, a grassy bank for cooking meals and lying in the sun but, above all, it offered privacy and peace. No sound from road or rail penetrated our sanctuary, nor did any fishermen. Absolute solitude and silence prevailed. We could do as we wished, wearing clothes or going entirely without them.

Farther north, after the first few locks on the Canal du Nivernais the hills start appearing, and the country becomes increasingly attractive. The canal's companion stream, the Aron, contributes to this with the little valley it has dug for itself ten to twelve feet below the level of the canal. The

fine feathery leaves of acacias overhang the steep banks, their rough striat-
ed trunks embellished with the tiny green leaves of climbing vines. This is
some of the best canal scenery in France, with a rare intimate quality,
unlike any other.

For most of its length the canal is a narrow thread of water surrounded by this beautiful landscape, but with water shallower than I would like
and some bridges that put *Lionel* on the threshold of collision. We went
aground often enough but more anxiety was caused by the bridges because
the results of misjudgment could be devastating even at low speed. I relied
heavily on Melodie in cases of doubt and she would stand just in front of
the wheelhouse from where I assumed she could judge clearances down to
an inch or two more easily than I could at the wheel. Before going under
one particular arched bridge, however, Melodie indicated no concern, nor
was I aware of any. But, after getting through it unscathed she commented: "That was lucky." I had clearly allowed the boat to wander slightly off
the centre line but Melodie seemed merely content to remark on our good
fortune. Perhaps, I thought, next time she'll think of a warning shout
slightly ahead of the probable impact.

The Nivernais continued to enchant us as *Lionel* moved slowly past
small fields, farms, intriguing glimpses of old stone houses through the
trees, and pleasant lock buildings, many built in the early nineteenth century. It is a canal made for slow meandering, and quiet enjoyment of the
countryside, the wildflowers and the birds. The Aron darts here and there
around rocks, Charolais cattle munch the day away in their meadows, and
farther away a cluster of red-tiled houses in a village play foreground to the
occasional proud château boasting towers and steep slate roofs. The country looked especially dramatic in the early morning mist with the sun just
breaking through the trees, and the brilliant white cattle taking their first
nibbles of grass, spotlit by the shafts of light on the hazy green velvet of the
cropped field.

We reached the summit of the Nivernais at Baye on Melodie's sixty-
sixth birthday and moored to a concrete quay at one side of the large lake
that feeds the canal with water, its long sparkling fingers stretching three
or more kilometres towards the north and west. The planned celebration
was washed out by the absence of even one small restaurant nearby and the
dreadful weather dampened the thought of a barbecue. Melodie, at least,
made sure of a good meal by doing it herself, and I opened a 1982 Fixin,
a good light Burgundy with fair flavour but hardly any bouquet and, oddly,

a waxed cork which I have not often seen on a wine.

Off early the next morning and through the rather scruffy tunnel, its portals festooned with climbing vines, and down the staircase of locks on the north side. Some of these locks are survivors from an earlier time, with gates operated simply by pushing or pulling a cantilevered wood beam. They are hard to work and rarely seen now except on small canals in Holland, England and Canada. Melodie took an instant dislike to them, but as compensation there was Eddie, the lock-keeper at Lock No.2, half Scottish and half French, whose lock-house and garden were scattered with the imaginative work he does to amuse himself during the winter. An interesting man, his surroundings had acquired a new life under his hand. He makes a few small oddments for the tourists who pass by but many others were, I'm sure, just for fun's sake—a meat grinder, coloured electrical wires tumbling from its holes into a bucket below, a laundry line hung with a dangling row of mad bright yellow fantasies, an outboard motor with rubber boots for a propeller, electronic bits from an old television chewing away like bugs at a photograph of the Mona Lisa. But perhaps his *chef d'oeuvre* was the Volkswagen grave with the car's roof as the centrepiece and a marker bearing the licence plate, a miniature French flag and the message: "Trop tôt partie" (Departed too soon). His next project was to be "Monday morning on Wall Street," for which we gave him a Canadian dollar bill to substitute for the American one he wanted. He also intended to work with curved mirrored glass but lacked information about the technique. I later obtained a description of how it was done and sent it to Eddie. It would be fun to visit Lock No.2 again and see if Eddie's garden

is now sprouting the curved mirror pieces he dreamed of making.

The bascule bridge occurs with some frequency on the Canal du Nivernais. Essentially a counterbalanced and hinged parallelogram, these bridges are useful for dealing with spasmodic water and road traffic and can be operated by one person if they are left in the down position. But even so, they can be hard to move and Melodie occasionally needed help. There are also times when the balancing isn't quite right and the bridge end tends to rise a few feet. Then, stones are sometimes placed to keep the end down flush with the road. If you are not alert to this measure, as once Melodie wasn't, you may find, as you start winding the bridge up that you have become the target of a rumbling, rolling row of small boulders.

Clamecy is one of the pleasanter towns on the Nivernais just south of Auxerre and a good place to moor for the night. Not knowing which might be the best restaurant to try, I checked with one of two men I met in a store. Since he was full jowled, ruddy faced and big about the belt, I judged him knowledgeable about local food. He recommended a restaurant and there we went. It wasn't superb but certainly adequate, and afterwards we strolled about the town, up flights of stairs to the church where we were surprised to find the door open. Inside only candles lit the small chapel in the chancel, and at the far end of the nave, lights came from above where the organ was being played. We stood in the dim nave listening to the music—short but lovely pieces played with the rare clarity found in an old organ. It was a wonderful but brief experience with no one else but ourselves in the church. Walking slowly back to the boat, down through the town, along its steps, alleyways and twisted streets we savoured the sounds of evening, the family chatter from open windows, the glimpses of rooms, the smell of cooking—the town, in fact, and the people of the town relaxing after the day and settling down for the evening. It has always seemed to me that this is the most enjoyable time to feel the quality of a place, the play of dark and light emphasizing the forms of things, and giving the town's whole fabric a character that one can never fully sense in the bald light of day.

And Baby Made Six

The Canal de Bourgogne heads roughly northwest from St-Jean-de-Losne through 189 locks and a two-mile tunnel to meet the Yonne River, which flows into the Seine. The canal's construction began in 1775 and continued in fits and starts for the next fifty-eight years, a period that saw the disruption of the Revolution, Napoleon's rise to power, his costly foreign adventures, final defeat and exile. Its numerous locks make the canal a demanding waterway but one of the most rewarding. It traverses landscape of great natural beauty, and one that has soaked up a rich brew of French history, leaving its mark everywhere in old towns, châteaux, monasteries and churches. Because the Burgundy provides one of the richest cruising areas in France *Lionel* has travelled it on two occasions, in 1986 and 1988. The next eleven chapters describe our experiences on both these trips but follow the route of the canal heading north towards the Yonne after starting from the south end.

Although the Burgundy starts at the Saône, it only blossoms beyond Dijon and one must be patient. After leaving St-Jean-de-Losne it goes north for twenty miles straight as a runway through flat, featureless terrain. All eighteen locks in this section are of the typical Burgundy type, different in their gate-operating mechanism from most, if not all locks in France.

The beam/lever arrangement makes them hard to open or close and places an added burden on the unlucky soul whose job it is. In our case that is usually Melodie and she felt eighteen locks was enough for one day. At the end of it, we were greatly relieved to reach the broad basin of the port at Dijon, with its lawns, flower beds, densely treed island, and sculling waterfowl. Of the last there were swans, whistling, mute and black; various kinds of geese; and ducks, domestic and wild, many with ducklings in small, closely grouped convoys under their parents' watchful care.

Our car, left behind in Amsterdam many weeks before was now needed for excursions in Burgundy and I set off on the long train journey to retrieve it. The second leg of this trip, five hours on the Paris-Amsterdam express, was spent in a six-seat compartment with an Israeli student, two American teenage boys and a trim, thirtyish Dutch woman, accompanied by her very young baby. Though attractive, she verged on the prudish. Her prim hairdo and facial expression were matched by her clothes: a small hat set on the top of her head, a severe dark suit and simple white blouse buttoned to the neck whose clever adaptability would soon be revealed. As the train rattled along through northern France we read our books or gazed out the window, not talking at all. Nor did we pay much heed to the woman or her baby, happily silent for the entire journey.

As we neared Calais, however, our interest picked up sharply as preparations got under way to feed the baby, not as I'd expected, with a bottle, but in the direct way, from the mother's own breast. That operation, I thought, might not be so easily or discreetly carried out in front of an intimate audience of four curious males. With the rest of us attempting to appear absorbed in other matters, the woman managed with care, skill and modesty to get the baby and the nipple of her right breast in suitable contact. It was deftly done, revealing little in the process. Though mildly disappointed, I was full of admiration for her no-nonsense attitude and the quiet dexterity she brought to a difficult manoeuvre. With the baby happily guzzling away, we covered a few more flat, bleak miles of Flanders.

Babies, as the novelist, Eric Linklater, once noted, are biological specimens with uncontrollable apertures. I was giving some thought to that statement when it became clear that baby needed urgent attention at its other end. Again the redoubtable mum met the challenge head on, unflinching and undaunted. Disappointingly, she had no thought of doing the diaper change in the washroom down the corridor. Perhaps the feminist in her thought that a little touch of basics might be beneficial for the mixed bag of males closeted with her. At any rate, right there and then on the seat in front of me she set to work on the unpleasant task. I thought it would be a demanding test for us all, but once its nature had become unmistakably clear, the younger members of our little group quickly found urgent business in the corridor. I stayed to weather the storm alone. As matters progressed, I too was tempted to escape and fervently wished that mum had opted for the washroom alternative. However, it was soon all over, barring the markedly altered environment in our little space, and, sheepishly, the cowards wandered back.

I spent a hectic few hours in Amsterdam seeing an old friend, picking up mail, rushing around the city to buy yet more boat supplies and twelve bottles of sherry (oddly scarce in France). I left the next morning to arrive very tired in Luxembourg seven hours later where I was delighted to find Canadian rye in the hotel bar. Adequately soothed by the rye, an excellent minute steak, *pommes frites* and a glass of wine, I wandered dreamily off to bed.

The next day was also long and tiring. I drove to Auxerre, and late in the afternoon, pointed the car in the direction of Dijon, joining the long stream of August holiday-makers in their campers and loaded cars, heading south on the autoroute. In spite of them I was making good time when I had a blow-out on a front wheel, fortunately a well mannered one, with only the noise of rapidly exiting air, followed by the tell-tale thump, thump, thump of complete collapse.

I faced the job ahead with distaste. The spare wheel and jack were, of course, at the bottom of all the cans of varnish, tar, wood bumpers, neoprene stripping, sherry bottles and innumerable bits of boating gear. Once unloaded from the car it looked like some kind of roadside sale and I was a little surprised that nobody stopped to buy something. I gazed at it all wearily and set about the messy business. By the time I reached Dijon I was exhausted, and again in need of strong drink.

Dijon

Dijon has long been an important place in France. The old capital of Burgundy sits on the much-travelled route from Paris to Switzerland, Italy and the Mediterranean. Its use stretches back from today's cacophonous traffic on rail and road to columns of Romans tramping through Gaul on Caesar's business. In the days when roads were little more than dirt tracks, the nearby Saône River, joining the Rhône at Lyon, would then have been a vital link to the south. In the early nineteenth century, freight-carrying barges began arriving on the newly built Canal de Bourgogne and further reinforced the importance of the city.

It was, however, the Dukes of Burgundy who, for almost one hundred years, gave Dijon its prominence in European affairs. Four of them, *les Grands Ducs d'Occident*, held sway between 1384 and 1477, not only over Burgundy but at times over a vast chunk of Europe as well. In less than a hundred years these great princes of the royal Valois dynasty acquired enormous wealth and influence, transforming Dijon with new buildings and a full cultural life, rivalling even that of Paris. In this brief, bright time, the capital of Burgundy shone with power and a princely brilliance it was not to know again.

After the Dukes, Dijon spent a few uneventful years until 1513 when an attacking force of 30,000 men arrived outside the city gates. With only a fifth of that number to defend itself, Dijon faced a serious dilemma. The Governor of Burgundy, however, rose to the occasion with a Burgundian solution, cunningly sending out negotiators preceded by wagons loaded with wine. The wine soon had its calming effect, everyone relaxed, the mere thought of fighting soon became completely idiotic, a deal was struck and the siege raised.

In spite of its long history Dijon is not richly endowed with remnants from its past. Some old streets survive with examples of half-timbering and roofs covered in the multicoloured glazed tile so loved by Burgundians for their more important buildings. A few parts of the Ducal Palace still stand, though they are now dominated by a larger and much later structure serving as the Hôtel de Ville. There are some worthy churches from the fourteenth century, particularly the Cathedral of St Bénigne, a fine example of Burgundian Gothic with a remarkable small crypt beside it. But Dijon is in some ways a disappointment for the pedestrian who expects greater rewards from the ancient capital of Burgundy. Each day, we explored the old city core on foot, constantly searching for the elusive vibrant heart of the place, only to return tired to the beautiful port, its boats, people, grass, trees and ducks.

One of my favourite buildings in Dijon is the fourteenth-century cathedral dedicated to the memory of St Bénigne who was tortured and martyred in Gallo-Roman Dijon about A.D. 200. The special agony chosen for him was to have his hands plunged into molten metal and subsequently crushed, giving him the grossly deformed fingers that are his personal symbol of martyrdom. His tomb became a place of pilgrimage, and in the eleventh century, the sarcophagus believed to hold the saint's remains was moved to what is now the crypt of the Cathedral. The three-storey Romanesque rotunda built over it had its upper storeys destroyed during the French Revolution, but the lowest floor still exists, and remains a place of pilgrimage each year on November 20.

Usually old, far older than the larger structures built over them, crypts are very often early Romanesque, a robust, direct architecture I have always liked. Being frequently also small, simple, and unembellished, they possess qualities not often found in the great churches. The crypt of St Bénigne follows this pattern, although it is unusual in being beside rather than below the cathedral. It is an impressive place: one round room with a roof supported on a dense grove of stocky stone columns, a small chapel to one side and an alcove to hold a sarcophagus at the other. From small openings in the roof, pale daylight filters into the space below but not a sound from the city overhead. Its peaceful, intimate atmosphere enfolds the visitor, womb-like, within its dark walls, making no attempt to dominate as cathedrals can. For its power it relies on simplicity, the concentrated focus on St Bénigne and the sense of timelessness to be found there. It is one of those rare, small, quiet places that casts a lasting spell.

Just south of Dijon is the Abbaye de Cîteaux. Founded in the eleventh century on swampy ground covered with *cistels*, the old French word for the reed growing there, it is a holy place with its own special atmosphere. In the twelfth century, Cîteaux was the home of St Bernard, who at twenty-one followed his strong religious inclination and joined the Cistercian Order. Nobly born near Dijon, Bernard's family objected to his religious vocation, but rather than give in to their influence, he persuaded thirty-two of his relations and friends to become monks and go with him to Cîteaux. Their arrival couldn't have been more timely. The monastery had few novices and was rapidly nearing its end. Bernard and his monks revived the failing abbey and brought new vigour to the Cistercian Order itself.

The Cistercians, like many monastic orders, follow the rule laid down by St Benedict in the sixth century. But they reacted strongly against its relaxation and the luxury prevalent then in the great Benedictine monasteries of their own time. Under Bernard the Cistercians observed the rule of St Benedict to the letter. Monastic life became an austere, rigorous affair of simple food, long hours of religious observance, study or manual labour, followed by a few hours sleep, fully dressed, in a cold dormitory shared with other monks. The only income the monastery received came from selling crops, animals and grapes raised on land acquired mainly through the monks' highly valued promises of eternal salvation. The monks introduced new agricultural methods unknown until then, and eventually became the leading farmers of their day. Their skills at the art of growing grapes and making wine were such that the first great wines of Burgundy came from Cistercian cellars. The order expanded to monasteries all over Europe as it grew in importance, and for one hundred years during the twelfth and thirteenth centuries, it was the major religious influence in western Europe.

On a calm, bright July day we drove to see what was left of the ancient monastery of Cîteaux. Only fragments of the old buildings now remain, but new buildings have been added, and Cistercian monks are still there, perpetuating the hard rule and the spirit of their predecessors. It is an inward looking monastery, closed to visitors except for the new chapel where the offices are sung. Though recently built, the chapel is a building in harmony with Cistercian ideas, a tranquil place with a cool white interior and no embellishment of any kind. At the time of our visit a full crowd of visitors sat on simple wooden benches at one end of the nave, while the white-clad monks stood facing each other in the chancel at the other. In this unadorned yet strangely elegant space we briefly lost ourselves in the glorious music of the chant—a thread drifting back almost 900 years to that small band of ascetics founding their new order among the reeds in that same place.

Soft, Perfumed and Delicious

Although Cîteaux lies in flat, featureless country, only six miles away to the west are the vine-covered hills of La Côte, the sacred grove of French wine making. We both like good wine but are not wine mad nor even skilled connoisseurs, rarely investing large sums on it. We certainly can't often persuade ourselves to visit remote vineyards for the purchase of a bottle or two or merely a *dégustation*. But La Côte was too famous and too close to be ignored.

Of all the wines of France, Burgundy is specially revered due to its qualities, and also to its relative scarcity. Against Bordeaux's annual production of over 100 million gallons, La Côte barely manages to produce eight million. Burgundy tends, therefore, to be an expensive wine, and the really good ones beyond the reach of most. None of this, however, deters its loyal fans who seem prepared to throw more money at the wine they drink than I am.

It was an abbot of Cîteaux who first gave the papal court a taste for the wine when he sent thirty barrels of Beaune and Chambertin to a pope, then in residence at Avignon. In the fourteenth century, Pope Urban V even refused to return to Rome because he couldn't live without his Burgundy, for which the poet Petrarch justly accused him of "an unholy fondness."

Later the Valois dukes made Burgundy the premier wine of Europe.

As one would expect in a country of wine drinkers, Burgundy has stimulated an unusual flow of extravagant prose. The late Camille Rodier, High Chancellor of la Confrérie des Chevaliers du Tastevin, described the red wines of the Côte d'Or as "rough and hard in their youth, divesting themselves, softening with age and when years have ripened them, shining bright, pure, soft, perfumed and delicious in all the splendour of a magnificent glory." Others talk of its "regal quality and power" for it is often a heavy wine. Napoleon treated his regal Chambertin casually by cutting it with water, but one of his colonels may have carried his reverence for Clos de Vougeot a shade too far by making his troops present arms when marching past the vineyards and shouting: "My children, it is to protect these beauties that you go to fight."

La Côte, stretching for twenty-eight miles southeast of Dijon is in two parts: the Côte de Beaune, south of Nuits-St-Georges, home of predominantly white Burgundies, and the Côte de Nuits to the north where the equally great reds come from. Both are sprinkled with villages bearing famous wine names, but our route lay only through the latter.

Lunch under an umbrella in Nuits-St-Georges was a noisy occasion, the small restaurant thick with French tourists busily chatting, eating and drinking their way through a two-hour meal. Neither of us was up to that kind of thing, so we chose an untried Burgundian *specialité*, *Oeufs en meurette*, essentially poached eggs on fried French bread, covered in a sauce composed of onions, garlic, leeks, cognac and a lot of red wine. In my opinion, this combination did little for the bread or the wine and certainly nothing for the eggs, which I tried unsuccessfully to separate from the clinging sauce. While I dabbled with my runny yolks in their wine dark sea, Melodie gobbled up hers with relish and we soon departed for our drive through wine country.

Following the little back roads as they dodged about at the foot of the eastward-facing slopes where the grapes are grown, we were soon in the wine lover's veritable inner sanctum. It is hard to go for any distance past the vineyards without confronting the familiar names on road signs and buildings: Flagey-Echézeaux, Vosne-Romanée, Romanée-Conti, Vougeot, Morey-St-Denis, Chambolle-Musigny, Gevrey-Chambertin, Fixin, and more. For the obligatory *dégustation*, and because it seemed almost boorish not to buy some wine in this venerated place, we stopped near the famous Clos de Vougeot vineyards, its château sitting like a grim stone island in a 125-acre sea of green vines. Owned by the Abbey of Cîteaux in the twelfth century, it is the largest of the Burgundy vineyards but divided now between eighty separate owners, each caring for his or her own little patch. Most are far smaller than Clos de Vougeot and arguably the greatest of all, Romanée-Conti, has made its name world renowned with less than four-and-a-half acres.

Oddly, the place we chose for our wine tasting was neither old nor picturesque but a very plain modern brick house with concrete steps leading down to a basement whose door announced *dégustation*. The house looked deserted, with shutters closed, and no hint of life anywhere. Since all French village houses look like this, especially in the summer, down the steps we went and pushed open the slatted wood door.

After the glare of the sun, we stepped into what seemed a small dark cave with vague human shapes standing around a little bar. As our eyes adjusted, I saw that the tiny room was crowded with people talking French, German and what sounded like Danish. An attractive, vivacious woman in her forties stood behind the bar, doing her best to answer queries. The French and Germans made their purchases and left. The Danes remained, bursting with questions which were directed at me in English since they spoke no French. I interpreted as best I could, and suggested some safe selections in the higher price range, not knowing at the time that some were far from ready to drink. The Danes finally decided on a costly (Massey recommended) wine and left, leaving Melodie and me to taste some wine and make our own choices.

After the departure of the Danes, Melodie moved rapidly down in price to buy a hundred-franc bottle of Clos de Vougeot 1982 and ten litres of a lesser wine, poured, alas, by hose into a plastic *bidon*. On the basis of a sip or two, the latter seemed preferable, but perhaps the '82 was still too young or, more likely, Melodie was the better wine taster. And she had, after all, laid down the cash to pay for it.

I then vaulted gamely into the higher reaches of price again. As a very special treat, I wanted to buy one bottle of a top Burgundy, an aristocrat of the species, preferably a Grands Echéseaux, a superb wine, full-bodied and smooth, described to me long ago as the "Queen of Burgundies." I had once drunk it in my youth during a memorable meal involving pheasant, at a small hotel between Geneva and Paris, as I was driving my father back to London after a League of Nations meeting in 1937. I'm sure he was indulging himself more than me, but at least he opened my palate to a regal

Burgundy, and I am grateful to him for that. It is a sad fact, however, that only very rarely have I been able to revisit that experience in later life.

In the dark little room there were many bottles on the shelves, including an Echéseaux and others of that exalted little band at the top of the Burgundy heap. On the point of taking the expensive leap, I was told the Echéseaux would not be ready to drink for seven years. With minor variations the same applied to all the best wines on sale in the little cellar. I thought about this for a few minutes. Then on the threshold of seventy, it occurred to me that, in seven years time, it was by no means an absolute certainty that a then very mature Massey would be in suitable shape to enjoy his mature Echéseaux at last ready to put its best foot forward. I sadly abandoned the whole idea.

Cornucopia

Justified or not, Dijon claims a reputation for gastronomy. As in any French city there is simple and often enjoyable food to be found in the *brasseries* and unpretentious restaurants at the lower end of the scale but their gastronomic value is slight. Several years earlier we once tried a more exalted table, one of the few establishments in Dijon honoured with one or more stars by Michelin. It had been a dreadful failure—an indifferent meal with duck tough enough to sole a shoe and a greatly elevated one-star bill. During our time in France we were to grind our teeth on much tough duck and had to conclude that these birds (with their brother the beef *faux filet*) were startlingly weak links in what was supposedly the world's outstanding cuisine. But it was in Dijon during a Vietnamese meal (including a delicious duck) that the waiter finally explained the reason for the strange oversight: the French shun the young tender birds in favour of the older, larger, tougher ones. Nevertheless, I stubbornly continued to order duck in French restaurants in the hopes of the occasional lucky strike but only very rarely was given what I hoped for.

Even forgetting about the ducks, however, the precious Michelin single star far too often guarantees high cost but seldom the food to match it. That exotic flower, haute cuisine, seems to flourish only in the highest realms of the Michelin hierarchy, and at last count, only one such restaurant graced Dijon. We didn't try it but were tempted because a major gear change usually takes place at the two-star level, and it is there one begins to experience what haute cuisine is really all about. It doesn't come cheap but is truly worth the journey of discovery.

Perhaps the city's reputation for good food lies in the wealth of its gastronomical resources. About these there is little doubt. For a city of 150,000 souls, Dijon seems particularly blessed in the number and variety of specialty food stores, each with its small but loyal clientele. These stores provide a dizzying range of choices, from the basic and inexpensive to the sophisticated and outrageously pricey. But this should not be surprising for a population that spends so much time thinking, eating and even dreaming of food.

One of the great pleasures of Dijon, indeed France, is shopping for food, not loading up a cart in the supermarket, but strolling through the town from shop to shop, examining what each little place has to offer that day. Questions must be asked, sometimes expanding into brief discussions with the *patron* or his wife. Shopping this way takes on a human, personal scale quite apart from the interest of the food itself. And in Dijon there were shops for every kind of food and every taste: a rare cheese, a plump pigeon, a guinea fowl, chicken from the minute to the large, from the battery or the farm, a box of hand-made chocolates, out-of-season vegetables and fruit, a special *galantine* from the *charcuterie*, a *tarte tatin* for dessert, a dozen quail for a special occasion, a bag of *cèpes* mushrooms for flavouring sauce, or even some wild boar, a traditional dish at *réveillon* on Christmas Eve. There was no end to it. Fresh seafood of amazing variety and quality can be found all over the country, even in quite small towns, and the villages with no fishmonger are supplied with fish twice a week by a travelling van. Although Dijon is many miles inland, the great fish store slabs were loaded with glistening shapes from sea and river, shining with such an unbelievable look of freshness we suspected they must be specially coated to keep them brighter than they really could be. Melodie and I would sometimes stand silently for several indecisive moments in front of gaping mouths and staring eyes pondering a choice and fighting the constant temptation to risk the shellfish displayed in such enticing profusion, regardless of the food poisoning that so often fells the French *gourmand*.

What goes by the unattractive English word, offal, is a popular food in France where many strange lumps of one kind or another appear in the appropriate shops. The French don't turn up their noses at much that can be eaten from the inside of an animal, including sweetbreads, tripe, heart, brains, and other nameless things. One day in Dijon Melodie spied such a nameless thing never seen before. Being an adventurous eater, she asked what they were. The *patronne* laughed and replied: "Ils sont rognons blancs, Madame." Melodie knew that the words meant white kidneys but what, she wondered, were they? At the time she lost courage and bought something else but a friend told her that *rognons blancs* was the delicate French name for sheep's testicles. Armed with that inside knowledge she then went off and bought some, found them good to eat and from then on occasionally cooked them for visitors on *Lionel* to their certain surprise and occasional shock.

And then, of course, you may not feel like cooking at all. To make the tired housewife's day easier, if more expensive, there is the handy *rotisserie* which will gladly sell her savoury tarts, intricate hors d'oeuvres, paella, intriguing pizzas, cooked chicken and other prepared foods all the way up to an entire Scottish salmon, prepared, decorated and ready to serve on a large platter. And for that little extra something there is always the local purveyor of costly delicacies to the wealthy. In Dijon it is the outpost of Fauchon from Paris, in food and wine terms, the French equivalent of London's Fortnum and Mason.

But Dijon is also known for three special things it likes to call its own. Mustard is the best known, coming into general use after it first appeared, in 1336, at a feast in honour of Philippe the Bold. As a crop, mustard was grown in Burgundy up to the Second World War, but needs soil rich in potassium. This used to be available as an offshoot of making charcoal, much used then by the small iron foundries scattered through the countryside. When these disappeared, so did most of the charcoal burners, the potassium and the mustard crops. Although there are still bright yellow fields to be seen throughout Burgundy in the spring, these are not mustard, as many think, but generally *colza* or rapeseed, and the seeds for French mustard now come largely from Canada. Mustard has been made in Dijon since the early nineteenth century, and is sold to tourists at high prices, in great variety and in containers as fancy as they want.

Although black currant liqueur is made in other places, the best known and perhaps the best is *cassis de Dijon*. Frequently combined with *aligoté*, a rather assertive white Burgundy, *cassis* is used to make the Burgundian apéritif *kir*, named for Canon Kir of Dijon, a Second World

War Resistance figure, who favoured the drink. His name now joins all those others whose surnames have become household words in France, including the unfortunate Monsieur Poubelle, his name forever synonymous in the French mind with garbage because as Prefect of Paris he was the first to put containers in the streets to collect it.

The third specialty claimed by Dijon is *pain d'épice*, a cross between cake and bread that is a cousin to the familiar gingerbread but made with quite different ingredients. Similar to a bread found in Arab countries, *pain d'épice* first came to France with returning crusaders. Made with rye flour, honey, spices and sometimes fruit or nuts, it has high nutritional value, and no fatty content, milk or eggs. Because of its "incontestable nutritious qualities" and the long life assured by its ingredients, *pain d'épice* is valued for Red Cross parcels and arduous expeditions. It is also good to eat, plain or toasted.

The French, ever keen to attribute therapeutic value to much of what they consume, claim remarkable properties for all three of Dijon's *specialités*. Mustard has medical uses as a decongestant; some may remember having mustard plasters stuck to their chests as children. Cassis blossoms with extraordinary benefits, and is widely reputed for its curative effects, its high vitamin content and nutritional value. The French also claim cassis is an antidote to poison, a treatment for the stings of bees, scorpions, and the bites of snakes and rabid dogs, a cure for fever and gout, and a remedy for limbs without feeling or movement. That is pretty hard to beat, and *pain d'épices* only claims to be a mild laxative. Voltaire, however, thought constipation caused some of the bloodiest acts in history, making the astonishing claim that Cromwell was constipated when he beheaded Charles I. It's an extraordinary theory which Jonathan Swift takes a step further by contending that Caesar and Henry IV of France would have died some other way if their assassins had only eaten *pain d'épices*.

It would seem, though, that *pain d'épices* can sometimes overdo its simple mission. Kaiser Wilhelm II is said to have once bought some in a Nuremberg bakery. He may have eaten too much of it for the *pain d'épices* vigorously and speedily went to work as he was driving in the country with friends. Caught short, he was forced to empty the imperial bowels in an open field, in full view of his companions. Not a man to treat such an embarrassment lightly, the humiliated Wilhelm found his scapegoat in the hapless baker. Venting his anger with a heavy Teutonic hand, he ordered the immediate removal of "Supplier to His Majesty," recently added to the baker's sign.

Of all the places one can buy food in France, its markets are the special pleasures, varying from place to place, reflecting the size of the town, the season, the character of the region and its people. After a while one becomes a sort of market connoisseur with personal favourites. One of mine is certainly the market held in Dijon three times a week. The food available in the stalls is everything one might expect or wish for, but my interest in markets lies only partly in the fruits, vegetables, flowers, honeys, poultry, cheeses, meats and all the unexpected odds and ends found in them. It is mostly the people that I enjoy, crowded together between the stalls, women with their two-wheeled shopping caddies, single men, everyone shuffling from one table to the next, examining everything closely, seeking the best price, chatting with friends. They are a marvellous mixture: poor and well-to-do, ancient, youthful and in between, mothers with children, office workers and farmers, the shabby and the elegant, short and tall, fat and thin, the beautiful and the plain, all milling together in a busy, bustling hubbub.

One day, after shopping, we took shelter from the rain under the awning of a café where sipping coffee and wine we observed the crowds hurrying past. Behind our backs, the café proper would have been quite at home in an Impressionist painting: a long thin room with marble-topped tables to one side, wet with wine and coffee spills. On the other, an elaborate dark mahogany bar of vaguely Art Nouveau design. A busty woman stood behind it. With only slight change, she could also have come from that period. Tall, clothed entirely in a body-hugging black dress, heavily made up, hair bunched high on her head, she was at her post drying glasses, completely in control, taking orders and shooting wisecracks off to the world at large.

As the rain continued, we ordered more drinks and watched people walking or running past, the lucky ones with umbrellas, others simply not caring, or using makeshift means, newspapers, shopping bags, bits of cardboard, and in the case of one unforgettable, dumpy, middle-aged woman, a blue plastic garbage bag. She had the situation well in hand as she walked slowly home in the pouring rain with the bag arranged over her head, its long translucent blue wings projecting here and there like the coif of a weird Fellini nun.

We shared the dripping awning with two other couples. Beyond us, sat a fat old man, wearing a full, floppy beret pulled forward over his forehead.

Beside him was his jolly bulging wife, with an equally bulgy shopping bag at her feet. Both sipped their wine, enjoying a brief pause between the crowded market and the bus ride home.

The man and woman sitting beside us were quite different from the older couple but also French to their fingertips. Both in their late thirties, they were clearly city types, drinking water-clouded *pastis*, the aniseed apéritif of French working people. The man was shorter than average, with cropped red hair, a ruddy face and full drooping moustache. His clothes were cheaply flashy: loud check suit, wild paisley-patterned shirt, open neck. The woman beside him had dyed black hair and a hard face layered with thick make-up. She might have been a tart but the conservative dress and hat she affected didn't quite fit the part. She was certainly a woman with years of hard life behind her and the necessary street smarts to deal with anything that might come along.

Her companion of the moment was, perhaps, one of those things. He had a face with a left eye larger than its mate, and eyebrows at different heights, a pugnacious face that had known violence in the past. They were a strange couple, yet belonging to the city that surrounded them as much as the market itself. I imagined that life had not been, nor was likely to be, an easy road for either. Yet, dressed in their market-day clothes, the hard, sparky woman and the strange silent man at least had each other for company and, with *pastis* on the table before them, could view their world for a while in contentment.

The Electrician

In the insufferably hot days of midsummer there seemed no way of getting cool in the port of Dijon. Melodie and I have long accepted French canals at their often unappetizing face value, and without further investigation, have often swum in them without clothes or ill effects. Contemplating the basin at Dijon, however, we were loath to commit our bodies, clothed or not, to its questionable mix of feathers, bird droppings, cigarette butts and whatever other nastiness might be hiding in its dark, uncertain depths.

But extreme conditions demand desperate measures, and noticing one scorching day that a breeze at twilight had carried much of the surface flotsam away from *Lionel*, we lowered the boat's ladder, stripped, and damning the consequences, dived in. Initial hesitancy overcome, it became easier in the hot days that followed to scatter the frightened waterfowl each evening at dusk, and perhaps some tow-path strollers as well, when we briefly pre-empted our small corner of the basin.

While in Dijon I had connected the boat to a power outlet on the quay, a rare luxury eliminating both the noise and fuss of running a generator. The task was routine but all *Lionel*'s cables were needed to reach the distant power point. Once plugged in, I thought no more about electrical matters until the following morning a voice announced from the kitchen: "There's no water in the taps." Another bloody water problem, I thought, as I went below to the engine room and turned on the light. In its death throes it could only manage a faint golden glow, then promptly died. It was not a cheery sight. The bad news was plain enough when I checked the batteries. Every one of the cells in the two big ones was completely and undeniably flat.

I have achieved passing competence at a number of things during my life but electricity, like a clever old trout, has always escaped my grasp. Willy-nilly, however, I am *Lionel*'s on board electrician and must struggle along, puzzled for much of the time by the phenomena I am faced with, and in dreadful ignorance of anything more than electricity's simplest rules. My first reaction on that particular day was plain dumb. I turned the charger up higher. The only effect of this, and I am truly grateful nothing worse happened, was to shoot the dial needle instantly to maximum charge, make the charger buzz uncomfortably for a second or two before the circuit breaker brought relief by shutting the whole thing down. Like a true idiot I did this once again before a small seed of understanding began its feeble germination inside my head.

The next step was a more sensible one. I tried charging the batteries with the boat's generator, thus eliminating the long run of cable which might be the problem. It worked. The cables were clearly the guilty parties in the system. One of them, an old 200-foot number, had breaks in its insulation and had obviously drained all *Lionel*'s precious stored power reserves straight into the ground. I threw the old cable away, and from then led a less troubled life with a new one.

In early August *Lionel* pulled out of the Port de Plaisance in Dijon, leaving behind its high stone obelisk marking the first boat's arrival from Paris in 1833, and its wild modern work recording the birth, one year earlier, of the engineer Gustave Eiffel, in a house overlooking the port. We would miss the strolling people and their dogs on the quay, the paddling waterfowl, the carefully tended flowers and the cunning *clochard* who slyly picked a few each day to sell on the streets of the town.

After only five locks we spent the night on the curving quay at Plombières. It is there that the Canal de Bourgogne makes a jog to the southwest as it follows the valley of the Ouche, and starts its long climb to the summit. The Autoroute, alas, clings to the valley for a few miles, its gross concrete structures and rushing noise disturbing the tranquillity and scale of the canal until the road shortly veers off to leave it in peace.

Moving along this canal one is acutely aware of how difficult its construction must have been. In those days only men, horses and primitive scoops were used for such heavy earth-moving work up and down the hilly route. Building began at the north end in 1775 and eight years later in the south but the Revolution soon brought an end to work on the canal and much else, including Louis XVI himself. But even when the dust had settled, work could still not have been pursued diligently against the background of the Napoleonic wars, and the first barge did not travel the full length of the canal until fifty-eight years after the first shovels of earth were moved.

Up to the end of the nineteenth century, load-carrying barges were pulled from the tow-path *à la bricole*. Men, sometimes women and children, wore breast bands with ropes tied to a short mast on the barge, which reduced its tendency to veer into the bank. Later came barges pulled by two, three, or four horses, able to do almost thirty miles a day, reducing the Paris-Lyon trip to about ten days. The animals worked in shifts, those off duty staying in stables aboard the barge. Then the self-propelled barge of today took over. It can carry greater loads at speeds considerably in excess of what is permitted now on the canals.

Free at last from the noisome Autoroute, the canal makes an even more determined effort to go south at Pont de Pany where there is a good restaurant, probably the best one close to the canal between Dijon and the Yonne. It is a favourite stop for a hotel barge whose captain is a friend, and mention of his name to the *patron* brought two large *kirs* to our table with his compliments and the promise of a pleasant evening. And so it proved. I enjoyed the meal that followed particularly for its main dish—an occasion beyond price when the yearned-for duck at last didn't disappoint as it had so often done. A carefully arranged plate was placed in front of me with six pink slices of breast, laid fan shaped in a reddish-brown pond of thin sauce, accompanied by a neighbouring archipelago of half a pear and little round potato cakes. The duck was tender and perfectly cooked, a most elegant dish, in preparation, design and flavour, not to be soon forgotten.

Sauntering home to *Lionel* beside the canal, I noticed some faint greenish-white lights in the grass at our feet. The tiny glowing beetles were new to me. I have often seen fireflies, the amorous males of the species, flitting about our garden in Canada, flashing love messages on warm summer evenings, but I had never met the so-called glowworm or non-flying female beetle before. They were engaged in some kind of group exercise, flashing away in a cosy female huddle, its purpose known only to them. There are about 2,000 species of this insect in North America alone where the males flash in flight and the females flash while stationary. In Europe, only the wingless females, the glowworms, flash to attract the flying males, but in the firefly division both sexes can emit light. One species of firefly can flash red and yellow light either separately or together, and sometimes seen is what must be the greatest display of all—the mass synchronized, rhythmic flashing of fireflies in their thousands.

The *Sénéchal*'s Castle

One of the strange features of travel on the Canal de Bourgogne is that locks are always prepared to favour boats going upstream. The Burgundy is the only canal I know that does this and results from its syphon method of controlling water levels which apparently does not work properly with the downstream gates closed. Nevertheless, having to empty every lock chamber after a boat has passed upstream seems like a profligate use of the available resources for a canal that is often short of water.

The locks themselves have the standard dimensions of 38.5 by 5 metres, as established by the Freycinet Act of 1879, and lock machinery that varies little from one end of the canal to the other. The normal paddles for filling or emptying the lock chamber are supplemented by an additional water flow control, mounted on a pedestal at the upstream end of each lock. The gates are not wound open or closed with a geared crank as on many other canals, but with a steel beam/lever arrangement, the operating end of which rears up above the ground in a sinuous curve remarkably like a frightened serpent about to strike. To open or close the gates requires effort with all one's weight against the round iron bar and a slow shove backwards or forwards along the arc of a circle.

From Dijon to the summit, the canal threads through countryside

along the bottom of a deep, narrow valley, views to either side confined to a close, intimate landscape. Moving slowly along, the canal held a fuzzy brown mirror to the trees overhead and, close beside it, the little river Ouche wound back and forth. Its umber water ran clear over sand and rocks, between the trunks of trees, alongside meadows where white cattle grazed, under old stone bridges, past lock-houses and little red-tiled villages, silent and sleepy in the afternoon sun. Beyond the meadows newly cropped wheat fields spread in golden folds to the dark green trees around their edges and beyond to the forest crowning the hilltops. At Pont d'Ouche, having struggled up through thirty-five locks since Dijon, one is not only no farther north but about seventeen miles southwest of the city. It is here, however, that the canal finally turns sharply right and decides at last to become serious about its northern destination.

Somewhere in the day's run Melodie had pulled a muscle near her ribs, a minor but painful business and a constant presence when moving, laughing, or even breathing. For her there could be no more jumping or climbing, so we reversed roles. I drove *Lionel* into the locks, and handed control over to her as I took a rope up the ladder and left her to manoeuvre the boat in the chamber. Although not fond of the task, she did it well, picking me up skilfully from the upstream ladder as the boat left the lock. Since I rarely had a chance to moor the boat, work the lock gates and chat with lock-keepers, it was all an enjoyable change for me.

At Pont d'Ouche a canal employee stopped beside us on the tow-path to enquire about a hotel boat just ahead. He said: "They ordered a whole salmon in Dijon and forgot to pick it up. I will take it to them if I can find the boat." I suppose forgetting an ordered salmon is not so extraordinary but having it delivered by the Service de la Navigation was. Some months later, not far from Auxerre, we encountered a man in a hire-boat who had been even more forgetful, having just discovered his dog was not on board and must have been left behind in Auxerre! Once again, a helpful canal employee came to his aid, driving the absent-minded dog-owner all the way back to the city to retrieve his pet.

At Vandenesse, after sixty-eight locks, only a short day's run remained to the summit of the canal. We badly needed a rest and the place was ideal. Spectacular views of Burgundy opened in all directions. A field and forest patchwork rolled away in great waves to the south. The old fortified village of Châteauneuf crowned a hill about a mile away, its reflection wavering in the canal's still water and a channelled stream gurgled away beside us, flopping over little waterfalls on its busy way downstream. All else was calm and peaceful, an arched stone bridge, a lock-house, a graceful row of trees reflected in the water.

From Vandenesse I took a bus back to Dijon to get our car. It was a marvellous way of seeing rural Burgundy. In the space of an hour the bus wandered the tiny back roads, round hairpin bends to the tops of hills, through old forgotten stone villages held captive by time, and down into valleys where the canal and bright little streams snaked along at the bottom. Through this lovely and secluded pastoral world the bus passed small fields of corn and wheat hemmed round by trees, diminutive meadows and their resident cows, farms and barns, compact stone houses with tidy vegetable plots, forest-topped hills and hedges sometimes so thick and high the road became a green trench. The constantly changing landscape just outside the bus window fascinated me so much, I tried to go back the same way by car, got thoroughly lost and saw a great deal more of back-country Burgundy.

The little village of Vandenesse, like the valley followed by the canal, is dominated by the rugged old *château* sitting like a rocky outcrop high on the hill above *Lionel*, its high stone walls and turreted towers forming a cliff on the edge of the slope. Built in the twelfth century by a local landowner, the fortress was altered and enlarged by Philippe Pot, *sénéchal*, or governor, of Burgundy. It was an important strong point dominating the surrounding plain and the road from Dijon to Autun, several miles to the southwest. Although it could never have been a very cosy dwelling place, its occupants at least had a magnificent panorama of the valley.

Now the *château* is partially restored and unoccupied, visited only by a few diligent tourists. The village behind it, however, still lives on, with picturesque old houses and barns jumbled together within the remnants of its ancient defensive walls. In the summer, Châteauneuf's life occurs at three levels. Most of the permanent residents are busy farming the surrounding fields but there are not enough of them now to fill the village. Affluent new arrivals have moved in to take advantage of the old houses, some with spectacular views and, through their restorations, have helped preserve much that might have been lost. Châteauneuf also has summer visitors. There aren't many, mostly tourists and holidaying young, but their presence is reflected in the newly spawned boutiques, craft shops and at the one café whose tables advance boldly into the village square during the warmer months.

The little square is fortunately the focus of activity for the transient young, containing most of their chatter and noise, and on one occasion, a Protestant revival meeting of earnest boys and girls singing hymns and passing out tracts. But the kinked cobbled lanes and back alleys winding through the village are largely undisturbed. It is there that we chose to stroll in the late afternoon, past old houses and stables jammed together in a tight stone matrix. It is in the lanes and back alleys of the village that one meets the life that carries on throughout the year. Something more basic than summer visitors anchors Châteauneuf to its hill, a continuum of rural life that gives it reality and contact with the earth. A few country people still live there, tilling the soil, pasturing their cattle on the sloping meadows, and sheltering the animals in village barns, or under their own houses in the time-honoured way.

It was this aspect of Châteauneuf that we most preferred. Walking through the village and, sometimes beyond it, into the park-like landscape to the north, we returned at twilight when everyone was settling down for the night. The village was best when darkness slowly fell, and the farmer's day was over. The dark narrow streets were full of familiar sounds and comforting barnyard smells. Half-open doors showed women in skirts, aprons and kerchiefs finishing off the milking in time-worn stables, dimly lit with single hanging lamps. I shall not forget one woman tenderly watching over a new-born calf as it noisily suckled its patient mother in the soft golden light of their straw strewn barn. It was a moving tableau, a timeless setting and a timeless task, that managed to exist and seem quite at ease in both the present and the distant past at the same time.

La Voûte de Pouilly

At the time of our passage, most of the last twelve locks on the Saône side of the summit were "do it yourself" affairs, an experiment to see how it worked. The lock machinery remained much the same with simple safety devices and colour coding added on vital parts. The canal authorities hoped that the colours and the slightly confusing instructions handed out to users would explain the simple operation to even the dullest hire-boat crew. If a success, and I suppose that will be judged by the number and awfulness of the "incidents" caused by summer boaters, one can expect more such locks on this canal. Without lock-keepers, money will certainly be saved, but the canal will lose much of its vitality if they go, leaving shuttered, lifeless houses behind. We worked our way through eight of these locks with fellow barging friends, Gordon and Sylvia, aboard, and finally reached the basin at the summit. We then faced the tunnel, one of the very few obstacles on the waterways of France that requires the demounting of *Lionel*'s wheelhouse. It was not a job we contemplated with much enthusiasm.

There are tunnels on many canals in France. Although my French dictionary says a tunnel is *un tunnel*, a lot of tunnels are called *souterrains*. You become familiar with these words and use them confidently in conversation with lock-keepers. Needing information about the one at Pouilly, I chose the most commonly used, and referred to it as "le *souterrain* de Pouilly." The lock-keeper surprisingly replied: "Oui, Monsieur, vous pouvez passer la Voûte dans une heure." *La Voûte?*

Although *voûte* normally means arch or vault, *la voûte* de Pouilly-en-Auxois is indeed a tunnel. It has no tow-path, no lights and is so straight that, on entering it, you can see the other opening two miles away. The trouble with this tunnel is its low headroom: only 3.1 metres on the centre line and descending rapidly to either side of it. It is even too low for unloaded barges that must pass the tunnel in a kind of caisson that is flooded for the barge to enter and then partly pumped out to float itself but keep the barge low enough for the tunnel. Other boats sometimes tie heavy branches or timbers in a vee at bow and stern to steer themselves through on the centre line. We elected to use simpler means.

There is a colourful and macabre legend about the tunnel, current on the canal, and still believed by some. The story goes that English prisoners from the Napoleonic wars were used in the tunnel's construction. Its more lurid and improbable version says that they were bricked up inside the tunnel, fed through vent holes in the roof and told to dig their way out to the other end, burying their dead along the way behind the masonry vault. It makes good telling, but seems most unlikely, if for no other reason than the dates are wrong. The tunnel was not started until 1826, eleven years after the battle of Waterloo, time enough to release all English prisoners of war.

I didn't believe this intriguing tale and tried to discover the facts about the tunnel's construction. At last, in Dijon's Bibliothèque Municipal a bright young librarian directed me unerringly to a paper in *Les Mémoires de l'Académie de Dijon*, *1936–1938* on the history of the canal. There I found what may be the seed of the story that time and imagination have embellished. According to M Hegly, the author, *civil* prisoners were used in the construction of the tunnel. They must have been a pretty rough bunch, hard to control and unhappy at the miserable task they had been set to do. In the late nineteenth century when there were still survivors of those times living in Pouilly, it was known that a certain *chef de chantier* (superintendent of works) who had been very hard on the men under him, failed to return home one day. It was apparently common knowledge at the time that he had been killed by the workers and his body concealed behind the tunnel wall. It's surprising that much more of this sort of thing didn't happen, in view of the nature of the work and the men who were doing it.

Until 1867 boats were poled through the tunnel or pulled by hand, using a chain fixed to the vault. After that a steam tug was used, but created so many fumes in the confined space that other means had to be found. The clever and resourceful M Galliot, engineer in charge at the time, made electricity from water power at the nearby locks, and then used it to drive a tug that dragged itself back and forth through the tunnel on an underwater chain, drawing power from a live exposed copper wire looped dangerously from the arch just above a boat captain's head.

Most boats now make the tunnel passage on their own and we set about preparing *Lionel* to do just that. With Sylvia and Gordon to help, the wheelhouse came down with remarkable ease, the roof panels all stacked on the deck and the window panels either hinged down or lifted off. The bow was then armoured with as many rubber bumpers as we could tie on it and the usual spotlights mounted.

Although I had driven *Lionel* through several tunnels, I had never been through *la voûte*. Being narrower, unlighted and without a guiding tow-path, it posed new problems for a boat of *Lionel*'s width—somewhere between a commercial barge and a hire-boat. I favoured sticking to the centre line and hoping for the best, but Gordon, with more experience than I, thought the boat would hit the tunnel walls whatever one did. He recommended accepting the fact, steering slightly into one wall, and doing all the wall hitting on that side only. I thought it was an odd tactic but, deferring to experience, said nothing and we prepared the boat accordingly, with more bumpers on one side than the other.

Once in the tunnel, the constant rubbing of the bumpers against the rough masonry was so unpleasant that I abandoned the "steer into one wall" plan and kept as much as I could to the centre line, guided by the wire running down the length of the tunnel. I hit slight glancing blows on both sides anyway, but it was a relatively smooth passage in spite of the poor visibility, made worse by exhaust fumes and a condensation mist. On a later occasion with better lights on the boat, I went through this tunnel without touching either side. But however it's done, the tunnel passage is a monotonous affair, relieved only by impacts with the masonry and the pale ghostly daylight sifting down occasionally from the eleven round vents overhead. It also requires a concentration that leaves one tense and slightly dazed from watching the masonry slipping slowly by in the spotlight's

beam. The light at the end of the tunnel is truly a liberation.

We remained at Pouilly-en-Auxois for several days to work on the boat, make excursions, and what seemed at the time most important of all, find a plumber to fix our hot water heater. It was a simple job involving the thermocouple, but it had defeated me several times. Professional expertise was called for. On making enquiries, I was directed to a large house on the town square, sitting proudly in a neat formal garden. It didn't look like your average plumber's residence, and I rang the doorbell feeling I must have the wrong address. It was promptly opened by a well-dressed middle-aged woman, to reveal a prosperous interior filled with expensive furniture and good antiques. The mistress of the house immediately summoned her husband, and a few minutes later Monsieur Hurtubise descended the grand staircase in a brown woolly dressing gown, slippers and, I would guess, nothing else. I thought it very strange to be meeting my plumber in this fashion, standing there in the wide front hall of his surprising house, barely clothed, hairy white legs showing below his dressing gown and, even at ten in the morning, certainly far from ready to face the day. When I explained the problem, I half expected him to say that he only worked on large projects and couldn't consider the tiny task on our boat, but he promised to come, and in spite of three failed attempts in other towns, I felt sure he would. M Hurtubise duly arrived after lunch, possibly the start of this plumber's working day. He struggled with but repaired our hot water heater, and for his half-hour's work, extracted a substantial charge, throwing a little light perhaps on how plumbers acquire such well-feathered nests.

While at Pouilly, the liberating car allowed us to explore territory beyond the canal. The nearby village of St-Thibault, once the seat of a priory, seemed to demand such a visit. Robert II, Duke of Burgundy, and his wife, Agnés, built a church there at the end of the thirteenth century to house the relics of St Thibault. It was a time when Gothic architecture was striving for a lightness and elegance that seemed almost to defy sound structural principles. The church at St-Thibault was such a building. Perhaps it went too far. Most of it, alas, is now missing after a series of catastrophes destroyed the nave. Whether the frail Gothic structure played any part in the collapse is not known but all that remains is a fragment of the original church, the chancel, and a chapel in part of the apse. But what a fragment it is. Eighty-eight feet from stone floor to a vault seemingly held aloft by nothing but an almost entirely glass wall and the thinnest columns and mullions, looking quite incapable of the job. After the chunky grey stone houses of the little town, the impression on entering the lofty, light-flooded space is extraordinary. The airy, delicate structure seems so out of character and scale with what surrounds it, it is like walking suddenly from one world into another, from a humdrum daily existence into an exciting, lofty stage set. It is almost as if someone had severed a bit from Sainte Chapelle in Paris and, for no special reason, plunked the delicate, soaring artefact right down in the centre of a country village.

Pique-nique

Pouilly-en-Auxois, the little town that sits on top of the tunnel, is about 1,250 feet above sea level. That's not very high, but in terms of the watershed, the area around the town is unique. In all of France it is the only place that is a three-way watershed, sending its ground water through little streams to feed rivers flowing to the English Channel, the Atlantic and the Mediterranean. *Lionel* was about to follow one of these streams, l'Armançon, as it dropped almost 1,000 feet from near Pouilly to its junction with the Yonne at the northern end of the canal. That meant a lot of locks.

At the start of the descent, more birds than normal began to appear. There were the usual canal standbys: skittering moorhens and coots, the lovely little European kingfisher, a blue-green streak darting down the canal, the occasional pheasant at the edge of a field, elegant broad-winged herons, but also soaring kites, first the black, and later, red kites with their distinctive V-shaped tails. All that is easy enough for a casual bird watcher but something is bound to come along that you haven't seen before. On our boat I am the keener bird watcher, but I'm also busy steering the boat. It is not easy to examine birds with binoculars, thumb through a book and avoid hitting the bank, all at the same time.

I simplified the job, occasionally, by handing the wheel over to Melodie, but any kind of bird watching from a boat is tricky. The bird watcher is on a moving platform and the birds are moving too. Flying in and out of trees, they offer only a flash of wings before they're gone. If the light isn't right, you can't be certain what it was and a second chance seldom comes, so you pore through your book only to find nothing that closely resembles the bird you thought you saw.

The big birds are easier. One day I saw a marsh harrier, with a wing span close to four feet, flying down the canal ahead of the boat. Then there was the only goshawk I have ever seen. It was flying above a field, its underside almost white against the blue sky, with wings broader than the harrier's and almost as long. It was a big bird. As the boat passed, it landed on a hay bale, presenting a noble sight as it folded its dark wings. Something like that once in a while is, I suppose, all your run-of-the-mill, floating bird watcher can reasonably expect.

A few locks farther down, the canal narrowed to a stone-edged slit cut through a low hill with trimmed grass and mature trees on the banks. After the wilder nature we'd recently passed, the 1,200-yard-long trancheé de Creusot made us feel we'd suddenly switched from a country canal to the silent manicured landscape of an urban park. Then we went through lock after lock down the valley in a typical Burgundy landscape of gently rolling hills, a patchwork quilt of field and meadow crisscrossed by boundary lines of dark green trees.

The fluffy, parchment-coloured plumes of meadowsweet were everywhere along the banks, their sweet perfume floating across the water, blending with the scent of newly mown hay. A friend told me of an English superstition that death visits any house that meadowsweet enters. But it is of interest apart from that. Once known as meadowort, it was used to flavour mead; the herb is also sometimes called Queen of the Meadow, perhaps because of its tendency to dominate a habitat. Linnaeus classified it as *spiraea ulmaria* because the fruit has spiral elements twisted together. From the flower buds of meadowsweet salicylic acid was discovered in 1839, and it was from these that Aspirin was later synthesized, the name recalling its origin.

In a little basin near the end of a staircase of locks we spent two days moored near a friend's rented lock-house. Such houses lack many amenities, and often, in spite of their charm and low rent, need a lot of work to make them liveable. However, Robin, then the captain of a small hotel boat, had returned his to a useful life with sensitivity and restraint. The basin beside it was a secluded and idyllic resting spot with no extraneous noise from road or rail—only the gentle sound of water from the nearby locks, pastoral Burgundy on all sides and no one around to worry whether we wore anything or not when swimming.

It was Robin who suggested the picnic. It's an odd word and the French version even more so. I have for years wrongly assumed that *pique-nique* was a quaint Gallic way of dealing with the English word, but as is so often the case, it is the other way round, and one really does wonder where it came from. Anyway, Robin's picnic or *pique-nique* was to be at a *lavoir* he had discovered near the Abbaye de Fontenay.

Before the days of efficient plumbing and washing machines, women in France washed their clothes in *lavoirs*, using water from springs, streams or canals. *Lavoirs* provided hard surfaces for rubbing and beating clothes, and can vary from the simplest place beside a canal to the large, sometimes imposing ones found in towns. The *lavoir* near Fontenay was unusual. Such washing places were normally near the people who used them, but this one, surprisingly, was right in the country with no village nearby. Built into a small hill below a country road, its one open side faced a pasture with a stream running through it. The stream was also unusual. Peacefully flowing in the meadow some of the time, it then dived underground into a limestone channel, to surface again farther on as a quiet pool, and, after falling noisily over little waterfalls, disappeared once more to do its trick again across the field.

Under the sloping tiled roof of the *lavoir* were two shallow stone basins about twenty feet long filled with cold, clear spring water which flowed in at one end and out at the other through miniature sluice gates. It was a simple place, with smooth stone walls and floor, covered by a sturdy tiled wooden roof. But someone a long time ago had given thought to details. The basins were pleasantly shaped, with slightly raised stone edges angled toward the water to ease the women's task. At one end of the *lavoir* stood a massive, altar-like stone table and it was on this that we laid out our picnic of bread, cheese, lettuce, raw carrots, cucumber, zucchini, fruit and wine.

When the picnic was over and the others were wandering off, Melodie, a keen cold water swimmer, decided on the spur of the moment to immerse her whole naked person in the chilly water of one of the basins. This she did, laying herself out in the few available icy inches of water like a pale, unclothed and slightly overweight Ophelia. She didn't stay submerged for long, but the sight of Melodie afloat full length in a *lavoir* will not soon flee from the memory of her sole observer.

The nearby Abbaye de Fontenay was founded by St Bernard in 1118 on the site of a hermitage, and moved twelve years later to what was then a marshy place with many springs and streams, as indicated by the root of the name in the Latin word, *fontanetum*, meaning spring. The buildings one sees today are little changed from the way they looked in the fifteenth century at the zenith of the Abbey's prosperity and importance, home to 300 monks and lay brothers. It had more buildings then but the essential ones are still there. The great church of the Abbey and the Cloister are as they were when completed in the twelfth century. The chapter house, dormitory, scriptorium, warming hall, infirmary, dungeon, dovecote, bakery, kitchens, forge, even the Duke of Burgundy's kennels, all still exist. In view of the fires, plunderings, near collapses, additions, revolutionary assaults, rebuildings, restorations and an eighty-six-year life as a paper factory, it seems remarkable that so many of its original parts remain at all.

The Cistercians are an austere order both in the rigour of their rule and in their architecture. As at Cîteaux, the monks at Fontenay slept on straw mattresses, fully clothed, in a common unheated dormitory. They had none of the customary cells found in other monasteries and knew no privacy in their lives, even during the night. Their asceticism was reflected in the buildings they used. They were basic, almost utilitarian, devoid of any but the most minimal decoration. It was the architecture that saved the abbey from the destructive excesses of the French Revolution, its plainness enough to mollify the wilder whims of its anti-clerical leaders.

Only after the monastery's material and moral decay began in the sixteenth century did decoration appear in a few of the Abbey buildings. The great nave of the church is almost exactly as it was in 1147 and it is, indeed, plain. The only things to be seen that could be called embellishment are a few slightly raised lines on the column capitals. Yet there is something magnificent about its simplicity, the physical presence in stone of St Bernard's beliefs, his reaction against the luxuries and distractions he found in other monasteries of the time.

Besides being undecorated and stripped to its essentials, the church was also empty, not just lacking people but what the people used to do there. It had become a great stone artefact with no animating spirit. It needed the monks not just because they were human beings, it needed them more for the focus of their ritual and their faith; the bare place seemed to offer no reminder of the purpose it once served. Perhaps others were conscious of this. As we stood on the steps of the chancel, Robin remarked that on an earlier visit a friend had chanted a mantra from the same spot. I had some reservations about that choice and perhaps Melodie did as well. Although now following the Buddhist tradition she had sung Slavonic Russian in the choir of a Russian Orthodox Church for twenty years, and a moment later I heard her clear voice singing a part of the Orthodox liturgy. The lovely flute-like sounds reverberated throughout that severe, unadorned place in a way that moved us all. Perhaps it was only a hint of what we felt lacking, but it was a glorious moment and for me, Fontenay will always be remembered for that small interval when the music of the ancient Russian church rang through the vast and empty nave.

Buffon's Forge

Boats have a fearful appetite for repairs. They never seem really happy without some part of their anatomy crying out noisily to be fixed. On the Burgundy it was the deck railings that needed welding, and I sought out a journeyman welder I'd heard about from my friend, Gordon. Monsieur Beaudet of Venarey les Laumes was reputed to be an artisan of reasonable competence and cost. He came to the boat by scooter to examine the job, wearing a helmet and dark visor, which after dismounting, he removed and replaced with a shiny, dark brown, fake leather fedora—a hat to which he was greatly devoted because, Melodie guessed, it hid the bald spot on the top of his head. A shortish man in his early forties, with a bushy moustache and bad nasal congestion, he fed the latter at frequent intervals with medicinal snuff, clearing his nasal passages each time with a very unmusical honking noise. Beaudet seemed quite convinced the medicinal snuff, brought by Gordon from England, was helping his condition but it did occur to me that the wretched stuff might very well be more the problem than the cure.

The next morning *Lionel* was poled backwards down the canal to a mooring beside Beaudet's workshop where he and a helper began replacing some of the boat's rusty railings. During the day it took, Beaudet's helper did most of the work while Beaudet himself stood around casually doing quite unnecessary supervision and smoking a cigar, which he lit off the steel, red hot from welding. Gordon reported that Beaudet's effectiveness as a welder was greatly reduced in the late afternoon by the vast quantities of beer and wine he consumed, but in the supervisory role he adopted on *Lionel*, it didn't seem to make much difference.

Having paid Monsieur Beaudet's bill, a notch or two above Gordon's idea of "reasonable," we moved down the canal to a better mooring. As I barbecued our dinner, I watched the animals of a travelling circus that was spending the night on the other bank. The more dangerous beasts—tigers and a large white monkey—were miserable prisoners in their small travelling cages, and gazed disconsolately out on a world they would never roam again. The herbivores were luckier. Tethered along the canal were horses, some with foals, and ponies of several varieties and colours, all munching grass with their incongruous companions, a vicuña, some llamas, a dromedary and a two-humped Bactrian camel. Later in the evening we watched, with some interest, several attempts to breed a large mare to smaller suitors who seemed not up to the task and despondently retired from the scene.

Montbard, eight locks farther on, is a small industrial town, which was the home of the eighteenth century naturalist, Leclerc, Comte de Buffon. His monumental thirty-six-volume *Histoire Naturelle*, was one of the first great works of its kind. But to canal travellers he is better known for la Grande Forge, which he built on the small river Armançon about three miles from Montbard. When the canal was constructed several years later, it followed the valley of the Armançon and now passes close to the forge. There, a curving stone quay offers one of the best moorings on the canal, with the eighteenth-century buildings and machinery of the forge only a few steps away.

After experimenting with local iron ores, Buffon built the forge on his own land between 1768 and 1772. It is remarkable today for being one of the few industrial operations from that period with most of its buildings still extant. Because of poor transport, forges of this sort were dependent on the immediate locality for everything they needed: a river for water power, easily accessible iron ore, and a large forest nearby for the production of the charcoal required in iron making. Buffon's chosen location had all these. Peasants from the vicinity were used for general labour, and skilled workmen were brought in from outside and lived in specially built lodgings on the site. At its peak the forge employed about 330 men, annually producing 360 tons of useable iron—much of it of the quality needed for gun barrels strong enough to resist the periodic explosions that had embarrassed the French army so frequently in the past.

The forge is also interesting for the physical presence of the stone structures, which in combination with the all-important water and an intimate enveloping landscape, produce a composition of great charm. I always enjoy visiting the forge if for no other reason than the simple pleasure of walking among the buildings clustered beside the river, looking at the huge trip hammer required for forging iron, and seeing the great wooden water-wheels that generated the power needed for all its operations: crushing the iron ore, working the great bellows of the blast furnace, and slitting and rolling iron bars.

Nearly all the buildings survive from the days when this was a working forge, and those that didn't have been meticulously restored to their original condition. The most impressive building houses the blast furnace. Its main room, with a ceiling twenty or more feet high, is entered from ten feet above the floor by a grand split staircase, curving down in two graceful wings. The massive vertical furnace, holding the iron ore and charcoal, extends thirty-five feet above the bottom opening. Out of this, the molten iron flowed onto a sand bed to form an ingot weighing almost a ton. There it cooled for seven hours before being treated and worked.

Each year the furnace was lit in the autumn and kept going until the following spring when work in the forge stopped for the warmer months. A huge pair of bellows brought the temperature in the furnace up to 2,700 degrees Fahrenheit, the fusion point of iron ore. These restored bellows have been superbly handmade from oak, to the pattern of the originals, and a similar high standard of craftsmanship pervades all the wooden devices used in the forge including the enormous water-wheels. Now privately owned it is being meticulously revived as a living record of the eighteenth century Burgundian iron forge. Buffon thought of his forge as a model factory and, for his time, it undoubtedly was, even to the simple housing for his skilled workers provided in a nearby building. Now the old forge has assumed a museum role, and in this new life it is also an outstanding model of how that should be done.

Ring of Kneeling Women

At Tanlay, Joss immediately leapt ashore to explore the local scene and do a thing or two she had on her mind. She had always been a live-and-let-live kind of dog, minding her own business and ignoring the rude advances of eager French males. She was aloof by nature and reluctant to get involved in what she considered rather dicey situations but mixed in with that was a large portion of plain cowardice. She was not a brave dog, retreat always seeming in her mind greatly preferable to bloody confrontation. Joss had already been brutally attacked without provocation by a huge black Great Dane bitch, who out of nowhere came charging at her broadside in the lobby of a Dutch hotel. In Dijon, an equally large hairy white dog had leaped off a boat and gone for Joss without warning. She was only slightly damaged but badly frightened on both occasions and was understandably wary of the same thing happening again.

Joss was, by then, fourteen, less sure-footed than in her prime and bothered with arthritis. One of us always kept an eye on her, even aboard the boat, but especially when she was poking about in enemy territory around our moorings. It was lucky that we did at Tanlay. Suddenly spooked by another dog, Joss made a dash for *Lionel*'s ramp, attempted to scramble up, missed her footing and plunged head first off the quay into the water,

disappearing rapidly beneath the boat. Although, like all dogs, Joss could swim, water was by far her least favoured element. She disliked it, didn't want to do anything but drink it, and when immersed, struggled in panic to get out of it. On surfacing, she started thrashing wildly between the boat and the high stone quay. There was no means of escape and Joss would certainly have drowned in a few minutes if Melodie had not quickly yanked her out, legs flailing, by the heavy leather collar worn for this very kind of emergency.

At Tanlay, and a little farther south at Ancy le Franc are two of the most important châteaux on the canal. Both were built in the middle of the sixteenth century but otherwise have little in common. It is almost as if they represented the male and the female of the species château. Ancy-le-Franc is a stern, macho block of a place, boring in its rectangular plainness and absence of architectural invention. Tanlay, on the other hand, is all fun and games. It is adorned with a decorative moat, balustrades, obelisk pillars, low wings embracing a wide entrance court, domed towers, fancy dormer windows and cupolas. The white stone château sits in a large expanse of cut grass looking gay and inviting, even a little frivolous.

I have always hated guided tours. You usually hear more than you want about something of only passing interest, in the company of listless, shuffling strangers, herded from room to room at an agonizingly slow pace. At Tanlay, however, a tour was the only means of seeing the inside, so we joined a mixed bag of people assembling for the next one. We soon realized it had been a mistake. The rooms were full of dreadful paintings, worn-out furniture, second-rate antiques and dusty photographs of dead European royals. Only the large principal room on the tour was mildly interesting, its walls and ceiling covered with grey *trompe l'œil* murals of classical motifs. Yet it was not even a fine example of this visual trickery and soon after, with the guide's attention distracted, we sneaked away down the stairs, to spend the rest of our time to better effect wandering in the garden and visiting an art exhibition in the old stables.

Tonnerre, probably more than other towns on the Canal de Bourgogne, is enhanced by water: not only the canal itself but the Armançon and its tributaries which nose their way between old houses in the lower part of the town. From *Lionel*'s mooring under a magnificent row of trees our daily walks into Tonnerre took us across the river and its branches each with vistas of old houses overhanging their banks, then up the main street past an unobtrusive but moving little wall plaque erected to the memory of a Resistance fighter killed on that spot by the Germans.

Farther along one passes the great bulk of the Ancien hôpital, built in the late thirteenth century by Marguerite de Bourgogne, and a survivor of the disastrous fire in the sixteenth century that destroyed much of Tonnerre. Although later shortened, the immense pitched roof still shelters the single great space of the Salle des Malades below, 260 feet long by 60 feet wide. Under its magnificent oak vaulting, forty patients could be cared for in wooden alcoves along the walls. The building continued to be used as a hospital until the seventeenth century, when it was then used by a parish church, not to care for the living, but to bury the dead. Their flat gravestones now partly pave the wide floor, sharing it with signs of the Zodiac, and the incised lines of an eighteenth-century sundial, using rays of the sun beamed through a small hole high up on one wall.

Whenever in Tonnerre, however, there is one place that I always make a special point of visiting. La Fosse Dionne is an unusual and remarkable *lavoir*, one of those old public washing places that still survive all over France. Although it functioned in its day as a place for women to wash clothes, La Fosse Dionne is in a class of its own if not unique. *Lavoirs* come in a great variety of forms and sizes: small, large, rectangular, U-shaped, round. There are grand urban ones and simple country ones to shelter two women beside a canal. There is a round one at Brienon, near the north end of the canal, an unbroken circle of paving and sheltering roof enclosing a round pool. The perfect circle is appealing but I found it a disappointment, having only roundness and none of the spirit that enlivens La Fosse Dionne, tucked away on a back street in Tonnerre, and the only other round *lavoir* I know.

La Fosse Dionne is unique, and I constantly return there for its seclusion and the silent beauty of the place. Almost concealed by towering old houses at the foot of a hill, this quiet, lovely eye in the swirl and clatter of bustling Tonnerre has qualities that transcend its simple original purpose. Built over an old spring, it was, strictly speaking, a place to wash clothes and, as a working *lavoir* it must have been quite different from what one sees now. It would not have been such a tranquil, deserted place then, but alive with a ring of kneeling women, chattering, slapping and scrubbing at their washing. Women don't go to such places anymore to kneel in the cold on hard stone. The old *lavoir* now sits unused and undisturbed, barring a handful of curious tourists wandering in off the beaten track.

But, whether used as a *lavoir* or not seems irrelevant for La Fosse Dionne. It has always been more than just that. The word *fosse* means roughly, "hole in the ground," and this *lavoir* is built over such a cavity or, more accurately, an underwater cave. Apart from anything else the setting is magnificent, but out of the cave comes an abundance of amazingly coloured water. In the round basin, its colour varies from the light blue/green of a tropical lagoon at its edge, becoming a dark green near the centre and finally a deep blue as the bottom falls away, finally becoming lost to sight in the cavern from where the water wells up.

Although La Fosse Dionne is remarkable for its incredible water, it is also remarkable for the care taken in its design. The pool is round, but the arms of the eighteenth-century shelter wrapped around the basin leave a third of the perimeter open to the south, allowing the sun to enter. When in use, women knelt under the roof, washing their laundry in a narrow channel of water, fed by the basin but at a lower level, so the clear spring water was never polluted by the washing. The dirty water was carried away around the basin and fed into a stream as it left the basin in miniature waterfalls. There are even little shelves built into the columns to hold washing materials.

The joining in this place of deep turquoise water from an extraordinary spring and the mundane job of washing clothes has been so thoughtfully handled that each can exist without hurting the other. It is a remarkable place. Its original usefulness has now gone, and a serene, still presence remains. Within the sheltering arms of its surrounding walls, the mottled blue and green disc of La Fosse Dionne is like a large dark emerald held within a setting of rough-hewn stone.

Barges and Spiders

St-Florentin is the last town of any size on the canal before it reaches its northern end at the Yonne River. The final miles are blighted by mainline railway tracks, yet there is still one beautiful stretch left where the canal is lined on both sides with large poplars. Their thick, grey, pole-like trunks, eight feet apart, form a continuous colonnade, following the gentle curves of the meandering canal. Each tree is loaded with mistletoe, like globes of green filigree spread throughout the branches according to some secret parasitic urge. Lower down, the trunks wear green sleeves of climbing vine, their small bright emerald leaves reaching twelve to fifteen feet above the ground.

On the Canal de Bourgogne, commercial barges are now rarely seen, although a few go up to Dijon from the Saône, and the larger towns at the northern end bring some into the canal from the Yonne. As a route between the Seine and the Saône, however, the more efficient Canal du Centre farther west seems to be preferred. It has fewer locks and more certain water than the Burgundy which is sometimes closed for lack of it. It is this very scarcity of barges that has allowed the Canal de Bourgogne to become shallow in places, for it is the scouring action of the loaded barges themselves that keeps small canals dredged.

The shallow water in the canal is a problem for the few barges still navigating it. Attempting to moor one evening, we encountered water so shallow that *Lionel* went aground some distance from the bank. While trying to sort this out, a loaded barge approached. Expecting its passage to cause *Lionel*'s bow or stern to swing out, Melodie and I held the boat with grapnels thrown into the greenery on the bank. As the barge slowly passed *Lionel* in a maelstrom of swirling mud, the *marinier* and I both commented on the shallow water. We were plainly aground and his barge, though loaded only to the permitted depth, was scraping the bottom.

Because of turbulence caused by the passage of loaded barges, *Lionel* needs solid things to put ropes around. There were no bollards about but trees would do and I decided to moor. We threw grapnels into a verdant tangle as high as elephant grass and drew the boat alongside it. The trees weren't quite the right distance apart but I used them anyway and drove in two additional heavy steel stakes for the spring lines, to stop back-and-forth movement. As I had resigned myself to expect there were stones under each stake. They always seem to be there, a little boulder, the size of a billiard ball beneath the point, needing several vicious blows with a heavy sledge before breaking through to softer stuff.

To do all this, I had to hack my way through growth higher than my head, thick with nettles that stung my hands, climbing vines that caught my feet and a whirling cloud of bloodthirsty mosquitos zinging about my head. Having struggled several times through this intertwined, malevolent ecology, beating little jungle trails from boat to tree one, boat to tree two, boat to stake one, boat to stake two and back again each time, I retired to the wheelhouse sweaty, stung, scratched and exhausted. I thought we were secure for the night.

Resting in the wheelhouse, I saw a strange craft approaching, or rather two, one pushing the other. It didn't look like the kind of boat that would disturb *Lionel* but it was going too fast, and I saw with alarm that the strange tandem affair displaced a lot of water for its size. The effect on *Lionel* was like that of a loaded barge. It sloshed violently one way and the other, disarranging the hard won moorings and pulling out a stake, nearly lost to the canal. So back into the jungle trails I went, got the moorings together again and once more returned to the boat. At this moment a young man came bicycling down the towpath on the far side of the canal. He had been driving the tandem rig when it had passed us. Perhaps unaware of the peculiar things that passing boats can do to each other in

canals, he'd had a useful lesson in fluid dynamics at our expense. Seeing what happened, he had come back to apologize for the trouble he'd caused. It was a courteous and rare gesture of concern which *Lionel*'s crew greatly appreciated. The boat was the *Leontyine*, and they were filming a journey from London to Vienna, which later resulted in both a series of television programs and a book.

In the misty morning that followed, with water dripping from the thick foliage of overhanging trees and the abundant growth beside the boat, our mooring took on the atmosphere of a dense rain forest. The spiders had been busy overnight, their perfect webs hanging from ropes and railings, clearly outlined with tiny crystal balls of dew. One couldn't walk anywhere on the deck without disturbing them, the wet filaments clinging to hands, arms, legs and unwary faces. I don't think it mattered much to the spiders for the webs had already done their nightly work and would be built again that evening.

Orb-weaving spiders are fascinating stowaways, and we often watched them at work. First came anchor lines, followed by radial lines like the spokes of a wheel. These were followed by a few spiral turns and the closer-spaced sticky spirals to trap insects, the earlier spirals being cut away in this last process. The silk itself is amazing stuff, coming in seven types from the same insect, some of it ten times stronger than Kevlar, the synthetic fibre used for bulletproof vests. The whole thing is built with amazing mechanical sophistication, and according to Fritz Vollrath of Oxford

University, even uses sliding joints, shock absorbers and spring-loaded cable drums. The web must be strong enough to withstand the impact of large insects without tearing. To achieve this the single layer web of the orb-weaving spider uses a silk that is a form of reinforced rubber. Its cunning trick is to transform the energy of an insect impact into heat which strengthens the silk and prevents it tearing.

What we could see of their habits was interesting enough but there is more than that. The mating alone is a tricky business. The smaller male must approach the female with extreme care, vibrating the web in a special way he hopes will inform his bride that he's not just another meal. But the bride hasn't seen anything like him before and could easily make a fatal error, so the courtship is a very delicate affair, and another female, a kind of chaperon, sometimes presides over the love dance that precedes the mating. Once the mating is over, the male retires quickly to avoid being eaten but dies soon anyway, his job done and all passion spent.

When the spiderlings emerge from their eggs, they perch on a twig or piece of grass. There they spin a fine gossamer a foot or two long and wait for something to happen. Soon a breeze will lift them off for a flight to the next field, the next country or even more exotic places. Such gossamers have been found in the rigging of ships at sea, even thousands of feet in the air. Darwin saw large numbers of spiderlings landing in *Beagle*'s rigging when she was sixty miles from land and they have been reported even 200 miles out to sea.

Melodie and I became attached to these fellow travellers aboard *Lionel*. They each had their own daytime living quarters, hidden away under or behind something, and their own territories to construct the delicate webs that supply their food. The bigger spiders seemed content to share their territories with far smaller ones under some sort of ladies' agreement. We and the spiders had a similar understanding. We welcomed them aboard and allowed them to do what they must, providing that was not inside the boat. The larger ones, wandering misguidedly into the wheelhouse, were gently removed and returned to a perch outside where food was more plentiful. It all worked very well. *Lionel* has been home to scores of spiders each summer. They have never been a nuisance but more a bonus, familiar shipboard colleagues who went about their work at sundown every day, in an intricate routine so fascinating we never tired of watching it.

Old Dog, New Tricks

In the intervening year between our two trips on the Canal de Bourgogne we returned to France as usual with the object of going to Strasbourg, a city far to the east in Alsace which we had not seen before. Black-spotted Joss was with us on the flight to Paris, travelling in her large cage, an unhappy and bizarre piece of baggage jammed into the dark belly of the aircraft, unfamiliar shapes and sounds her only companions on the long journey from Toronto. She had been given a tranquillizer against the stress of air travel and arrived at Orly stoned as usual, but physically none the worse for the ordeal.

Joss was then in her fifteenth year, old for a Dalmatian, and suffering from a recurring ailment that demanded special food. In Canada this was available in cans, but the logistics and cost of transporting the dead weight of more than two hundred cans across the Atlantic by air were too much to contemplate and attempts to have the cans sent to France from Belgium by the only source in Europe failed utterly.

The eventual solution was a made-up formula specially prepared by Melodie for the four meals Joss was required to eat each day. Some of the scarcer materials for this occupied much of the space in our luggage. Apart from numerous boxes and jars of this and that, there were several large plastic bags of a white powder that I felt certain would put the Orly *douane* on red alert. They appeared, however, to be quite disinterested, neither checking our bags nor even looking at Joss's papers. The three of us sailed through the critical zone without the least hassle and onward to our rented car.

A night in a hotel south of Paris restored lost sleep, but on the way to an early morning walk, Joss's disturbed insides tossed Melodie a challenge she was loath to face at any time or place, but especially in a hotel. Going down a corridor, our old friend, now an incontinent and indisposed old friend, couldn't wait for the greenery outside and simply did what she had to do, right there on the carpet. It was not an easy crisis to deal with. Melodie did what she could, but acknowledging defeat, went in desperation to the kitchen for extra materials. She got what she needed, with some nasty comments as well, and returned to our room determined that from that time on, Joss the ticking time bomb, would go only to hotels providing rapid egress to the great outdoors.

Leaving Joss's mark behind, we went to the little port of Mailly la Ville, where we'd left *Lionel* moored for the winter. Once again water made its presence known in places where it didn't belong. The gentle sound of the stuff running from a hidden source under the kitchen counter was only the harbinger of more to come, but it, at least, explained the mysterious emptying of *Lionel*'s main water tank and one should, I suppose, have been grateful for that. This first leak from a frozen pipe was followed quickly by a leaking water pump, the long overdue replacement of the water pressure tank and a large wet spot on the floor of Melodie's cabin. I thought the last had been put there by Joss in one of her more insouciant moments, but it turned out to be a gusher from a pipe under her bed. However, these watery problems were soon fixed, and seemed relatively tame when compared to the drama of the previous start of the season in Holland.

My next challenge was to wade through French bureaucracy in order to get our small car properly registered and licensed. The car had been bought many months before in the south of France and its registration document (*carte grise*) obtained there. Because of this I couldn't acquire the annual registration sticker (*vignette*) in the north and resolved to change the *carte grise* to give me "residence" in the Yonne Department where *Lionel* was then based. For a boat dweller, with no permanent address, this is not always easy, but with a letter saying I resided in the port of Auxerre, I advanced with shaky confidence on the outer fringes of the departmental bureaucracy. The first skirmish went well. Although the letter was a minor deception, it was not questioned and I was told that the new *carte grise* would be forthcoming when the office computer was fixed.

Several days later I was the first to arrive at what I thought was the right wicket in the *prefecture*, and was joined there shortly by a pushy crowd, intent on getting ahead of each other and me. When told we were at the wrong wicket, the others all easily beat me to the right one at the end of the hall. By the time I got there too I was at the end of a long line. There was nothing to be done but wait patiently and gaze in wonder at French bureaucracy in action beyond the counter, foot-high stacks of files randomly littering every desk.

The more fortunate members of the waiting group got their *cartes grises* in what looked like a bureaucratic lucky dip, but the precious documents for ten of us could not be found. Flustered women riffled through files and piles of papers, finding the missing documents one by one until our small impatient band finally dwindled down to me, the sole remaining witness to the paper chase. Thirty minutes passed. Then someone sheepishly appeared with a large brown envelope, clearly marked with my name. At last, with the *carte grise* in my hand, I bought the *vignette* at the Hôtel des Impôts and with new licence plates stamped out in a matter of minutes, the car was finally ready to face the *gendarmerie* of Burgundy.

Once established on board *Lionel* again, it was obvious that Joss could no longer deal with the boat's steep stairs in the carefree ways of her youth. Back then, with four good legs, she handled these stairs with almost excessive abandon. It always looked haphazard to me, bounding leaps up, and descents like barely controlled falls. Now weakened by old age and arthritis, Joss was fearful of the stairs. It hurt her to climb them, and since she was no longer able to make it on her own, one of us was there to give her a shove from behind. Without help, going down became a Dalmatian avalanche, ending in a crumpled, hurting heap on the floor below. To prevent this, we held her back by the collar so she could land under reasonable control and dignity at the bottom. Poor old Joss needed a lot of care in those days, but we loved her very much and begrudged none of it.

Our time at Mailly la Ville always seemed to be shorter than we would like, but barely had we arrived than we felt the urge to leave. In the spring, at the beginning of a new season, there is an almost irresistible itch to get underway again, and we shortly headed north down the Canal du

Nivernais towards Auxerre, a familiar old friend for us both. After buying our barge in 1982, we spent a winter there converting it while moored on the Yonne. During that winter and a few months the following year we came to know Auxerre well. Moored on the opposite side of the river we delighted in the magnificent view of the town climbing up to its summit crowned by the Cathedral of St Etienne and the excitement of it when floodlit at night. From that time on, returning to Auxerre was like putting on a favourite old coat with its easy fit, familiar smell and warm associations. During those few days we wandered the well-known streets again, saw old friends and stocked up *Lionel* with food and wine for the trip ahead.

When moored against the quay at Auxerre a reporter from a local newspaper came on board one day. We could hardly be the source of interesting hard news but she may have been intrigued by the Canadian flag at *Lionel*'s stern and needed a little story to fill a corner of her paper. We had a brief conversation after which she left and I departed for London to see a publisher. On my return I was surprised and a little concerned when Melodie told me she had been interviewed by the reporter. Mon Dieu! I thought. What did she say? Melodie must have known I might be worried for she was quoted in the paper as saying: "Il pense que mon français n'est pas bien et que je parle tout le temps." The reporter went on to wind up her piece with a little romantic thought *à la française*: "Ils promènent sur l'eau une éternelle jeunesse. Avec cette seule recette: vivre d'amour et d'eau vive." The article was headed in bold type: **Deux amoureux au fil de l'eau** and carried a four-column-wide photograph of the lovers standing on their boat. We were overwhelmed.

We left these romantic thoughts behind in Auxerre and headed down the Yonne on a fine warm day. The following afternoon, after an overnight stop at Joigny, we arrived at Sens, a town we had always liked. Although long familiar from earlier visits, the great Cathedral of St Etienne invariably drew us back. Built in the twelfth century, it was the first of the great cathedrals to appear in France and expressed the daring, freshness and vigour of early Gothic. It was also a strong influence on William of Sens, the architect/builder who later reconstructed the choir of Canterbury Cathedral.

Beside the cathedral, a little museum housing its treasures had recently been re-opened. It contained the usual chalices, reliquaries, vestments and archaeological odds and ends that one would expect in such a place. They were well displayed, all of interest and a few exceptional, but there was also something unexpected. In 1164, Thomas à Becket had come to

France as an exile after his dispute with Henry II and lived in Sens for four years. In a room of the museum, there is a case holding some of Becket's liturgical vestments. While interesting merely for their historical importance, what struck me most about them was their size. Contrary to my image of the man, he was not of medium height, but, judging from his cope, very tall, and if his slippers provide a clue, the owner of enormous feet!

On a day of sun and scattered, puffy clouds we reached the Seine at Montereau. There we took on 540 litres of gasoil, largely without the help of the service station's *patron*, half-drunk, red-faced and far from jolly after a boozy lunch. Then through one of the large, efficient Seine locks to spend the night at Samois, an attractive little town at the northern edge of the Forest of Fontainebleau, with roses hanging over its stone garden walls. Elegant Parisians have weekend houses there and the less affluent come for an extended Sunday lunch in a riverside restaurant or a boat trip on the Seine.

Almost the entire focus of our stay in Samois, however, had to do with our mooring and the problems it posed for Joss. The Seine, like most rivers, offers few places where boats can be safely tied, and in spite of friends' assurances to the contrary, this was true of Samois where all the best spots had been taken. The only place remaining was a steep overgrown bank and a few trees to put ropes around. It was secure enough, but access to the road above would not only be difficult for us, but quite impossible for Joss. So we went to work with two hatchets, the only available tools, and cleared the brush out of the way and cut steps in the bank.

Joss eyed the finished project with some mistrust, but gamely allowed herself to be pushed and cajoled up the precipitous slope, straining to bring into play as many of her increasingly deficient legs as possible. While the ascent required power, which Joss lacked but we could easily provide, the descent needed brakes. A human substitute for these was more difficult to contrive, and with the Seine at the bottom of the slope, the hazards considerably greater.

With Melodie down below, Joss and I launched ourselves from the top, her leash and tail firmly gripped in my hands. Joss didn't want any part of it, and once committed to the descent, simply sat down on her collapsed rear legs. Having become a kind of canine toboggan, with me still hanging on to her tail, she slithered to the bottom where Melodie stopped her downward rush before she plopped into the Seine. It was an arduous and nerve-wracking business that was hard on us all and only the most dire necessity could persuade us to attempt it again.

Under grey and showery skies the following day we cruised down the Seine through all but two of the remaining locks before Paris. After an overnight mooring at an old stone quay near Viry Chatillon we started our final day's run into Paris. Approaching Melun, large, fanciful houses decorated the riverbanks, romantic turn-of-the-century concoctions, set on wide, carefully tended grounds. The architects had clearly enjoyed themselves. Given understanding clients, lots to spend and few constraints, they had played with all the tricks of the trade, in a time when every architect's bag was full of them: steep pitched roofs, fancy dormer windows, slender high chimneys with corbelled tops, half-timbering, elaborately decorated balconies, turrets, towers, cupolas and a fantasia of materials and patterns.

After the frivolous riverside houses, the grim prison at Melun was an especially depressing sight, its inmates enclosed within stone walls, thirty feet high, armed men in guard posts along its top. Then on down the river, past a lone cormorant sitting on a post, an unusual sight so far from the sea, and after two more locks, Paris closed around us. Its bridges jumped the Seine ever more frequently, steel ones, stone ones, train ones, road ones, until finally a small, dark opening appeared in the high river wall on the starboard side. This was the entrance to the Arsenal, our Paris destination.

Paris by the Back Door

Mooring near the centre of Paris can be a problem. Boats may use some of the quays on the Seine for short periods, but there is risk of theft, break-in, vandalism or a bottle casually tossed by a passing youth. Some *gardiennage* seems essential, whether by a *marinier* living on his barge or in a marina.

Mooring to a barge is a solution if you know the right person, have his permission, and accept the nuisance of clambering over another boat to get to the shore (in our case with an infirm dog) and back again with loaded shopping bags. It would also be prudent to find out when the barge is departing, in order to avoid what happened to the boat a friend was aboard two or three years before. It was tied to a commercial barge whose captain decided to leave early one morning. He had unfortunately omitted to inform his neighbours about this. They woke up later to find themselves underway, on a trip to God knew where, alongside a 350 tonner!

There is a lot to be said for the marina. Paris has at least two well-known possibilities in its centre. One at the Place de la Concorde, once run by the now defunct Touring Club of France, has serious drawbacks, being on a narrow section of the river where the wash of heavy barge traffic creates random choppy waves that constantly rock the moored boats.

Moreover, it is a long way from shops selling basic supplies, separated even from the Rue de Rivoli and fashionable Faubourg St-Honoré by cars sweeping around the Place de la Concorde, a hazardous asphalt desert at the best of times.

So it was to the other that we decided to go, the Port de Plaisance de Paris-Arsenal. I had called them twice earlier by telephone and VHF radio to make sure there was space, and spoke to the *capitainerie* again when *Lionel* was waiting in the Seine just below the entrance lock. This lock, under the broad riverside road is not only deep but dark as a cave. Coming from the bright light outside, it looked and felt like a black hole with few discernible features. We entered hesitantly, not knowing what we'd find inside. Fortunately equipped with floating bollards which, after a good deal of shouting back and forth, we got ropes around before the water poured in. When the gates opened at the top we sailed into the calm basin of the port and tied up with some difficulty to a tiny floating pontoon, far too short for *Lionel*. After reporting to the *capitainerie* the boat was moved farther down the basin to a mooring alongside an unoccupied barge, oddly enough a familiar one, last seen in the Midi with friends aboard.

After the cavernous entrance lock, arriving in the Arsenal is like slipping into the centre of the great city by a hidden back door. One is speedily and magically transported from the separate, hurly-burly world of the Seine into the very heart of Paris. Notre Dame is just around the corner downstream, and at the far end of the long port, the great monument marking the opening act of the French Revolution rises from the Place de la Bastille, where the new Paris Opera, designed by a Canadian architect, was then under construction. After several days on the river, we were suddenly in the midst of the city's life, its buildings, its people, its noises, smells, cafés and movement. It was an arm's length contact, however, for the port is about twenty feet below the level of the streets, protecting it from much of the noise, and offering excellent security for over 200 hundred boats moored in its length, with guard dogs even patrolling the quays at night.

The present Port de Plaisance is a newcomer to this part of Paris. There was no water there until the Canal St-Martin was built in the early nineteenth century to link the Seine with the Ourcq (both canal and river), which wanders off to the east of Paris. The boats are now moored in a widened part of this canal almost half-a-mile long. Much earlier, it was the site of a royal arsenal with a foundry for cannon and seven mills producing gunpowder. The latter blew sky high in 1563, making a bang heard even in Melun, thirty miles away, and the dangerous explosives operation was moved to la Saltpêtrière, later to become, under the same name, one of the city's great hospitals.

In the next century Cardinal Richelieu established a court of justice at the old Arsenal to deal with unusual crimes. Nicolas Fouquet, the *procureur général* to the parliament of Paris under Louis XIV, was tried there for embezzling state funds. Towards the end of the seventeenth century the Arsenal was still a place where criminals of a special sort were dealt with. Starting with the Marquise de Brinvilliers who had been executed in 1676 for poisoning her father and two brothers, an epidemic of poisoning swept through the Parisian upper classes. A finger was finally pointed at a woman called Voisin, thought to be responsible for the commerce in poisons. At her trial she implicated several figures in the aristocracy, even the court, and before things went rapidly from bad to worse she was summarily condemned and burnt alive.

Today the Arsenal is a generous urban marina, attractively landscaped, secure and well serviced by the humming city close at hand with its Metro, restaurants, galleries, cafés and plentiful shopping just a climb up from water level. Although Melodie found the twenty-foot vertical trip between quay and street a chore with shopping caddy added, there were enough delights to be found at the upper level to obscure concern about the physical effort needed to get there. In every way, it was a convenient and pleasant place to spend two weeks in Paris and though hardly cheap, cost far less than most hotels.

The first part of our route to Strasbourg was not the more direct one up the Marne. The river had been closed for months because of repairs to a weir, and we had to go the long way, down the Seine and up the Oise, before turning east. Rather than leaving the Arsenal via the Seine, we chose the Canal St-Martin and the Canal St-Denis, winding through the back streets and northern suburbs of Paris before joining the Seine again in St-Denis. Together, they cut off a big bend in the river, shortening the normal barge route through Paris by almost twelve miles.

Toward the end of June, with our Canadian friend, Joe, aboard, we finally left the port and headed for the gaping maw of the tunnel carrying the Canal St-Martin under the Place de la Bastille. It is a one-way tunnel, a little over a mile long, controlled by traffic lights, and has unusually generous, comforting dimensions. The tow-paths on either side increase the feeling of space but it is dark—only dim shafts of daylight from above occasionally pierce the gloom—and we had to navigate through the tunnel with the usual array of spotlights mounted on the bow.

Lionel emerged into a sun-splashed Paris street scene. Plane trees lined both sides of the canal and delicate iron pedestrian bridges arched elegantly over the water at the locks. It was full of colour and life, and the backdrop of old buildings was so well composed and picturesque, it was easy to see why this location had been popular with French film-makers who had used it to shoot parts of both *Les Enfants du paradis* and *L'Hôtel du nord*. Alas, this delightful canal soon came to an end as we turned left onto the Canal St-Denis for an entirely different experience. Passing largely through the industrial zones of the northern suburbs, it was a down-to-earth working canal with twinned locks, heavy barge use, little to enjoy, nothing to attract film-makers, and we left it without sorrow.

Seventy Days in Auvers

Rejoining the Seine again in the industrial wilderness of St-Denis, boatyards lined the banks. We were by then far downstream of central Paris, even below our original Paris berth at St-Cloud, and the great Bois de Boulogne. By this point the Seine had become a very busy river. Commercial craft plowed up and down in all their ponderous variety, resolutely carrying their cargoes between the ports of Paris, Rouen, Le Havre and the north. It all seems remarkably easy these days. Powered boats, adjustable weirs, and huge electrified locks allow the heavy traffic to flow back and forth, with few of the problems that plagued the Seine in the past. Flooding still occurs, but the water level never drops below the required minimum, as it sometimes did in the nineteenth century. In those days steam tugs pulled as many as fifteen loaded barges upstream, using a chain laid on the river bottom stretching all the way from tidal waters near the English Channel to Montereau, the junction with the river Yonne about sixty miles above Paris.

Melodie and I have very different views about waterways. She dislikes rivers for their traffic, feared hazards and scarcity of mooring places, much preferring the calmer world to be found on canals. She wasn't, therefore, anticipating the crowded lower Seine with any pleasure, while I looked

forward to it as a stimulating and mildly exciting experience. We patiently accepted this difference between us, knowing that water travel in France
demands voyages on rivers as well as canals.

With so many large boats, all intent on important business, the lower
Seine is indeed a demanding river, requiring constant alertness. But I
enjoyed being in such company. Apart from the Rhine, there are few rivers
to match it for the sheer number and diversity of boats. There were tugs,
tankers, floating cranes, workboats; there were barges, from 350 tonners
to the giants of their species; and there were push-tows, some with four
barges tied end-to-end, and the monsters of the river, immensely powerful pushers churning the water behind barges the size of several playing
fields. They were all coming and going with great determination and much
"blue flagging," the signalling method used by boats wishing to pass on the
"wrong" side, an allowable exception to the normal rule of the road, permitting boats struggling upstream to get out of the main current.

On the outskirts of Paris, due north of Versailles, we stopped overnight
at Bougival. Berlioz lived there at one time, as briefly did some of the
Impressionist painters, giving the village a reputation as a centre of art and
bohemian life. Corot, Meissonier, Renoir, Berthe Morisot and Monet all
painted at Bougival, drawn there by the countryside and the endless fasci-
nation of the river, its life and ever-changing nature.

At Conflans Ste-Honorine, the river Oise joins the Seine. The name
honours both the third-century martyr, Ste Honorine, and the merging
rivers, Conflans being a corruption of *confluent*. Most of the barges going
to or coming from northern France, Belgium and Holland use the Oise, and
the Seine generates its own heavy traffic. It is small wonder that Conflans is
one of the great barge towns of France. Barges line the banks of the river,
rafted out, in places, six or seven deep. There are boatyards for repairing
them, shops for supplying them, a floating chapel for their crews and a
small museum to record the history of this ancient means of transport.

Then we headed north up the Oise to spend the night at Pontoise. On
first acquaintance the river was surprisingly pleasant, similar in size and
terrain to the Yonne, but with a stronger current and less overgrown banks.
The locks, however, are very different from the wretched things on the
Yonne, with their sloping walls and slow manual operation. The Oise is a
business-like river with locks that are large, mostly in pairs, even triples,
electrified, efficient and fast.

Not far beyond Pontoise is the small riverside town of Auvers-sur-Oise.

I couldn't pass it by without spending a little while walking its streets for it was there that Vincent van Gogh spent the last seventy days of his short and restless life. As a boy, I had become familiar with this strange man through my mother's enthusiasm for his painting. I read about him and grew up with his sunflowers, his irises, his cypresses and the interior of his bedroom in St-Rémy. They held a special place in my early life, and although the man himself was too complex and strange for a boy to count a hero, his presence came so strongly through those paintings, he was close to being one for me.

Like Bougival, Auvers also attracted artists in the late nineteenth century. It was a small town then, thinly spread between the Oise and a ridge of rocks where stone was quarried. With a normal winter population of 2,000, Auvers attracted a thousand more in the summer, some of them artists. Daubigny, of the Barbizon school, lived in Auvers, and Pissarro in a village nearby. Cézanne, and several others painted at the village. There was also Dr Gachet, a doctor and amateur painter, who knew many of the artists and had a good collection of their work in his Auvers house. He was one of the main reasons van Gogh went to Auvers, and when they came to know each other, thought the doctor "one of the liveliest and most sympathetically original of men."

During two richly productive years in the south of France van Gogh suffered attacks of what may have been a form of epilepsy, possibly aggravated by absinthe, glaucoma, digitalis poisoning or syphilis. Some think van Gogh was a manic depressive, but no one really knows, and whatever the cause, the attacks were becoming more frequent and lasting longer. He had a row with Gauguin in Arles, threatened him with a knife, and then in remorse, cut off his own ear. Later in the asylum at St-Rémy he attempted suicide by swallowing his own paints, and again later, by drinking stolen kerosene.

Through all these troubles his brother Theo, then working with the art dealer Goupil in Paris, was van Gogh's sole support, both moral and financial. It was Theo who established the contact with Dr Gachet in Auvers so that Vincent could go north, as he wished, to live and work in a place where the right medical care was close at hand.

Van Gogh arrived at Auvers in May 1890, finding it "profoundly beautiful, the real country, characteristic and picturesque." He took a room in l'Auberge Ravoux on the Place de la Mairie and settled down to life in Auvers. He saw a lot of Dr Gachet who became to him "a true friend, something like another brother." He painted steadily, turning out a canvas every day while he lived in Auvers, a remarkable outpouring of his unique vision. Then in July something went wrong. He became very upset and wrote an incomprehensible letter to Theo, who feared another attack was imminent.

On Sunday July 27, van Gogh walked into the countryside beyond the town, set his easel against a haystack, went behind the Château de Léry and shot himself clumsily in the chest with a revolver. The wound was not immediately fatal. Bleeding and in great pain, van Gogh stumbled back to his room in the inn without speaking to anyone. When discovered, Dr Gachet and another doctor were summoned, but decided against removing the bullet. Eventually Theo arrived from Paris and remained by his brother's bedside. In the early hours of July 29 his brother said: "I wish I could pass away like this," and died half an hour later.

Because van Gogh had taken his own life, the Auvers priest refused the use of the parish hearse. Another was found, but the church service was cancelled. Van Gogh lay in a closed coffin at the inn. His paints, easel, brushes

and palette were on the floor nearby and his last canvases nailed to the walls. Sunflowers brought by Dr Gachet rested on the coffin beside other yellow flowers brought by friends. In the hot sun, Theo, Dr Gachet and the small party of friends walked up the long hill to the cemetery. At the grave side, Dr Gachet was so overcome that he could only stammer "a very confused farewell." Theo was broken with grief.

Auvers is a larger place now, with three times the population, but I imagine, not greatly changed. Many of the buildings and places van Gogh knew or painted are still there: the Mairie, l'Auberge Ravoux, l'Eglise Notre Dame, Daubigny's studio, the Château, Dr Gachet's house. And the memory of this troubled man lives on in the town and in the park that bears his name, now with a memorial statue by Ossip Zadkine.

I walked through the streets of Auvers, past many of the landmarks, then up the hill by the church and out of town, beside the wheat fields that van Gogh had loved to paint. Once in the country, I saw something red lying in the middle of the road ahead. As I came closer, I found two red roses joined together, in their prime, not yet fully opened. I carried them to the top of the hill and laid them on van Gogh's simple ivy-covered grave against the east wall of the cemetery, the exact twin of Theo's lying beside it. On van Gogh's grave there were other flowers, some dry and faded but a few fresh red poppies to accompany my two roses.

Vincent van Gogh was only thirty-seven when he died. His entire re-markable production was accomplished in only ten years of that short life.

The Bomb and the
Buttonhole Knot

As *Lionel* progressed slowly up the Oise I was deep in musings about Auvers and the tenant of l'Auberge Ravoux. It was a tranquil summer day, perfect weather for a quiet cruise, but suddenly my reverie and the whole mood of the day was utterly shattered by an explosion, as if from nowhere, very loud and very close. Two sharp bangs, louder than a 12-bore shotgun, exploded just outside the wheelhouse, scaring us out of our socks. *Lionel* was going under a high bridge at the time but I'd no idea what had happened. All I could see was blue smoke drifting away from the boat. Melodie, suspecting an attack of some sort, shouted: "Someone's shooting at us, Hart, do something!" It wasn't clear what she expected of me, although I was greatly touched by her sudden faith in my ability to pluck both boat and crew from imminent peril.

I remained at the wheel, thinking it sensible to put some distance between the boat and its attackers, whoever they were. It was then that we discovered on the deck, just in front of the wheelhouse, two golf-ball-sized stones, sloppily tied with string to a bundle of burnt, shredded paper. It was immediately clear what had happened. French boys buy very powerful and noisy firecrackers, and throw them around casually. *Lionel* had clearly been targeted by some *garçons méchants* on the bridge who must have been thrilled with their bomb-aiming for it had been fiendishly accurate. The weighted explosive had hit the boat squarely and presumably exploded on impact. Luckily it missed both the thin-skinned wheelhouse roof and an irreplaceable plastic skylight, only inches from the target.

Continuing more calmly up the Oise, we found it, like many rivers, quite miserly with its mooring arrangements. Although one can usually find a few that hold out promise, you cruise slowly past, examine them carefully, reject most as hopeless and forge on until something better comes along. At last, in the village of Le Bac, a possible mooring appeared, enticingly near a restaurant. It was small and difficult, with hazardous steel projections sticking out here and there, but the thought of a restaurant meal cast these concerns aside, and we made the attempt.

Mooring *Lionel* has never been the simple, quietly efficient operation that I have hoped and longed for. It is not for want of experience, because we've had quite a lot of that. Nor is it from lack of persuasion and basic training. God knows, I have tried hard to instil the concept of calm, swift, silent efficiency aboard our boat. Yet, after years on the waterways, the reality is, regrettably, more languid than swift, hardly ever quiet, and once in a while, plainly ineffective. It most certainly is far removed from that epitome of silent competence said to have prevailed on the Royal Yacht *Britannia* where I'm told orders were given by hand signal only and no shouted commands. On *Lionel* we simply do the best we can, in a casual, noisy, sometimes argumentative way.

There was a strong current running at the chosen mooring. The ropes were put ashore at bow and stern but the bow line, suffering from a knot malaise that annoyingly recurs from time to time, began to unravel and come away from its bollard. Immediately the current caught the boat, carrying the bow away from the quay in the first stage of a slow unpremeditated turn into the middle of the river. In desperation, Melodie got another rope fixed to *Lionel*'s middle bollard, where the mechanical advantage to prevent the impending fiasco was very slight. It was clearly well on its way to being another of *those* moorings and would have to be abandoned for a second attempt.

I asked Melodie to release her rope. Still holding it, she started to argue about the merits of what she was doing. I didn't think it was a moment for debate. I asked her again to let go her rope as the current pulled the boat farther from the quay. Still determined, she stubbornly hung on. I knew my word was not always law to her but something had to

be done—*fast*. Although Melodie finds the Bligh approach distasteful, I thought it might be the very thing right then—pure high-volume sound to weaken her resolve in the struggle against both Oise and me. One peremptory bellow did the trick, and reluctantly, Melodie let the rope go. *Lionel* then retreated into the Oise, got itself in order and advanced on the mooring once again.

Melodie's knots are unknown territory to me. They are unlike anything you might find in a book on knots or even on any other boat. What she does with ropes is each her individual creation, according to the whim of the moment, owing more to her training with needle and thread than the long traditions of the sea. Some of them are truly bizarre but surprisingly effective. Others look more or less right but are not. These have an alarming tendency to unravel themselves at critical moments. Not one of them is easy to untie when its job is done.

I have preached the gospel of the simple, time-honoured knots every seaman knows but Melodie refuses to be converted. I had high hopes that she and the clove hitch would get on friendly terms, and for a long time she practised it with heavy string and a candle in the saloon. It sadly faded from her repertoire, which finally boiled down to three basic knots. There is the standard two half hitches that one *will* find in a knot book. Then she has a bollard knot of her own devising, one half hitch with the loop dropped over the bollard. It is easy to do, holds well but is too slow and entails fiddling about to find the loose end when the time comes to leave. Finally, there is something Melodie calls her "buttonhole" knot, its origins lying somewhere in the craft of stitchery. I don't trust this knot. It looks a little like a clove hitch but is erratic in performance, sometimes showing an unexpected and alarming self-release capability. I suspect it was one of these little numbers that so neatly undid itself at the attempted mooring on the Oise.

On a dull grey day sputtering with showers, we ran the remaining short distance to Compiègne, passing on the way a large and rotund collared turtle dove who watched us glumly in the rain from its perch on a dead tree. When we arrived in the city, it too looked cold, damp and unhappy. Although some important things have happened in and around Compiègne, the city itself is not a place where I would wish to spend much time. More than a thousand years ago, Charles the Bald built a palace there, hoping to emulate Charlemagne's in Aix-la-Chapelle. Six hundred years later, in May 1430, during a siege by Burgundian and English forces, Joan of Arc was unseated from her horse during a skirmish outside the walls and taken prisoner by the Burgundians. Philippe the Good, not averse to making a quick profit on the side, promptly sold her for a good price to the English.

The thread that runs through the town's history is its use as a place of royal residence, starting with Charles the Bald's ninth-century palace. Louis XIV had stayed in this old palace but felt it much below seventeenth-century royal standards, and complained: "At Versailles I am housed as a king, at Fontainebleau as a prince and at Compiègne as a peasant." Louis XV corrected this gross deficiency in royal accommodation by building an immense new palace on the foundations of the old. It was in the new palace that the Dauphin, later Louis XVI, was paralysed with timidity when faced with the young Marie Antoinette for the first time. Not, however, the impatient Napoleon Bonaparte. When his future bride, Marie Louise, arrived at the palace, he rushed outside through driving rain, jumped into her carriage, soaking wet, and smothered her with warm embraces. But it was Napoleon III and Princess Eugenie, who made it their favourite residence, and it was they who put this great renaissance palace to extravagant use in the month or more they lived there each autumn, hunting in the nearby forest and entertaining European royals and VIPs of the time. However, accommodation for the large court, their guests and accompanying retinues was a problem even in such a grand palace, and many of the visitors, accustomed to more sumptuous quarters, had to make do with rooms in the attic. The hours, however, were so filled with hunting, theatrical evenings, *tableaux vivants*, balls and intrigue, amorous and political, one would think that there couldn't have been much time left for wondering why you hadn't been given one of the better suites.

On the Aisne north of Compiègne we passed the forest where the Armistice was signed on November 11, 1918, bringing the four-year war to an end. The formal act took place in a converted railway dining car drawn up on a siding. Years later, after the defeat of France, Hitler took pleasure in humiliating the French by using the same railway car in the same place for signing the armistice of June 1940. The carriage was subsequently moved to Berlin where it was destroyed by bombs and has now been replaced by a replica.

There Are No Sabbaths on This Boat!

The river Aisne and the Canal des Ardennes farther east are really the same waterway, linking the Oise and the Meuse. As one moves from one to the other there is no noticeable change. Both go through similar country with few locks, except near the eastern end, where the Canal des Ardennes climbs steeply to the summit. Past forest, overgrown river banks, and small fields of corn and wheat we travelled up the Aisne to Soissons. Bird life was plentiful on the river: collared turtle doves, mallards, little teal, grey herons, moorhens, black-headed gulls and great crested grebes floated warily hull down. On the quay at Soissons were birds of an entirely different kind—racing pigeons, hundreds of them, their baskets filling five large specially built trucks. We enjoyed the massed choir of cooing birds which sent its complex warbling chord across the water, and it would have been marvellous to see them go—a mass of pigeons, in one great soaring cloud, beating their wings hard to gain height for the long journey to home coops all over Belgium. Their release, however, was dependent on weather and radio communication with Belgium, both delaying departure until we could wait no longer.

The fourteenth-century Cathedral of St Gervais and St Protais in Soissons was a Great War casualty, so gravely damaged that much of what one sees now is the result of rebuilding. Only the choir and transept remain intact to show a little of what the whole once was. As I walked in the hushed nave, I noticed a modest plaque fixed to the stone, such a small, unobtrusive thing in the dim light, most visitors would pass it by. Yet, this understated memorial to the one million men of the British Empire who died fighting in France during the Great War had a startling impact, and a power far greater than anything more elaborate could hope to achieve. What more moving tribute could there be than that simple record of the awful, stark fact.

In the late afternoon, at the end of the next day's run, I selected a mooring place covered in nettles and bracken, but the attraction of a small lake nearby made it worth the trouble. Apart from the aggressive plants, it had another familiar drawback: not enough things to tie the boat to, and such as they were, in the wrong places. We moored with stakes (the inevitable stones below them) and a complicated system of ropes designed to prevent what soon happened. A loaded barge came by, *Lionel* did its usual uncontrolled tango and the stakes were plucked from the ground. Gathering up the mess of ropes, we moved on to a more secure mooring not far from the same lake. When will I ever learn?

It was a beautiful spot: the shade of nearby trees, views of the green countryside, the lake only a field away and perfect summer weather for the enjoyment of it all. I heard a few rumblings from the crew about a free day which finally came to a head with Melodie's plaintive cry from below: "There are no Sabbaths on this boat!" That settled it. The following day would be a holiday.

It was a good decision. Our moorings held well against the passing of more loaded barges, even two passing each other and *Lionel* at the same time. Although the others didn't seem interested, the lake just across the field drew me like a homecoming mallard. I swam often in its deep, clear water, under the overhanging willows, especially at the extremities of the day. In the evening, I joined the fish jumping around me and the stars dusting the smooth surface of the water with flickering sparks of light. In the early morning, perhaps the best time, I swam out farther than before, with the day's new sun rising slowly above the willows and bouncing its brilliant, undulating image off the lake.

Joss, as usual, had to go for walks. We could jump from boat to shore, but it was too much for her and each time she needed the boat's ramp to reach the grassy bank. Being a nine-foot aluminum ladder with plywood fixed to its rungs, it was awkward to handle. Because female Dalmatians are not heavyweights, I later substituted a single piece of plywood as a "dog only" ramp, much simplifying the frequent chore. This had a close resemblance to the sturdier ramp, being the same size but minus the supporting ladder and Melodie, forgetting this vital fact, tried to go ashore on the thin plywood. It broke in two, pitching her into the water, and forcibly against the stones below. The result was a painful separated rib which took weeks to heal and kept her from any but the lightest jobs on the boat. Luckily, with the help of friends we were able to continue the journey.

Joss

Joss and I first met in the spring of 1973. I was at my workshop in the old barn near our house when Melodie came walking up the path with a small white bundle in her arms. As she got closer the bundle turned into a puppy, a Dalmatian puppy, almost pure white with black spots just beginning to show. She was my birthday present. I was then newly fifty-five and Joss was entering the ninth week of her life. I didn't know much about her and she knew nothing of me. We would both slowly discover more.

When she was old enough I began to train her. Morning and afternoon we'd go onto the old croquet lawn and fumble our way through the basics over and over and over again: sitting (easy), lying down (more difficult), walking properly at my side (unwilling and erratic), staying and coming when called (also erratic and basically unreliable). By no means a willing pupil she did give the impression of knowing what I wanted most of the time but gave way only reluctantly in the running battle of wills that it all became. Even after several months of daily lessons, Joss always seemed to comply with commands because they fitted in with her own current plans rather than some idiot idea of mine. Much of it was undoubtedly my fault, but her independent thinking and my shortcomings as a dog trainer meant that we went through life more as friends and equals than as master and dog. That was all right with me because I liked to think that her spirit meant more than mere canine docility ever could.

Early in her life Joss was imprinted on Melodie and me. She was with me all through the day, slept on our bed at night and was miserably unhappy, bored, perhaps even depressed when deprived of this companionship. In her teenage phase, she had demonstrated this in decisive terms by inflicting massive damage on upholstered furniture more than once and even in middle life was quite capable of trashing a screened verandah in an attempt to be with us. In her maturity, she might still chew casually on this or that to pass the time away and howl pitifully when left alone.

She went everywhere with me, even into local stores where she usually behaved impeccably. In her youth, however, there were some memorable lapses. I recall in vivid detail, being in a hardware store, waiting, with others, to pay for my purchases. The other customers may have been shocked at what was happening at their very feet, but not the store owner, who calmly handed me a shovel. Shovels, however, aren't always handy. As Joss and I were strolling through the frilly white drifts of women's lingerie in another store, it happened again. No shovel was in sight or anything else of any use. After that miserable event, I became more cautious with my unpredictable young Dalmatian who may well have sparked the rash of NO PETS signs that started appearing on the fronts of local stores.

Joss would put up with an awful lot for the companionship she so desperately craved. The noise of machines in my workshop never seemed to bother her. At times, she lay very near me while I worked, gradually almost disappearing under a fine layer of sawdust. She even stayed close by, quite undaunted, when I welded or cut steel with a torch, the flying sparks and hot metal far more frightening and dangerous than sawdust. But there were those special times, twice a day, when I'd hit a hard rubber ball with a baseball bat to send grounders bounding fifty yards or more across the lawn. Joss went after the ball like a bullet, quickly catching up with it to grab it in her mouth and dash back for more. In the winter it was sticks, the thrown stick slowly turning as it arced against the blue sky, her long legs plunging through the deep, powdery snow, nose snuffling under it to find the stick and then dancing back, covered in ice crystals, with the long bit of wood clutched in her mouth and a look of utter delight on her spotted face.

Life on *Lionel* was very different from anything she had known before.

First came the fears and isolation of air travel, confined for eight hours in a cage. Then the boat and strange places with all their hazards and new sensations: falling in the water, falling down stairs, almost daily explorations of new territory, strange dogs to be wary of, being attacked by a few of them, the incredible smells and occasional titbits of French markets, confronting cows and horses for the first time, staying in hotels, and trying hard to be good in restaurants.

It had been a long and happy time, but by midsummer of 1987 Joss was in her fifteenth year, an old dog, suffering from the typical problems of advanced age: weak back legs, arthritis, occasional incontinence. She also had infrequent but recurring attacks of what the vets call "bloat," a twisting of the stomach which blocks the escape of gas from fermenting food, the result finally being a dangerous and sometimes fatal pressure on vital organs. In an attempt to prevent this happening, Joss was fed a complicated formula involving rice, pablum, yeast, calcium and two other chemicals four times a day. Although hoping for the best, we knew a serious crisis might have to be faced on *Lionel*.

One evening at the end of June, that crisis came. Then in isolated country at the start of the Canal des Ardennes, we were a long way from the kind of help that Joss required. While out for a brief walk she became ill and wandered up and down retching, before collapsing on the grass beside the boat, breathing rapidly and in great distress. We got a blanket under her and moved her into the wheelhouse. She was clearly in bad shape but there seemed so little that we could do. We made her comfortable on the soft seat where she normally sat, covered her with a blanket and stayed close beside her during that evening and night.

After suffering through five hours, poor Joss died at two in the morning. Early the next day Melodie and I dug a grave in the clay soil at the edge of the nearby cornfield and buried Joss in her old pink blanket. Neither of us will ever forget our feelings the next day as we left that sad mooring and pulled slowly away, to leave our dear friend of so many years behind.

C'est le drapeau du Canada!

It was a sombre cruise the following day. The death of poor Joss lay heavily on us both, and the war-damaged, much rebuilt town of Rethel did little to lighten our spirits during a slow climb to the watershed. The canal became less crowded by bankside greenery, opening up long views of spacious fields sweeping away on either side. It was the kind of country that is good for mechanized farming and the movement of the armies that have doggedly tried to destroy each other over this terrain so often in the past. Almost as a grim reminder of those times the fields were speckled with bright red poppies, even dense vermilion splashes, in the light ochre of the ripening wheat. The landscape changed to high pasture land near the summit broken by forest into segments with occasional glimpses of country recalling alpine foothills.

In the last five-and-a-half miles to the top, the twenty-six locks of the staircase come in a tightly compressed bunch. They were automatic, with the hateful activating arms which had caused us trouble in the past and would do so again. Earlier we had resorted to the boat-hook but feeling it the last resort of an amateur, I was determined again to do it properly with the boat. I removed all *Lionel*'s bumpers so they wouldn't interfere with what had to be some pretty precise pilotage where a matter of inches would be crucial. With Melodie to guide me from the deck, I tried, as before, to bring the boat into the lock no more than four inches from the lock wall. Once again, it was beautiful when it worked smoothly and dreadful when it didn't. After several jarring collisions with the stonework, Melodie confessed she couldn't tell when the boat was too close. With our friend Joe as my guide, the result was much the same, and reluctantly we returned to the boat-hook. *Lionel* got banged up, scraped and dirty in these locks, and the last straw was our treatment at the top lock by a drunken keeper who let the water rush in before the boat was secured. I tried to counter this with throttle and wheel, but the boat swung wildly from side to side, smacking into the lock walls with resonant booms. What little ability I had to swear in French sadly failed me utterly at the very moment when I needed it so badly to curse the wretched lock-keeper. He certainly got no tip or even a *merci*.

At Sedan on the Meuse there was a change of crew. Joe left and Ian, another Canadian friend, joined us for the next few weeks, a fortunate replacement for the still disabled Melodie. After treating us to a farewell dinner, Joe departed the following day, leaving behind a present of a shiny new set of *boules* for the boat and the recollection of some memorable knots. We stayed in Sedan until the following day, but lazily made no effort to explore the town. As another casualty of war it might have been a disappointment anyway.

The Germans crossed the Meuse at Sedan on May 14, 1940 at a point north of the fortified Maginot Line where the French thought the Meuse and the Ardennes hills discouraged attack. They were wrong. The Germans did the unexpected, attacking on a fifty-mile front between Dinant and Sedan. It was a dreadfully uneven struggle—French cavalry against German tanks, poorly armed and trained French reservists facing élite German regiments. The Germans quickly crossed the Meuse, captured Sedan and continued their lightning advance towards the west, leaving the smoking town behind to recover as best it could. Seventy years earlier, in the Franco-Prussian war of 1870, Sedan had been the scene of another French fiasco. An indecisive High Command and miscalculations about German strength had allowed the French army to be trapped there. The resulting *débâcle* caused the capture, death or wounding of a hundred thousand men, the overthrow of Napoleon III, the collapse of the French Second Empire and the loss of Alsace-Lorraine.

Sedan holds a grim place in French history as the scene of two humiliating defeats, but the name of the town is known to most due to the alleged origin there of the "sedan" chair, the one-person covered chair carried on poles by two bearers. It was popular in the seventeenth and eighteenth centuries, and oddly, we know the bearers were usually Auvergnois in Paris and Irish in London. The chair's origin, however, is obscure. It may have evolved in Sedan, or even in Italy, though a likely source of the word is not the town at all but a seventeenth-century English gentleman, Sir Sanders Duncombe, who is thought to have made it up from the Latin verb, *sedere*, to sit.

Moving slowly up the French Meuse in seductively warm weather, a filter of haze softened the lovely tree-covered hills, and I was struck again by the quiet beauty of this river. Although lacking the drama of the Ardennes farther north and the more active river life of the Belgian Meuse, it had a soothing pastoral quality, greatly enhanced by the small number of boats using it. Then, somewhere in a canal cut, the quiet of that benign summer's day was shattered by the sudden pulsing racket of a military attack helicopter. The sinister presence remained hovering forty feet away, ten feet off the ground, flashing strange lights, apparently aimed at *Lionel*. These were not the normal navigation lights carried by all aircraft, but had another purpose we could only guess at. It was briefly unnerving. Both Ian and I, having been shot at in the war, felt more than a hint of those old sensations and were much relieved when the pilot finished what he was doing and left us in peace. It's not nice to be a target, even in a training exercise.

During our leisurely progress up the Meuse, Ian proved to be an excellent travelling companion as well as a skilled and vigilant crew member. Because of Melodie's damaged ribs, it was our good luck that he came when he did. Ian took over from her, doing all the jumping, climbing of ladders and tying of ropes. With Melodie out of action, she had lost the contact with lock-keepers she so enjoyed but Ian assumed this part of the job as well, enthusiastically chatting to the young ones, many of them students on summer jobs. Since he was shortly to buy a boat of his own, Ian also gained experience by taking over *Lionel*'s wheel occasionally and acquiring the feel of a large boat in different and increasingly demanding conditions.

Although our boat is registered in France, it flies a large Canadian flag at the stern in defiance of rules which dictate it should be a *tricouleur.* Nobody has ever questioned this but even if they do, the Canadian flag will continue to fly as long as Melodie and I are aboard. Canada only acquired its new flag in 1965 but it is widely recognized in France. In the rural backwaters of the country, however, there can still be uncertainty in the minds of some. Ian, as enthusiastic a Canadian as one could find, decided to leave nothing to chance. Whenever there was an audience at hand, even a solitary, unsmiling lock-keeper, he wished to make unmistakably clear what flag it was. Standing at the stern, holding the flag out straight, he would announce in a clear voice to anyone paying attention: "C'est le drapeau du Canada!" or challengingly, to students working the locks during the summer: "C'est le drapeau de quel pays?" His otherwise happy face was suffused with sadness by the rare wrong answer he hoped never to hear.

Bastille Day in Toul

Not far from Commercy the Canal Marne au Rhin takes over from the Meuse, passes through the short tunnel at Foug and drops down in fourteen electrified locks to Toul. The only mooring there was full of Dutch boats, leaving little place for us. Ian, however, skilfully negotiated a bilateral agreement with the Dutch, who moved some boats so *Lionel* could squeeze in between them. It was still a tricky business, requiring a 180-degree turn with our bow nuzzling a tire held against the quay by Ian.

Like so many towns in the east of France, Toul has a mixed German/French past. It is a small, old fortress town, bound tightly within the corset of massive defensive walls, on one side rising sheer from the still waters of the canal. Yet Toul seems to offer fewer interesting historical titbits than other towns its size. But probably one of Toul's lesser claims to fame is Hilaire Belloc, the French-born author who did his military service with the artillery in Toul before going on to Oxford and writing *The Bad Child's Book of Beasts*, one of his first books of nonsense rhymes.

As dusk fell on the night before Bastille Day, we joined a crowd of local citizens beside the water of the large basin in the town. A military band was thumping out heavy-footed stuff from a floating platform at one end, and at the other the *pompiers* were making a water arch with their fire-fighting hoses. Closer by, radio-controlled model boats were scooting about in the water, one a model of a Canadian Coast Guard ship. Seeing this, Melodie rushed back to our boat and returned with a diminutive Canadian flag, which the boat's owner promptly tied to his radio antenna. All this resulted in a remarkable flowering of bonhomie, hugging, kissing and an all-round display of Franco-Canadian goodwill. Then the fireworks burst into the night sky, one after the other in a dazzling spectacle that went on and on, the stunning bursts, coloured showers, glittering traces and bright arching stars all above our heads, and in the water as well, a mirror to the airborne brilliance in the sky.

The following morning, Bastille Day itself, Ian and I observed the town's formal ceremony marking this special day in France. Compared to the jolly evening before, this was serious business, largely military in nature, but carried out in that uniquely French way that gave it a flavour rather lighter in tone than the participants may have intended.

On one side of a road, the Mayor, local VIPs and senior military officers were carefully arranged in precedence under a covered stand. Beside them stood a motley collection of uniformed men and women, mostly khaki-clad army officers, but also a sprinkling of air force men in navy blue uniforms and white spats. Immediately beside me a tubby young lady of unknown service stood rigidly to attention in ill-fitting slate-blue tunic and

skirt, the last hanging markedly stern high. Drawn up on the other side of the road in a loose military arrangement were a band and four veterans carrying flags, one a short and very plump old fellow wearing baggy pants, large, floppy beret and oversize dark glasses.

The first event of the parade was the presentation of medals or honours of some kind. Three officers appeared from the right in line astern, casually executing a shuffling attempt at military precision. One carried a small cushion bearing medals. They were shortly joined by a civilian, who stood at attention facing the reviewing stand. A medal, perhaps some grade of the *Légion d'Honneur*, was pinned to his chest by a senior officer who then kissed him on both cheeks. When he retired, two more appeared and the procedure was repeated but without the kisses, leaving one to wonder at what level in the French system of awards the kissing stops.

The medal-pinning ceremony was followed by a march past, led by a carefree army band wearing white gauntlets, white spats and ragged red epaulettes. After the band, an army unit followed also wearing white gauntlets, but carrying guns, giving them the appearance, at least, of being real soldiers. Behind them, another white gauntletted and spatted bunch ambled past, also carrying guns but their jaunty forage caps, pale blue shirts and navy pants marked them as *Armée de l'Air* and probably for that reason, not too familiar with the weapons they carried.

The *pompiers* were next. It was not a large contingent, just one small, bright red pick-up truck, bringing up the rear of the parade. The limited space behind the cab was packed with big men, all in full dress, wearing the heavy leather jackboots and shiny metallic helmets favoured by French firemen. There were only four of them in the back of the truck, three in a row at the rear, one holding a flag and the rotund fourth, undoubtedly the Fire Chief himself, saluting from a raised platform in front of them. All four figures were working their hardest to inject what dignity they could into a situation that bordered on the comic. The fire department of Toul thus condensed into one shiny red, pompous little package, brought the day's military parade to an end with an unwitting but welcome bit of humorous relief.

The Funeral and
the Builder

After many years of travelling European canals and rivers, it might be reasonable to assume that we could avoid the major pitfalls and cruise peacefully about the countryside without the crises that booby-trapped us in earlier days. To some extent this is certainly true, but it is also true that nobody is immune to unpleasant surprises. The unexpected always lies in wait on a boat, even for the experienced. Crises happen, and when they inevitably do, even to an experienced captain, it is like being tapped on the shoulder by the finger of some ghostly dominie with his usual irritating reminder: "Ye have a few things to learn yet, boy."

We had all got up at six to get a jump on the Dutch party at the next few locks. After a brief passage through a section of the Moselle near Liverdun, we joined the Canal Marne au Rhin again at Frouard. This meant going through the twenty-three-foot-deep Ecluse de Jonction. A hire-boat, alas, had joined us in this lock. To give it room, I took *Lionel* to the front of the chamber, the hire-boat then placing itself only a few feet behind our stern, thereby leaving *Lionel* no room to move forward or back. In addition, the lock was so deep that the only way of securing a boat was to tie onto small bollards set at different heights in the lock wall. Ian fixed a bow rope to one of these, the boat being held in place by the thrust of the slowly turning propeller working against the restraining rope's tension. So far so good.

The boat rose as the water poured into the lock. Foreseeing the coming problem, I asked Melodie to move another rope to the port side so it could be used for the next bollard on the wall as the boat moved up. It was a reasonable plan, but as the water rose rapidly, the rope tightened around the bollard. Ian struggled unsuccessfully to release it, but its bollard soon disappeared below the water. There was only one thing to do. I shouted: "Cut the rope!" After a frantic search, Ian found one of the hatchets always kept handy for such emergencies, and with a few sharp blows, severed the rope. While all this was going on, the lock-keeper, seeing our difficulties, closed the paddles to stop our ascent. It was too late to do any good but lowering the water allowed us, at least, to recover the end of the nylon rope. It was small consolation.

Lionel and its rather subdued crew arrived soon after in Nancy. There we found a convenient but grubby mooring amongst barges at a quay in the old industrial part of the city. The absence of bollards forced me to drive a large mooring stake into unpromising terrain between a railway track and the water's edge, using a sledgehammer of great weight. I had taken several energetic swings at the stake, when my hands lost their grip. The sledgehammer flew through the air and sank rapidly out of sight in seven feet of opaque canal water. We marked the spot as best we could, but I feared the port of Nancy had acquired yet more useless scrap metal. I had, however, underestimated the power of *Lionel*'s strong magnet, carried for such salvage jobs. Fishing methodically, with the magnet tied to a string, Ian finally made contact and brought the sledgehammer to the surface. And so ended the second and last crisis of that day.

Nancy is the historic capital of Lorraine, a part of France rich in iron ore, and partly for that reason, swept frequently by tides of war. It was lost to the Germans in 1870, regained in 1918, lost again in 1940 and finally won back in 1944 by Free French forces who had adopted Lorraine's double-barred cross as their symbol. It used to be said in Lorraine that the three most magnificent ceremonies in Europe were the coronation of an emperor at Frankfurt, the coronation of a French king at Reims and the funeral of a Duke of Lorraine at Nancy. If the Duke of Lorraine's funeral in the seventeenth century is a sample of what was meant, it may well have been more than mere boasting.

This particular Duke died on May 14, 1608, but there was to be no

quick burial for him. His passage from deathbed to grave was an extended process. First the Duke was embalmed, an essential first step so that he could last the course without causing offence to others. He was then laid out in the Ducal Palace, draped with gold cloth and rich velvets. There he remained for nearly a month, watched over by priests. Later, a sequence of banquets was served to the Duke's courtiers with his effigy in full-court regalia reclining on a bed in the dining room, and his empty chair at the head of the table. Periodically, in elaborate court language, a herald announced to the empty chair the arrival of each new dish.

These macabre banquets went on for four days, and were followed by two more days of religious offices and prayer in a black-draped, candlelit room. At last on July 17 the *cortège* finally started off. It consisted of court nobles, priests, 300 town merchants and 300 poor people. Still not anxious to hurry things along, the funeral procession stopped for the night at Eglise St-Georges, arriving the next day at Eglise des Cordelièrs, the dead Duke's final destination, two months and four days after his death.

Yet, showy funerals, even such displays of ostentatious splendour, make no lasting impression. It was Stanislas Leszczynski, in the eighteenth century, who gave Nancy much of its architectural heritage and the magnificent square that bears his name. When the dukedom became vacant in 1738, Louis XV offered Lorraine to his father-in-law who had recently lost his own throne in Poland. It was a wise choice. Stanislas was a man of peace who ruled Lorraine well for thirty years, accustoming it, for the first time, to French domination and through his love of building, greatly embellished its capital. Stanislas loved good living and beautiful women, but above all, he wanted to build. He had a passion for architects' drawings, for the step-by-step process of construction, and especially for watching skilled artisans at work in their *ateliers*.

La Place Stanislas, the main showpiece of present-day Nancy, is the evidence of his enthusiasm and his love. The rectangular paved square is a highly formal composition typical of the late renaissance, its perimeter formed by stone buildings of the same period. The monochrome stone of the buildings and the paving is relieved by complex, highly decorative wrought iron grilles and gates. Partly gilded and oddly feminine in character, this elaborate ironwork plays more than a minor role in the total effect. The square is a good one, although it suffers from an aridity often present in French urban design of the period, and the surrounding buildings seem unable to give it enough of the city life that would make it truly vital.

Through the Vosges

Barely beyond the outskirts of Nancy the enormous chemical plant of the Solvay company dominates a stretch of the canal, towering over it on both sides and crisscrossing it with pipes, conveyors and bridges. This giant undertaking produces chlorine, salts and carbonate of soda in a complex operation spread over more than two hundred acres. The canal passes through its heart, immediately below the massive furnaces, claimed to be the largest of their kind in the world and fed by limestone brought fifteen kilometres on elevated belts from quarries to the north of Nancy. As we cruised slowly under the furnaces, cranes, and entwined intestines of the industrial monster, many of Solvay's large fleet of barges were evident everywhere in their company colours.

On the Canal Marne au Rhin, many of the locks are completely automatic, but fortunately now use infrared beams rather than the wretched arms that had earlier become such a nuisance. Yet even automatic locks are fallible. Occasionally, they simply didn't work, much to the irritation of commercial barge captains and ourselves, forced to phone for help. Mostly, however, they worked obediently as they should.

The lock that finally raised *Lionel* to the summit level had a lift of fifty feet. We have been in some monsters with much greater lifts but not one like this, combining a big lift with the ungenerous dimensions of a standard canal lock. Entering the lock through a small rectangular opening at the bottom of a high concrete wall was like sailing into the hearth of a large, sooty fireplace. Coming into the dark chamber from the sunlit day outside temporarily blinded me, and I brought the boat into the lock dead slow for fear of hitting the practically invisible end wall. Once inside, the lock became more a chimney than a fireplace with a small rectangle of blue sky far above. I was grateful, however, for its floating bollards, avoiding the awkward business of moving ropes up from bollard to bollard as the boat rises.

At the top, the lakes that form a reservoir for the canal were unfortunately hidden from the canal by high dykes. The Souterrain d'Arzviller came soon after, and there we endured a two-hour wait while loaded barges slowly made their way through it from the other side. When *Lionel* finally emerged into daylight again at the tunnel's eastern end, we broke through into the most dramatic scenery of the canal. It is at this point that the canal cuts through the Vosges hills and drops down the Zorn valley west of Saverne. In the deep valley, cliffs and steeply wooded slopes squeeze canal, road and rail together in close company at the bottom of the gorge.

After the tunnel, the old staircase of seventeen locks needed to overcome the 145-foot drop, appears on the left. The trip up or down this precipitous part of Alsace used to take eight-and-a-half hours. It is now accomplished in less than thirty minutes thanks to a new boat lift, a caisson of water rolling on railway tracks fixed to a concrete inclined plane. Although its lift is not a patch on the giant slope at Ronquières in Belgium, the Plan Incliné d'Arzviller has a more spectacular view and a beautiful basin of dark turquoise water at its foot.

It was an exciting moment as I brought *Lionel* into the caisson at the top, with the inclined plane sliding away below us to the basin at the bottom. A magnificent view of the valley hugging hills stretched out ahead, and close at hand, Ian had a ready-made audience of tourists for his lesson in flag recognition. The water of the basin at the bottom looked so enticing and the place so peaceful that we moored there for the night. Melodie swam but even she, a daring cold water bather, found its frigidity excessive. This news quickly decided the matter for the rest of us, and an athletic young friend told us later that even he had been daunted by the chill of the water. Having swum across on a dare to collect a bottle of champagne placed on the opposite quay, he had immediately rejected any thought of swimming back, and returned overland with his prize.

It was a short run down the lovely wooded valley to Saverne, past picturesque little Lutzelbourg, as Alsatian as they come, with steep roofs, black and white half-timbering and flowers at most house windows. We were joined that night for dinner in a local restaurant by an old friend (the swimmer) who had once, in the south of France, re-built *Lionel*'s wheelhouse roof. It was a good meal, but the only detail about food that remains in my head is Ian's courageous decision to have *choucroute garnie strasbourgeoise*, a true Alsatian dish. Predictably, a monstrous heap of food arrived on an oversized platter: poached Strasbourg sausage, a substantial hillock of sauerkraut, fatty pork, smoked bacon rind, goose fat, ham, and a heaping mound of mashed potatoes laden with thick gravy—sheer bulk amply compensating for anything else that might be lacking. His choice struck me as rash but Ian attacked the edges of his food mountain bravely and perhaps, in the beginning, even with enjoyment.

The cooking of Alsace is hearty fare but capable of far more delicacy than Ian's *choucroute*. It owes as much to German as it does to French influence, as with Alsace itself, where one can hear not only the languages of both cultures but the peculiar blend of the two that many Alsatians use. The cooking follows a similar pattern: most of the Alsatian dishes like *choucroute* and *tarte à l'oignon* have strong peasant roots, as does *kougelhof*, which a Strasbourg friend brought to the boat one day. She had talked about it earlier as a sweet Alsatian bread but we were not prepared for the giant round loaf she gave us, twelve inches in diameter at its base formed by a thick projecting brim, it rose twelve inches in a squat, ribbed mound to a flat summit. Made by her mother in a special *kougelhof* baking dish, it turned out a huge round loaf looking like a child's crude drawing of a hat. It was delicious, especially toasted, but what do two people do with a loaf that would keep a large farm family munching happily for days? We gave much of it away, but even the small portion kept on *Lionel* lasted for weeks.

Always searching for new and interesting food experiences, Melodie wandered around Saverne and discovered a *patisserie* of a very superior kind, the sort one doesn't expect to find in a small town. The establishment of Muller-Oberling was also a *glacier*, a *chocolaterie*, and a *salon de thé*, all looked after by attentive handmaidens in identical flowered dresses. As a preliminary test, Melodie brought two sample *gâteaux* back to the boat. They were packed in the elegant and practical way the French have devised for carrying such delicate things home, a little paper-wrapped box, supported in a sling of ribbon tied with an intricate bow. The *gâteaux* themselves were deceptively simple little blocks to look at: laminations of coffee cream, chocolate, buttercream and a thin layer of cake, topped with a light chocolate icing of exceptionally delicate flavour.

Words do not come easily when describing what it is like to sink one's teeth into such a thing. The tongue registers the consistency and taste of each layer, breaks down and analyses them in the mouth, which absorbs the subtleties of its multi-flavoured sweetness and parts with it reluctantly to the throat. In our own ways, we have all experienced something like this but there are degrees of excellence. What Melodie found in Saverne was at the haute cuisine level of pastry with all that implies in the exploration of quality and subtle flavour. We were both transported by the delights of Saverne's unexpected goodies and were tempted back seven times before we left Alsace. They were of a quality quite rare, even in France, and so addictive one might easily think that Mephistopheles himself was working away at making those things with one's personal downfall in mind.

Ian finally left us at Saverne and was much missed as we continued our journey to Strasbourg, reached two days later after a night spent at a dreadful bug infested mooring. The final stretch of the canal was quite straightforward, except for a few sharp corners which experience has taught me to approach with caution. At one of these, where the abutments

of a bridge made the canal even narrower and the corner sharper than usual, I gave a long blast on the boat's noisy horn. Hearing no answering toot from an approaching boat, I started into the corner. Once under the bridge, the blunt nose of an advancing barge confronted *Lionel.*

On these occasions there is never any doubt about who must give way. A loaded barge cannot be quickly stopped nor can it wander far from the centre of the canal. So, in a dense cloud of blue exhaust from *Lionel*'s long suffering engine, I put it hard in reverse. Once halted, I had to get our boat out of the way. Backing up is an unpopular manoeuvre with *Lionel*, but that time the boat did exactly what was needed. I persuaded it to go backwards in a straight line close to the bank, and remain there obediently as the barge squeezed past.

The final approach to the city of Strasbourg was up the River Ill and under five bridges. The river current proved unexpectedly strong, requiring more and more throttle as we went upstream. My main concern, however, was the bridges, about which I had been able to get little information. Would *Lionel* be able to pass under them? I didn't know but the only way to find out was to try. There was no problem with the first three but the next ones looked doubtful. With Melodie posted on the deck to warn me of trouble, I approached them cautiously. They were both constructed with wide sweeping arches, far too low at the sides but possibly high enough if I kept to the centre. And they were, just. Clearing the last bridge, we moored safely at the Quai des Pêcheurs, right in the centre of the city.

Strasbourg

I didn't know what to expect of Strasbourg. Distrustful of glowing reports, I had resigned myself to anticlimax, if not disappointment. First impressions, however, confirmed all I'd heard. On my first walk in the city, I followed the River Ill upstream from the Quai des Pêcheurs, through the tangle of water as the river breaks out of the old city, and on to the railway station where I bought a ticket for Auxerre so I could fetch our car. It was a captivating stroll beside the narrow, fast flowing Ill as it curled around the heart of Strasbourg. Bright green weeds waved about in the umber shallows below moored punts and paddling swans. Old buildings lined the river's banks, many elaborately half-timbered in the Alsatian way with stark white stucco panels, and their steep roofs patterned from eave to ridge with dormer windows. The old domestic architecture of the region reaches a kind of black and white frenzy in La Petite France, where the Ill divides into four narrower channels, forming a watery confusion of little locks, waterfalls, sluices and mills. Ancient houses cluster drunkenly together on the narrow, torturous streets of this old district of Strasbourg which was home in the sixteenth century to tanneries, mills, fishermen, and also a place of refuge for Huguenots fleeing persecution in France. Now it has become largely a focus for the teeming tourists.

Heading away from the River Ill with its paths, trees, parks, boats and riverside restaurants, the casual stroller finds other rewards in the city of Strasbourg. There is pleasure to be found in its buildings, both grand and humble, in little squares, some bright with life, others green islands of peace, in dormer dotted roofs, in glimpses of alleyways and private courtyards, in old houses and shops cheek by jowl along the streets, in its window boxes, in its lively cafés, and especially in the great red stone cathedral sitting in its busy square at the city's hub.

Built on the foundations of a Roman temple, the cathedral of Notre Dame was started as a Romanesque church in 1015. Destroyed by fire thirty years later, construction resumed in the Gothic style and completion finally achieved in the fifteenth century. Because of vicious anti-church sentiment, Notre Dame was under great threat during the turbulent years of the Revolution, as were many ecclesiastical buildings in France. At Strasbourg, the damage could have been more severe. Although over 200 statues were destroyed by angry mobs, the building itself remained relatively untouched. There was grave concern, however, for the spire, which the revolutionaries considered an offence to the concept of equality. But a resident of the town came forward with a clever idea. An enormous Phrygian cap, an important symbol of the Revolution, was made of metal, painted bright red and placed over the threatened spire. The gesture satisfied the mob and the spire was saved.

Above all else, the important influence on Strasbourg's long history has been its location on the Rhine, at the juncture of two conflicting cultures and on a strategic point in an early system of roads and river crossings. For these reasons it was coveted from its very beginnings, fought for by many, and like most old towns in Europe, also had its share of sieges, fires, pillagings, earthquakes, plagues, persecutions, repeated rebuildings, frequent changes of ownership, and religious squabbles.

During the Reformation, feelings were at fever pitch in Strasbourg, with Alsace split into two opposing camps. To relax tension and forestall a confrontation, the town held an archery contest in which Alsatians, Swabians, Bavarians and the free towns of Switzerland were invited to compete. The contest was won by men from Zurich and to celebrate their victory, forty-eight citizens from that town made the long voyage to Strasbourg by boat. Rowing down the Limmat, the Aar and the Rhine they made a record passage, carrying with them a huge pot of millet porridge, kept warm in hot sand. It took them seventeen hours to cover the

125 miles, the porridge still warm on their arrival. At the concluding dinner of the contest, the leader of the Zurich delegation told the Strasbourgeois: "Now you know that if you are in danger we can come to your aid in less time than it takes a millet porridge to cool." In 1870, three centuries later, descendants of these men kept that promise by coming to help Strasbourg when it was under siege by the Prussians.

Strasbourg was wholly German in language and culture from early times until long after it came under French rule in 1681. Johann Gutenberg was there for a few years in the fifteenth century when he fled from Mainz and associated with three Alsatians to develop his printing process. That collaboration eventually broke up and Gutenberg moved back to Mainz where the printing technique was later refined. It was also due to Strasbourg's German cultural traditions that the young Goethe studied law at the university there in the late eighteenth century, some years before he dramatized the legend of Faust and established his reputation as an outstanding German poet. He does not seem to have made a great impact on Strasbourg, but he got his degree in law there, fell in love with the daughter of a poor country pastor, searched unsuccessfully for the grave of Erwin, the architect of the cathedral's west front, and forced himself to overcome vertigo. His way of doing the last was to climb to the top of the cathedral, and clutching the stone balustrade at the edge of the roof, hang fearfully over the awesome void below, refusing to give in to his fear.

It is hard to imagine that one could be in Strasbourg for long without being affected in some way by the cathedral. The red stone mass and its companion square are at the core of the city's life. Strasbourg's Notre Dame is, however, very different from the great Gothic cathedrals in other parts of France. On the outside, at any rate, Notre Dame seems to lack the strong, pure expression of the Gothic idea found in Sens or Bourges or Metz. On the west façade and spire, at least, it has a delicate, almost fragile character expressed in the filigree-like decoration standing free of the walls. It seems like a false note in a building that has so many other strengths, particularly its nave and chancel. Inside, Notre Dame is totally different, having an unsuspected power. In the dimly lit great nave, with massive columns soaring to the vaults high overhead, its atmosphere is so serene that even a shuffling throng of tourists seems to have little effect upon it.

Promenade gastronautique

Some of the rare and unusual surprises of France are what I can only think of as weird time shifts, brief moments when one seems to experience the incongruous occurrence of an event that leaps into the present from some quite different time. This has happened to me on several occasions, and it is a strange sensation, this awareness of both the past and the present happening at the same time in the same place.

One of these shifts occurred during a short cruise down a small, forgotten river. Like a voyage into another time when a simpler life prevailed, there was little evidence of the modern world, no noises of car, train or tractor—only an all pervading pastoral peace and little sign of life apart from birds, trees and fish. The mood of that river was so totally different from any other I have travelled, its memory stays with me still. A similar impression of time warp occurred at Châteauneuf when Melodie and I were looking through the door of an old stable at twilight where a woman was watching over a cow and its newborn calf. The woman's clothes and the dimly lit stable were identical to what would have been a typical, everyday scene in a country village hundreds of years ago, but just down the lane, the present day leaped suddenly into a surprising and totally contrasting life. And yet again under quite different circumstances I saw a man walking along a towpath on a quiet summer day. This man could have come right out of the nineteenth-century art world, dressed as Monet might have been when sketching, with wide brimmed straw hat, shirt, tie and dark trousers held up with braces. He looked incongruous, quite out of place and time, a misplaced figure wandering in a century not his own. It is odd events like these that make it hard to dismiss the occasional chance mingling of past and present as a possibility. Perhaps it is not so surprising and especially noticeable in an old civilization like France.

Another candidate for this possibly crazy notion occurred one evening in Strasbourg. In spite of the summer tourists flooding through it in waves during the day, the cathedral square drew us back frequently because of the cathedral itself and the life surrounding it. But at night the square took on a more subdued character. With the day's bustle gone, the sound muted and light dimmed, it seemed to transform itself into something else. The lively daytime presence of the surrounding buildings had faded into featureless dark forms, then only spotted here and there with points of light. And the great cathedral had surrendered its Gothic detail to the night, becoming a huge anchoring mass, its sombre presence silently dominating the square. There was a special drama and an air of expectancy there after dark.

One evening, we were having drinks on the second floor of a café, and quietly enjoying the square's night-time transformation, when a troupe of travelling players made preparations to put on a performance against the wall of the Cathedral. Their stage was nothing more than the paving stones in front of a rough-and-ready tent. Costumes and props were rudimentary, the lighting primitive, the only music their own voices and a guitar. But they needed no more than that. For as long as we were there, the five of them entertained a small crowd with a blend of boisterous melodrama, lusty songs, juggling and low comedy. In the subdued light of the square and the backdrop of the dark cathedral, the little band of players and their engrossed audience resembled a scene from medieval times when travelling players would almost certainly have done the same thing, in the same way, and perhaps, even in the same place. Was time playing its tricks again or could it only be imagination?

Moored near *Lionel* in Strasbourg was an old British-built plastic boat, retired from a hard life with a hire-fleet, and then about to depart for the Black Sea with a French family of four aboard. It would be a long and daunting journey for anyone and only possible then for boats light enough

to be trucked over the forty-odd miles that still separated waterways linking the Rhine to the Danube. When we met Francine and Georges they
hardly seemed prepared for such an adventure. Francine had a recently
damaged hand with two fingers broken and one minus its top joint. She
didn't know how it had happened, possibly because she had fainted dead
away, and the severed tip could not be found for re-attachment. One of her
two sons also had a broken finger. The boat was underpowered, under-
supplied with water, had no generator or charger and couldn't even be
started in Strasbourg because the boat's one battery was flat. They had no
river charts, could speak a little German but no Slavic languages. It didn't
look highly promising, but the family was in great spirits and ready for
whatever fate was going to toss their way. We gave them a bottle of champagne for celebrating their arrival in the waters of the Black Sea, if they
ever got there.

Almost a year later we saw this pleasant family again at Chalon sur
Saône, at last on their way home to Valence on the Rhône and moored in
the same marina as *Lionel*. Francine and Georges appeared one afternoon
at the wheelhouse door with a bottle of champagne, the same bottle we'd
given them in Strasbourg. "We are returning it," Francine said: "because
we never reached the Black Sea." I replied: "That doesn't matter, you must
keep it." And there the matter was left for the moment. They had not
done badly. Fifteen miles south of Vienna, their engine broke down in a
terminal convulsion. After seven weeks delay, inefficient mechanics, the
delivery and installation of a new engine from France, they sadly decided
against going the additional 1,200 miles down the Danube to reach the
Black Sea. After spending much of the winter in Greece, partly to escape
the cold on their boat, they had reluctantly returned home in the summer
via Germany, Holland, Belgium and northern France. The next morning
we said goodbye to our intrepid friends, gave them a book I'd written, a
jar of Canadian maple syrup, and returned their special bottle of champagne, which I insisted they should soon open and drink to celebrate the
end of their long journey.

During our stay at the Quay des Pêcheurs it had become crowded with
later arrivals, all it seemed badly in need of water, all with short hoses and
all looking longingly at the one tap in the distance at the far end of the
quay. Hoses were joined together to reach it but fell short. *Lionel*, however, being an experienced European water traveller had equipped itself for
most unusual situations and supplied extra hose to reach the tap where

another problem arose. The faucet on the tap was an unusual one. No normal fitting seemed to work but one is always meeting such awkward problems in France where individuality governs uniformity in things plumbing and electrical. *Lionel* was also prepared for that and magically found the right device in its travelling box of tricks. All the thirsty boats were at last tanked up and a crew member of one boat was so delighted he presented *Lionel* with a forty-ounce bottle of Bermuda rum with the high potency of 50 percent alcohol by volume. "More bang for the buck,"said the donor.

The Quay des Pêcheurs was the terminus for most boats coming up the Ill, since farther upstream the river became shallow and restricted by low bridges. Yet the tour boats, designed for the conditions, could go where they pleased. Of these one stood out from all the rest, passing us two or three times a day. It was a strange craft, long and low like the others but innovative in design, with a catamaran hull and modular construction shown by vertical joints every few feet down its length. Although hardly beautiful by traditional boat standards, it had a certain high-tech chic that I found appealing. While the other tour boats served only as floating buses, the *Alligator* offered *promenades gastronautiques* through the waterways of Strasbourg in most elegant surroundings.

It sounded irresistible, and appropriate since the following day was our thirty-ninth wedding anniversary. Looking back all those years, our wedding did indeed have some odd features. The preliminaries comprised a sequence of lawyers, each setting up their own special obstacle. First came the one in Ottawa who told us Melodie's Reno divorce was not acceptable in Canada and suggested we marry in the United States. So off we went to Vermont where the second lawyer revealed that his state only married its own residents. He was ignorant of the situation next door in New Hampshire but a phone call to the first lawyer in Ottawa confirmed that this state was more lenient in matters of divorce. In New Hampshire, however, the third lawyer refused to deal with our problem on religious grounds because of the Reno divorce. Then on to the fourth lawyer who only set up the minor hurdle of Wasserman tests to ensure neither of us had venereal disease. Feeling confident this minor obstacle posed no problem we waited the required four days camped in a pup tent beside a little stream running over a white marble bed.

At last, feeling pure and ready for a New Hampshire marriage, we presented ourselves at the office of the local town clerk who, conveniently, was also a justice of the peace. Then, naturally, the ring had to be retrieved from our motel where I had left it and the essential paperwork completed before the ceremony could begin in, of all places, the minuscule walk-in office vault, a dusty and cramped little room with a broken window, jam-packed with filing cabinets, piles of paper files and an oversize safe. Although it seemed almost impossible the wedding party of town clerk a stenographer witness, bride and groom all packed ourselves into the tiny space. Then, as we stood in a tightly compressed little group, the town clerk read the required words, Melodie and I responded at the appropriate moments and the long awaited wedding was over.

With that memory as strong as ever, I made reservations on the *Alligator* for a dinner cruise the next night. Our dining room for the two-and-a-half-hour cruise was a space surprising for its cool, smart elegance, restraint and high standard of design, a combination of qualities rare enough at any time but especially on such a boat. As we and a few others sipped our *apéritifs*, we slid slowly and sedately up the Ill through old Strasbourg and La Petite France, where ancient half-timbered houses overhang the water, and the river splits into four channels, the navigable one with a lock. Passing through this lock with the sound of tumbling water all around us, we started on our delectable cold tomato soup with its accompanying flotsam of croutons. Coming out into the broader waters of the upper Ill, our water restaurant turned left and glided past the grim Caserne Barbade, the old military barracks now serving as the departmental prison.

South past the hospital, *Alligator* emerged from another lock into barge country as grilled lamb came to the table, with a bottle of St Emilion '78. We had by then entered the outskirts of Strasbourg's great inland port, second in size only to the one in Paris. It took a while to go through it, passing a complex steel clutter of barges, tugs, cranes, boatyards and all the paraphernalia of a busy port lying along the darkening shoreline. By the time our cheese arrived it was night. Eating it, we drifted past the dim forms and flickering lights of the Bassin des Ramparts, the heart of the port's life.

Turning northwest, *Alligator* slid past the Parc de l'Orangerie, where a pavilion designed by le Nôtre had been built in 1805 for the Empress Joséphine. It seemed the right moment for the arrival of plates bearing three balls of sorbet, lemon, raspberry and *cassis*, garnished with red currants, and all awash in a wild strawberry sauce. Around the next corner and up the Ill, the new building for the Council and Parliament of Europe glittered brilliantly through the dark evening. Disappointing in daylight and housing a body with little real political power, it makes a brave show at night, its many lights dancing across the water. With a Cointreau for Melodie and an Armagnac for me, we sailed on up the familiar river, past the Quai des Pêcheurs, to bring the exceptional evening at last to its end.

That short cruise brought together in one agreeable package several pleasurable experiences that are rare enough on their own. In retrospect, it is hard to find a flaw in any of it—the boat, the route of the cruise, the meal, or the service. While the food wasn't exciting or different, it had an unpretentious excellence. No fancy sauces, nothing tricked up with a pastry overcoat, no outrageous combinations. Simply the best raw materials, cooked perfectly to emphasize what they were. Such understanding is seldom found. Add to that, service both efficient and unobtrusive, an agreeable dining room slowly drifting through an ancient city in the gathering dark of a summer evening, and the bill concluding it all becomes nothing but a trifling detail.

Roman Irish Baths

During the late 1980s, France started demanding visas from all visitors outside the European community, supposedly to make life more difficult for terrorists. I doubt that any determined ones would be greatly deterred by such a minor bureaucratic obstacle, but tourists certainly were. People waited patiently in long lines at understaffed offices all over the world, or in exasperation went elsewhere, deciding that France didn't seem anxious to have them. *Lionel*, after all, was *in* France so *we* had no option. At the end of a long wait, we obtained a three-year visa with the odd stipulation that every ninety days we had to nip across a border somewhere and re-enter France again. It didn't make any sense and we later learnt to ignore this aggravating requirement. In 1987, however, we played strictly by the rules, and while at Strasbourg made a short trip by car across the Rhine into Germany.

I had been through the Black Forest before but never in such dreadful weather and never when its name seemed so apt. Although gaps in the trees sometimes revealed hazy views of distant valleys, the journey was mostly a passage up and down winding roads, through an endless nave of dark, dripping greenery, with moss-covered trunks wreathed in damp, ghostly mist. It was a relief to break out of the gloomy wood and arrive at last in Baden-Baden, the old spa at the western edge of the Black Forest where it meets the plain of the Rhine.

Because there are several other towns calling themselves simply Baden (baths), the extra Baden was added to make the town's name distinctive, and I suppose a town calling itself Baths-Baths has made a point of some kind. Regardless of the name, however, the fame of Baden-Baden rests on its reputedly therapeutic hot springs which dispense a chemical-laden water, drunk and/or swum in for as many reasons as there are people doing it. The ubiquitous Romans had, of course, been here too. After a hard march through the Alps, Roman soldiers used to have a long soak in the hot springs there but it was really in the nineteenth century that Baden-Baden had its high time. It was then one of the fashionable centres of Europe where royalty and the rich bathed, drank and played. The gloss has gone, but the old baths remain; prices are still steep in the *grande luxe* hotels and people come to do what they have always done but certainly with less style than before.

It is a pleasant town to saunter through, but the main point about Baden-Baden is all that hot water below the ground and those special places where it surfaces in a controlled, useable form. Having come to Baden-Baden, it was unthinkable to leave without experiencing one of the baths. Of these there seemed to be two main establishments: the recently built Caracalla Baths where a younger bathing-suited set frolic in mildly radioactive water, laced with sodium chloride. It had the look of a sporty health club, so we chose the Friedrichsbad, a far older place where the long tradition of naked bathing still prevailed. These baths were time-honoured, authentic and serious.

Melodie and I had only once before done anything like this. In Tokyo, several years before, a spur of the moment decision had taken us to some public baths. Once there we found a wide range of options, many uncertain or mysterious, perhaps even questionable. Certainly none were clearly understood, but we finally chose the individual, one-to-one arrangement, wished each other happy landings, and went to our respective rooms. When I opened the door of mine, a short, fortyish Japanese lady faced me, dressed in white shorts and top with mixed hospital/gymnasium overtones. We stood looking at each other for a moment but since clearly nothing could start without a naked Massey, I took everything off, even my glasses, and at her insistence, the stainless steel Medic-Alert bracelet on my left wrist.

Then, bare as it is possible for me to be, I was seated in a small cubicle whose heat was so intense I doubted my chances of survival for more than a few minutes, certainly not the twenty demanded by the little sand-filled hourglass. Getting hotter, sweatier and weaker, I watched the sand dropping to the bottom, grain by little grain, apparently almost immune to the force of gravity. On the point of expiring, the door opened. Thank God, I thought, this is the end of it. A hand pushed a cool, wet cloth in my direction and closed the door again. It was only half-time, with ten more minutes to go but that cold cloth saved me. The ordeal over at last, I was led in a state of near collapse to a rubber covered bed where I lay on my back, with a small damp cloth placed daintily over my genitals by the unexpectedly prudish masseuse. Scrubbing came next, from head to toe like a baby, with important omissions left to me. I rinsed the soap off with a shower and was told by gesture to immerse myself in a nearby bath of tepid water.

After drying, the main event began. Lying face down on a bed in the adjoining room, the masseuse set about *shiatsu* massage on my frail person. The Japanese word means "finger pressure," the massage using the pressure points on the body similar to acupuncture. It was to be an amazing experience. That small woman truly worked me over. I will never forget the unremitting exploration of every muscle that I seemed to own, even some quite unknown before, the extraordinary energy and strength of her probing fingers, the occasional pain she inflicted, and the final phase when she seemed to be walking down my spine, propelled along with her toes. And while all that was going on my little Japanese masseuse was watching television on a set fixed to the wall across the room!

What happened in the baths at Baden-Baden was very different, interesting in its way, a good deal more relaxing but certainly less exciting. Melodie and I presented ourselves at the grand old neo-classical Friedrichsbad, the home of the traditional form of hot-spring baths in Baden-Baden. Although there are special days for mixed bathing, our chosen one, alas, was not one of these, so we went off to separate locker rooms and baths.

The Friedrichsbad is a nineteenth-century building with a grand staircase, the rich and pretentious ornament of the period, and a monumentality that the Romans would find familiar. You don't just wander casually through its spaces sampling at whim the features offered, but follow a specific routine, one step following the next with recommended times allotted for each, all carefully calculated and suggested by its German management.

After leaving my clothes in a locker and attaching its numbered key to my wrist, I picked up what the management called a towel but was really a thin cotton sheet. Then it was to the shower, "stage one, shower/cleaning the body, five minutes" the instructions said. Once that was done, I wandered off, feeling exposed and vulnerable, into a damp world peopled with naked men, youthful and virile to aged and creaky. Having left my glasses in the locker, I discovered I couldn't read the locker number on my key, and without help, I was cut off from my clothes. Like the overture to a bad dream, I found myself naked and helpless in a public place. After stumbling about for a while, an amused masseur told me my number, and I then followed the entire regime of the baths with restored peace of mind.

Stages two and three in the Friedrichsbad are two rooms: a warm air room of 130 degrees Fahrenheit and a hot air room of 160 degrees. This is the Irish part of the Roman Irish Baths. Since Ireland was one of those rare places the Romans never went, the Irish were not exposed to Roman bath sophistication, and simply used hot rocks in specially built rooms to achieve high temperatures needed for a dry sauna. Fifteen minutes is supposed to be spent in the first room and five minutes in the second, lying on slatted wood benches, not designed for comfort. The heat was no match for the Japanese cubicle but was oppressive enough, even unpleasant, especially in the hotter room, and there was boredom to contend with as well. Sleep seemed out of the question and not much was going on except the slow circulation of naked figures and the barely discernible progress of the minute hand on a wall-mounted clock. To pass the time I studied the vaulting above, which was decorated with idealized country scenes populated with wildfowl, but that was only a minor compensation for my discomfort. I waited patiently, willing the clock to hurry along and release me from the heat.

After the allotted time it was a relief to go back to the shower again (stage four), and after that, to add my own to the bare prostrate flesh on the massage benches (stage five). The Friedrichsbad does not go in for any kind of boisterous pummelling but a far gentler routine involving soap, water and a brush. I am not a massage addict nor even a connoisseur, but I found this extremely pleasant and was disappointed when it came to an end after what seemed too short a time. By then I had given up my towel and was told to remove my rubber slippers before having yet another shower (stage six) and advancing into unknown territory.

Without even the comfort of a towel or slippers, I slopped across the wet floor and through a door into the next room where I was met by a cloud of hot eucalyptus steam. For me, this room (stage seven), and the even worse one next to it (stage eight), were the torture chambers of the Roman Irish Baths. At temperatures of 110 to 120 degrees, they were not excessively hot, but the relative humidity of a room full of hot steam must be at least 100 percent. The combination of heat and moisture created an environment I could stand for only a few minutes.

In the middle of the first room there was a tiered marble seating arrangement on which the higher one sat, the hotter one got. I stuck it out on the lowest level for about half the allotted time and moved with foreboding to the next, hotter, room. Here one was meant to remain for five minutes only. It also had tiered seats. I cannot imagine what it might have been like sitting on the top level with all that hot steam hissing about one's head. It was bad enough at the bottom where I remained for a minute or two before escaping to more civilized pleasures in stages nine to eleven.

Then I discovered the real glories of the Friedrichsbad: three thermal pools with temperatures starting at body heat and descending gradually to 83 degrees Fahrenheit. All were lined with marble or glazed tile, some were deeper than others, and one had underwater jets to massage the body. For Grand Duke Friedrich von Baden, the Romans showed the way, and it was a pleasure to relax in each of the pools, but to do so amidst the grandeur of the largest pool was splendid. Here the Grand Duke's architect created a magnificent giant arcade circling the round pool, with arches rising twenty-five feet above the marble floor, its walls embellished with swags, Greek key decoration, and sculpted neo-classical half figures, for some odd reason all holding their hands behind their heads. Surmounting it all, rose a great coffered dome, gilded and enriched with classical decoration. This is no ordinary pool. It is worth visiting the Friedrichsbad just to lie back in its water, enjoy the setting it has been given, and if you've chosen the right day, the bathers of both sexes sharing the pool with you. After that, everything else would have been anticlimactic. I declined the management's suggestion I also bathe in a colder pool with a temperature of 64 degrees, and then retire to another room for thirty minutes rest. Neither much appealed to me so I withdrew to the locker room and got dressed.

We returned to France the next day, after buying some sherry and German white wine, both almost unobtainable in France at the time, and persuading the French *douane*, almost against their will, to stamp our passports on re-crossing the border, which was, after all, the main point of the exercise.

The Cardinal's Palace

After more than three weeks moored on the fast-flowing Ill, we left Strasbourg on a fine morning in the middle of August with another Canadian friend aboard. It was Thelma's first trip with *Lionel* and after what happened in the ten minutes following our departure, she may well have wondered what kind of a cruise lay ahead.

Ever concerned about the low bridges just downstream, Melodie and I carefully monitored the level of the river, timing our departure to avoid the high water caused by recent rains. Thinking there might be problems with the second bridge, I also studied the currents there and the behaviour of other boats as they made the passage. Most of them, however, were long low tour-boats, and it might be quite different with *Lionel*'s high wheelhouse. I soon found out.

With the help of the current, the boat turned well in the narrow river and we headed for the first bridge, passing easily under it. The second bridge was not only on a bend but at a fork in the river, both creating currents that were complex and unpredictable. To make matters worse, the bridge's shallow steel arches only offered clearance for *Lionel*'s wheelhouse near their centre. Danger lay only a few feet to either side of it.

I stupidly approached the bridge with confidence, thinking I knew how to deal with the problem. But I was suddenly alarmed to find *Lionel* being carried inexorably sideways by the current. Impact with the bridge appeared imminent. This was bad enough for any part of the boat but in greatest danger was the wheelhouse, a fragile glass-and-wood demountable construction that is sensitive to rough treatment. There were only two things I could do and I did them both frantically, fearing we were going to hit anyway. By pushing the throttle forward to maximum power, I lowered the stern (and the wheelhouse roof) by roughly six inches. That would help but it might not be enough, so I spun the wheel to steer the boat towards the abutment of the bridge. Contrary to what one might think, this had the effect of swinging the stern, along with the threatened wheelhouse, away from the abutment and the dangerous part of the arch. It worked, but only just. We came through shaken but unscathed, missing calamity by the barest of margins. Perhaps only an inch or so saved us from the broken glass and splintered wood of a shattered wheelhouse. With grateful thanks to St Nicholas, the patron saint of mariners, we followed the Ill through its remaining bridges and turned west onto the Canal Marne au Rhin.

As we faced the first locks I began to think about our new crew member, totally unfamiliar with ropes, knots, locks, even boats. While friends are nice to have aboard they can sometimes make captains nervous, and once in a while, when left on their own, spring nasty surprises. Although they don't happen often, such events are each burned deep in my memory, like a brand that lasts for life. One of the first incidents of its kind occurred long ago during our very first cruise in France. We had rented a boat for two weeks on the Canal du Midi in the south of France. It was very small but offered a temporary home of sorts for Joy, a Japanese-Canadian writer, my erstwhile architectural partner, John, Melodie and me. The four of us were packed together in a minute space which never left much doubt about what was going on at any time of the day or night. The boat was at once christened the good ship *Intimate Relations*, and it proved quite fortunate that at least two of us were small and that Joy, true to her Japanese inheritance, seemed to occupy no space at all.

The diminutive Joy had absented herself from crewing duties for most of the trip, but one day saw a chance to play a minor role in marine affairs. Ashore, as *Intimate Relations* made a slow but determined entrance into a lock, she found one of the boat's ropes on the towpath. There was an appealing loop on its end and a handy bollard nearby. Feeling the two were made for each other, she mated them, feeling happy it had been so easy. In the middle of my carefully judged approach, the boat came suddenly and unexpectedly to a jarring halt. I was thrown forward over the wheel and the loose objects dislodged below clattered, clanged or thumped onto the floor. Investigating what had happened, I was surprised to find the rope still in one piece, attached to the bollard at one end and the cleat it was fastened to at the other end not removed from the deck, complete with its stainless-steel roots. In the stunned silence that followed, I heard a quiet male voice say, "Joy, please don't do that again!" She didn't do it again, or anything else with a rope again, poor Joy deciding there and then to remain a non-playing member of the crew.

Fortunately Thelma showed no inclinations towards such creative initiative and we arrived without incident in Saverne. We moored opposite the château, an impressive if pompous pile of substantial dimensions. Its long, formal red sandstone façade seemed to go on for ever. It was as if scruffy old *Lionel* was gatecrashing a grand event soon to take place. Cardinal Louis de Rohan had lived there for a time in great splendour, and rebuilt it after its destruction by fire in the late eighteenth century. But grandeur no longer reigns at the palace. Napoleon III made it a residence for widows of senior public servants, and from 1870 to 1944 it served as a barracks. It now leads a pretty humdrum municipal existence.

As we arrived, however, preparations were under way to stage a theatrical production at the château. Avid fans of their own history, the French flock with enthusiasm to spectacles all over France in the summer. It was Saverne's turn in late August, but since all seats were taken we had to be content with glimpses of the excitement through gaps in the stands. This was no half-hearted pageant put on by amateurs, but a full-scale professional performance dramatizing the history of Saverne and the Rohan family in a complex production with music, sound effects, a hundred or more in its cast, elaborately costumed and well-rehearsed, their voices carrying clearly across the water of the basin. Our blinkered view of the action revealed real horses and carriages, firing cannons and sword fights, but the burning of the château was the sensation of the evening. Remarkably simulated, the flames roared from windows and along the roof, reaching up into the night sky from its entire length. One wondered how the extraordinary effect was achieved without causing yet another disastrous conflagration.

The Angry *Pêcheur*

Leaving Saverne and its splendid *patisserie* behind, we climbed through the steep, pine-clad hills of the Vosges, up the inclined plane and along the summit pound to turn north on the Canal des Houillères de la Sarre. Built, like so many canals, in the prosperous nineteenth century, it serves the coalfields (*houillères*) near the German border. Twenty-seven locks lower boats to its present terminus at Sarreguemines. From there, the canal continues north to join the German Mosel near Trier.

After the hilly, coniferous Vosges, we entered an open, pastoral landscape of undulating fields. Large lakes were often close by, at first ten to twenty feet lower than the canal, but as it stepped down lock by lock, soon on the same level. At the height of the summer holidays, they were alive with windsurfers, fishermen, sailboats, water skiers and campers gathered in bright little flapping settlements along the shore. Sarreguemines proved to be a disappointment, revealing little of interest and not even a sign of the coal which comes from farther north. We left early the next morning for the return trip.

Because our passenger needed to catch a train, we had to rush the trip on this canal, having to do too many locks in the available time. Melodie, upset and tired, fell on the return trip and sprained her foot, rightly accusing me of pushing too hard. Once again we switched jobs. She became the pilot, and I the jumper, climber and knot man. Melodie didn't like driving the boat and had not done much of it before, but did remarkably well in spite of the unusual demands she inflicted from time to time on items of boat gear. Two bumpers neatly plucked from *Lionel*'s hull in a lock suddenly vanished with loud popping sounds and a heavy nylon rope was once stressed to twanging musical effect and near destruction. To be fair, I have done a little of this sort of thing myself.

On this canal, as on most in France, commercial barges are a dwindling species. Although still the cheapest method of transporting bulk goods, road and rail are gradually reducing the loads shipped by water on the French canal system. For some *mariniers* and their families this can only mean the end of the line. On our way south an unloaded barge had allowed *Lionel* to pass. This isn't normal behaviour for a busy barge and I was told later that the *marinier* was on his last trip before leaving the waterways. He had found, as so many have, that he could not support his family with the barge and was going to find work in a factory. His boat would be sold, either privately or perhaps to the government who would insist it be broken up. Both man and wife would be abandoning a way of life they knew, the special skills they had acquired to live it and a long inherited tradition. The *marinier* would no longer be master of his own boat, making his own decisions, as he and his wife travelled the canals and rivers. It is admittedly not an easy life; the partners must work long hours to suit the opening and closing times of locks. Yet, there is freedom in it too, more than in the tedious daily grind of an industrial job, and it is a pleasanter working environment than the pollution and noise of a city. It may be too easy to argue for the life of the working *marinier* when, in France at least, with high costs and low returns, it borders on poverty for many. Clearly, some must make this kind of drastic change for the sake of their families, but I still lament their passing. The canals will be poorer places when the vital presence of the working barge has finally gone.

Continuing west to Nancy on the Canal Marne au Rhin, there is a fork in the canal after the short tunnel at Foug. At this crucial junction in the canal system of France, where the right decision is vital, one would expect an informative direction sign, showing, at the very least, the canal names, the general direction of each, or the names of large towns on the two routes. Instead, all one sees is a small board on the left fork with an enigmatic "DIRECTION VOID." For a few moments I was puzzled. Depressingly, it seemed to hold out little hope of getting anywhere that way. What could it mean? In a kind of daydream, I pondered the implications. The end of the line for *Lionel* and all aboard? If foolish enough to proceed were we to drop off into some limbo just around the corner? It was a mystifying message. There was no *void* in my French dictionary. In English, "empty," "invalid" or the medical term for a natural function occur to one, but it seemed unlikely that the canal authorities had any of these in mind. So, I forged bravely ahead to find the explanation a mile or so farther on in a little town with this strange name. Why it had been chosen for the sign over one of the important towns to the west, I will never know.

On the Canal Marne au Rhin, as on all canals, one comes across the ubiquitous French fisherman. Normally a peaceful species, he appears content to contemplate a sagging line and motionless float for hours at a stretch. His patient vigil produces few tangible results, and perhaps, he doesn't expect many. It is a populous breed, generally lone males, although sometimes with a companion knitting in her camp chair, or in family groups, and occasionally in a long competitive row. Most of the time they only catch little tiddlers, enough of which, fried whole, make a kind of *friture*, and, infrequently, something a good deal bigger, like carp. Canal fishing has

always struck me as a strange pursuit, with few rewards other than the peace and quiet to be found beside the water, and perhaps that's really what it's all about.

The men who fish in canals and those who operate boats have quite different attitudes towards the medium they share. For the man in a boat the canal is his highway; for the fisherman, boats are an intrusion into his fishing ground. There is not much love lost between them, little mutual understanding and small effort made by either towards a more harmonious coexistence.

Perhaps, in a boat, one can't do a lot anyway although we have always done the little we can. I slow *Lionel*, stop the screw turning as we pass fishermen, and keep as far away from their lines as I can. However, they are a solemn, uncommunicative lot who often don't even respond to a wave, so I devised some simple little signals that might evoke at least a smile. As we pass, Melodie or I hold up our hands, palms facing each other at different distances in a mime question about the size of the catch. It usually works, breaking the fisherman's trance, often triggering a grin and a return signal to tell us of his luck; thumbs down or a head shake for nothing, two fingers apart for tiddlers and (rarely) hands apart for something big. I doubt that our silent little game with fishermen changes anyone, but it does seem to relax tensions along the canal as we pass.

It isn't always as pleasant or easy. At an overnight mooring on the Canal Marne à la Saône, I once woke late in the morning to find the boat aground and a fishing competition under way on the opposite bank, fifty or more whip-like rods hanging out hopefully over the canal. To get free of the mud holding the boat I had to power it away with the screw, churning up enough of the bottom to turn the calm canal into a swirling opaque brown soup. The fishermen were understandably not pleased, nor was I happy about what had to be done. We set off with despatch down the canal, leaving behind a grumbling line of *pêcheurs*, entrenched more than ever in their resentment of boats.

Then there is the isolated fisherman with a chip on his shoulder. This man claims the canal as his personal fish-pond. We encountered such a fellow on the Marne au Rhin. He was in his thirties, wearing a pink and white baseball cap over an assertive red face, with pointed nose and bushy moustache. As a fisherman he had extended himself. Three of the longest rods I have ever seen hung like antennae over the canal, their lines reaching right across it. Apparently not content with these he had two or three shorter ones sticking out of the canal bank. Even before *Lionel* was near him, he had begun making gestures that we should hug the far side of the canal. I knew the water was shallow there, and although I slowed the boat, I couldn't meet his every wish. The *pêcheur* didn't understand my problem, as *pêcheurs* rarely do, and left a line stretched right across our path. The man must have had a martyr complex.

As we got closer, he began shouting and waving frantically. With the boat slowed down and the throttle in neutral, I could do no more. We drifted slowly past as "angry" spat awful French expletives at *Lionel* from the bank. Then I heard a tinkling sound like the steady faint ringing of an aged bicycle bell. His line had snagged on some part of the boat and was running out from the reel. The poor man, now almost demented, waved both arms wildly and swore, "merde, merde, merde, merde..." in a long dwindling repetition, and then shouted, "*Stop!*" I put Lionel in reverse but a forty-ton boat can't be stopped quickly. The line continued to run out, the damage already done. There seemed little point in backing up to try and make amends with "angry" who was certain to be unpleasant about his lost hook, sinker, float and line. So, with his fishing gear assuredly wrapped snugly around *Lionel*'s propeller, we headed down the canal with "angry's" shouts getting fainter and fainter as we put some distance between us.

Encounter with *Tulipe*

The flying lock-keepers of the Canal Marne au Rhin pro-
pelled *Lionel* at speed through twenty or more locks a day towards the west.
After a final run across a flat plain where corn, wheat and sunflowers
stretched to the horizon, we reached Vitry and a tranquil mooring under
big trees on its outskirts. Before setting off again, we took on a load of
gasoil and began to eat our way through an enormous bowl of ripe, yellow
mirabelle plums. The plums, picked for five francs from a lock-keeper's
tree, were the sweetest we'd ever eaten and a constant temptation on the
wheelhouse table, before disappearing in a piggish display of summer glut-
tony, and questionable benefit to our insides.

Although one meets the youthful Marne as it ducks under the canal
near Vitry-le-François, the navigable part is not reached until Epernay,
about forty miles to the northwest and a hundred miles from the river's
source near Langres. The lateral canal from Vitry to Epernay is straight,
boring and busy with barges. The land on either side is flat, but even that
is largely concealed from the canal by its high, heavily overgrown banks.
Only grain elevators raise themselves above the wide, flat fields of wheat
and corn, or a cement works, their even less attractive neighbour, busily
powdering the surrounding houses, trees and cars with a fine layer of pale

grey dust.

Lionel's arrival in Châlons-sur-Marne was marked by going aground, not, as one might expect, at the edge of the canal but in the middle of what was supposed to be the port. As we rounded an island and headed for the quay, with propeller turning, *Lionel* very slowly and quietly stopped moving forward. Backing away, I tried again with similar results. Frustrated in this attempt to moor in the "port" of Châlons, I attacked the mud again, got stuck again, and by then fed up, powered *Lionel* through it. Tying up at last to the quay, the stern was held well out using a pole to avoid further entrapment in the gooey bottom.

Châlons lies at the southern fringe of the wine growing district famous for its champagne, twenty to thirty miles southwest of its twin centres, Reims and Epernay. Wine has been made in this part of France for almost two thousand years but Châlons also brews beer, refines sugar, makes chemicals and watches. In addition it is home to an enormous military establishment, making it the Aldershot of France. Of its famous sons, one stands out for a discovery with such far-reaching effects on our daily lives that it would probably have astounded him. Nicolas Appert, the *père de conserve*, born at Châlons in 1749, was the man who first discovered that food could be preserved for long periods in hermetically sealed containers, opening the way to today's common can.

Napoleon III, one of France's least inspiring leaders, established a huge military camp at Châlons, spread over 25,000 acres. Fond of playing soldier, he visited the town occasionally to enjoy a luxurious life in his pavilion, and entertain guests with lavish hospitality. When it came to the serious business of war, however, he was clearly not the man for the job. As commander of the army when the Prussians invaded France in 1870, he failed utterly as a strategist and tactical leader. Largely because of him, the French army was trapped near Sedan, France capitulated, and Napoleon III never played soldiers again.

Two little streams, the Mau and the Pau, wind their attractive way through Châlons under ancient bridges, and past old houses, restored to new life. But it is the two churches at Châlons that are the more interesting survivors from earlier times when the spiritual climate and the hazards of life focussed attention on them. Neither church is outstanding, but still deserves attention. The Cathedral of St Etienne has welcome breathing space around it, unlike many urban churches in France, which are crowded by the surrounding town. Largely thirteenth-century Gothic, some of it is pure and strong, but the whole effect is spoiled by the Renaissance west front added four hundred years later.

The more interesting church is Notre-Dame-en-Vaux, its high spires visible from many points in the town, one of them the original lead-sheathed wooden structure. Notre Dame is an honest thirteenth-century church, very nearly as it was built. It is what one expects from a church of this period, a harmonious blend of robust Romanesque and early Gothic, a peaceful uncluttered nave, fine stone carving in the wonderfully direct manner of the period and good glass lighting the nave with a blaze of colour.

Under way again, we came at last to the Marne near Epernay. We had particularly looked forward to seeing this town, renowned as one of the two principal headquarters of the champagne industry and home to several of its great houses, but we were thwarted by trouble on the river. For many months repairs to a weir two miles below Epernay had closed the river to all barge traffic. It might well have closed it for *Lionel* too, had it not been for the lucky arrival of rain upstream which increased the water depth an inch or two in a critical lock cut. A lock-keeper explained the problem, urging us to forget about Epernay and hurry through the trouble spot before the water level dropped again. Sadly, we abandoned our plan to visit Epernay and, moving dead slow, squeaked through the lock cut. Expecting any moment to hear the grating sound of steel on stone, *Lionel* made it all the way without touching, even over the final hurdle of the lock sill, with what could only have been a finger's thickness of water under its keel.

As always, my spirits rose to be on a river again. In the days that followed we sailed through the beautiful valley, the hills on either side covered with vines bearing white Chardonnay and red Pinot Noir grapes, all soon to be harvested for champagne. The vines climbed up the slopes beyond clumps of riverbank trees, each laid out in precise parallel rows, the small vineyards slightly angled to one another and looking like a patchwork of bright green corduroy. Narrow roads zigzagged between the vines, a château sometimes crowned a little hill, and villages hugged the valley side between the vines and the forest at the summit. Farther downstream, the Marne valley flattened, the vineyards gradually usurped by forest and the large fields of mechanized farming.

The Marne is no different from other rivers in its scarcity of mooring places. Because of this, we sometimes stopped for the night against the long quays at the upstream end of locks, but always leaving space for a late arriving barge. Moored this way one evening, we were quietly sipping *kirs* and playing rummy when a bedraggled private barge named *Tulipe* hove in view. It was about *Lionel*'s size, and though hardly possible for such a heavy thing, approached in an undecided, tentative way. We sat in the wheelhouse trying to fathom what *Tulipe* might do. Was it going through the lock? Moor against the rocks behind us? (A poor choice.) Moor ahead of us in the space left for a barge? (Not a wise choice.) Moor against *Lionel*? (Perish the thought!) During this preliminary indecision, *Tulipe* had drifted close to *Lionel*, and for reasons known only to its captain, threw me a heavy barge rope. I caught it, noticed it was not tied to *Tulipe* and I was left standing on *Lionel*'s deck, holding one end of the rope, with the other dangling in the Marne.

Sad-looking *Tulipe* then made a feeble pass at the rocks, failed miserably, tried another manoeuvre whose purpose was unknown, failed again at whatever it was and retired upstream to reconsider matters. There, after a great deal of to-ing and fro-ing, in what looked like uncertainty about how to turn the boat, it finally did so and pointed its bow downstream again.

Tulipe then set course at speed for the lock in general but specifically aimed at *Lionel*. I found this worrying. Not knowing what was about to happen, I held *Tulipe*'s rope to throw at the appropriate moment and Melodie had our largest bumper deployed for what I thought would be a certain collision. Instead of hitting us, *Tulipe* swept past, with the apparent intention of mooring in front of us, but approached the quay at such a sharp angle, no one could get ashore from the boat. It was fortunate that Melodie caught a rope thrown by one of *Tulipe*'s crew as it went by.

By then it seemed inevitable that *Tulipe* would have to moor for the night alongside us. With much pulling on ropes, shoving of boats, tying of knots and exchanged broadsides of *bonhomie*, our new neighbours were finally made secure in a rough-and-ready kind of way. Luckily they had not succeeded in mooring ahead of us. A barge soon arrived and occupied this priority spot with the consummate skill of a professional crew, a lesson in how it should be done that was, I'm afraid, lost on *Tulipe*'s captain. Surprisingly, he had owned his boat for five years but still seemed totally inexperienced. To be fair, however, he lived on his boat in Paris, only cruising in it for a two-week holiday each year and he had, after all, not been greatly helped by his motley crew of wife, very young baby, baby's grandmother, two callow teenage girls, a Cairn terrier and a cat.

Tulipe's captain later came aboard for a glass of wine, giving me a

chance to explain as nicely as I could that turning a barge requires a special technique. Several years before I had a similar problem and was taught
how it was done by a friend. I, therefore, passed on the simple rules to our
guest: stop the boat moving in the water, put the rudder hard over and
apply lots of throttle. It sounds easy and is, but most new barge captains
don't know it and I fervently hoped *Tulipe*'s would find his barge more
manageable from that time on.

At Meaux, the capital of the Brie region, famous over 500 years for its
cheese, we left the river to chug along behind two loaded barges down the
eleven miles of canal that bypasses a section of the river. As compensation
for the plodding pace, we enjoyed the lovely country that slid slowly by
outside the boat. Lagny, however, was neither beautiful nor welcoming. I
have never known a town of its size so unconcerned with the convenience
of river travellers. We scanned the banks in vain for a decent mooring,
went aground trying one and settled for another that was marginal at best,
requiring much fiddling with ropes, rings, chains and shackles to make it
work at all. At the end of the long business, Melodie was near to tears and
I went into town to shop for basics and hunt all over unlovely Lagny for a
place to buy her a large bunch of flowers.

At last near the end of the Marne, large old houses, legacies of an earlier,
ampler style of life, appeared here and there along the river, but the country's
green pleasantness was soon engulfed by the urban sprawl of Paris. Entering
the Seine, we went downstream to spend a few days in the Arsenal before
returning to Auxerre, almost a hundred miles to the southeast.

Posthaste to Bruges

In 1989 *Lionel* spent the summer moored in its home port at Mailly la Ville, a few miles south of Auxerre. We too had a break from the waterways, remaining in Canada to enjoy the pleasures of its warmer months, and pursue the interest in our respective crafts. But that time also offered a rare chance for Melodie to go on a trip she had dreamed of for years. In the fall of that year she and a small group travelled the ancient Silk Route from Russia through Mongolia and China to Hong Kong. It was a long, arduous journey but she still had enough stamina at the end of it for a dive trip in Indonesia. She later joined me in Europe where we had been lent an apartment in Venice through an architect friend. We spent several weeks in what was a perfect base from which to explore in more detail than ever before the intricacies of that fascinating and much loved old city.

It was not, however, to be a year entirely without boating of some kind. I was committed to be the cox of a four-oared boat in a regatta on the Serpentine in London's Hyde Park. It was a strange regatta and a strange place to be rowing. The serious part of it was sprint races in quadruple sculls entered by Russia, France, Italy and Great Britain. Then, as a less serious crowd pleaser, several dragon boats thrashed across the water in their own races but the event in which I played a part had nothing whatsoever to do with speed, quite the reverse. 1989 was the 150th Anniversary of the Oxford University Boat Club, and was to be celebrated with a row past on the Serpentine by a crew of five pre-war Boat Race veterans—four oarsmen and cox. As celebrations go it was a rather lame affair with not one man aboard under seventy. There should have been eight in the crew but old age and illness had whittled our effort down to four plus cox and the course to be rowed only 500 metres long with periodic pauses to catch breath. At one time there had been talk of a Cambridge crew also taking part but even the mere suggestion of competition alarmed the Oxford crew so much that they insisted on a sedate side by side row with an agreed dead heat with Cambridge at the finish. Though two university boats would have made it a more interesting event, the Cambridge boat unfortunately never appeared.

In 1990, after arriving once again in France, we found Polly, our new shipmate, already gazing anxiously out of her wire cage. Although a female Dalmatian like her predecessor, Joss, Polly had a bouncier, puppyish temperament which, even several years later, she seemed loath to abandon. Although eight hours at 35,000 feet in a pitch dark cargo hold surrounded by strange shapes and even stranger noises can't have been fun, she arrived in France so full of beans she could have swallowed a whole bottle of pep pills rather than the pre-travel tranquillizer she'd been given. In-flight boredom and perhaps resentment had driven her to attack the eighteen-inch high denim skirt on her cage which I hoped she'd falsely interpret as a modest amount of security in her scary airborne ambiance. So much for that kind thought. On arrival at the airport it lay about her in small, ragged fragments.

In Mailly la Ville the following day, *Lionel* appeared to be surprisingly free of the worrying and expensive problems faced in previous springs. The reason was the presence on board all winter of a friend's son, Simon, an experienced and skilled young man who knew about boats. In return for paying the modest mooring charges he had used *Lionel* as his winter quarters and kept everything in working order. With nothing to worry about we settled down to enjoy spring arriving in the beautiful country around Mailly. Alas, it was not to last for long.

The hulls of all boats must be inspected from time to time. For barges, whose metal hulls rust, the average time between inspections is three to five years. In 1990 *Lionel* was at the five-year point and arrangements had been made for a visit to a boatyard in Belgium near Bruges, reputed to be competent, and cheaper than most in France. Only some of this turned out to be true but we didn't know it then and a date was fixed for the boat-yard to take *Lionel* and *Thetis*, a barge of the same size belonging to Ian, our Canadian friend. And then, our spring idyll at Mailly was shattered by a sudden change of plan. The Belgian boatyard wanted the two boats in their yard earlier than planned. The trip we had to undertake was a long one. To meet the new timetable *Lionel* must leave for the north immediately. Melodie pleaded for a leisurely cruise, but I feared it could never meet her definition of "leisurely" and would more likely turn into a mad dash. It did.

Leaving at the end of May, we travelled down the familiar waters of the Canal du Nivernais, the Yonne and the Seine. There was no time to enjoy Paris except from an overnight mooring on the quay of the Jardin des Plantes across the river from the Arsenal and a river police station. Melodie was sure the police would tell us to move, but we were allowed a peaceful night, and the next day in lovely weather cast off to wait for the lights to turn green, allowing our passage around the Île de la Cité. But we waited and waited with the stubborn red light burning steadily just ahead. It must have been about half an hour before one of us had the bright thought of checking the river guide and found the small note explaining it all. Ah! The upstream and downstream traffic on the one-way passages is confined to certain times of the day. If you arrive, as *Lionel* did, at the wrong time, you may indeed have a long wait. It always pays to check the manual.

Once through Paris it was clear sailing down the Seine, up the Oise with fuel tanks full, and into the Canal du Nord, fresh cruising territory for *Lionel*, but through flat farming country with little scenic variety. A rel-atively new canal, reconstructed in 1965 after severe damage during the Second World War, it is built for commercial use, with nineteen locks, two tunnels and concrete-lined banks. The locks are unusual in being ninety-one metres in length, long enough to take two small barges or one large one, and in having side ponds to save a third of the water in each locking. In spite of this last feature, however, we still endured long waits at many locks due to water shortage on this canal.

The Canal du Nord was neither attractive nor clean. Going farther north it was increasingly polluted, especially in the industrial areas, vari-ously coloured effluents casually emptying into the canal through pipes in the canal walls. And mooring was unusually difficult. Because sloping canal banks discourage mooring we often tied up for the night to high factory quays. They were convenient for commercial barges, but were as high as

Lionel's wheelhouse roof. To reach the nearest flat surface on top a ramp had to be temporarily rigged from the upper deck to the top of the wall between the wash of passing barges. But the water was rarely still so Polly and her companion of the moment had to navigate the ramp's very steep and usually moving slope to reach land. In addition to being tired from days of hard running, this routine became tedious for me, and was the last straw for Melodie who was plainly exhausted. In view of past experience she was close to that critical point when tears or even accidents can happen and rightly insisted on a rest. So we stopped to allow her what was clearly needed, for she slept almost solidly for a full twenty-four hours.

Through much of the Canal du Nord, *Lionel* cruised in tandem with the huge Belgian barge *Soraya* carrying a cargo to Antwerp. While waiting for the lock-side ponds to fill, the captain of the *Soraya* and I often had a chance to chat. He was clearly proud of his family-owned boat and one day invited me aboard. I jumped at the chance for their boat was of a new type being seen in greater numbers on the waterways and its young crew was from the new generation of commercial barging. Though smaller than many of the modern giants, *Soraya* was just short of 300 feet long. The enormous craft was handled by the young Belgian couple with a subtle skill only possible with all the mechanical and electronic aids that are now available to such large boats. A bow thruster with its own engine, invaluable for manoeuvring in tight places, can move the bow to right or left, power steering with electric controls eliminates the normal wheel and frees the captain to steer his boat from wheelhouse or deck, depth sounders give vital information as does radar, permitting navigation on rivers even in a fog and radio communication of various kinds for talking to locks and other barges. Technology has taken over the traditional barge in every way. The wheel, that age-old symbol of things marine, is gone from the wheelhouse, which is now a marvel of modern labour-saving technology looking like a cross between an executive's office and the cockpit of a long-haul jet. The modern large barge is conned entirely with levers, switches and buttons by the captain sitting in a luxurious black upholstered armchair in the wheelhouse, or by remote control from the deck. It is the pattern of the future.

Going through lock after lock we came to know this couple a little in spite of language problems. He spoke Flemish and "some English," she Flemish and "some French." Since we mostly talked with her it was the "some French" that had to serve. Soraya, the captain's wife aboard the barge named after her, was an attractive and helpful woman who had come from a barge family following the tradition and practice of the trade. The daughters of barge families are brought up on barges and know the life and their responsibilities as a captain's wife. It is not a life for every woman, being hard and demanding with long days divided between domestic chores and playing a vital role as a working crew member when docking or entering locks. It is rare that the wives of *mariniers* come from families without a barge background, and interestingly, it is also rare for the *marinières* to wear anything but a dress even working on the deck and climbing ladders. Soraya thought it perfectly normal to be wearing a skirt, blouse and high-heeled shoes as she came down a filthy ladder to visit *Lionel* in a lock.

When the Canal du Nord came to an end at Arleux we turned east onto the capacious reaches of the Liaison Dunkirk-Valenciennes, a large canal running east from the channel port, linking with the smaller canal networks of France and Belgium. It is built with generous dimensions to take heavy barge traffic ranging from the standard thirty-eight-metre barges on up to 3,000 tonne push-tows, the giants of those waters. We felt very small and vulnerable mingling with such leviathans, but the wide spaces of the canal and the enormous electrified locks made for speed, an important factor in our lives at the time. And there was much interest travelling this busy waterway, with barges of wildly varying sizes, types and countries of origin, some from as far away as Poland.

On entering Belgium it was forcibly driven home again that its water-ways are quite different from those of its neighbours to north and south. Belgian canals and rivers are so badly polluted that many of them have that distinctive cloudy blue/grey look of running drains. And to judge from their smell this is what they are. As an additional reminder of Belgium's abuse of its own environment, everything in contact with the water is left with an unpleasant reminder of the experience, particularly in locks where ropes and ladders are coated with the black tarry substance that results from casually spilt diesel fuel. Melodie, who was the rope handler and lad-der climber, came face to face with this problem more than I and often returned to "civilization" on *Lionel* with ropes that had to be cleaned and hands and clothes besmeared with the stuff. If she had been more prone to swearing *Lionel* would have resounded with her curses.

There is nothing very nice to say about the Upper Schelde. It is not really part of the Schelde River as the name implies, but a Freycinet-sized canal, meaning it takes no boats larger than the standard thirty-eight-metre commercial barge. It runs north from the Belgian border to Ghent through flat, uninteresting terrain. In addition, it is badly polluted, smells and offers more of the mooring problems already experienced on the Canal du Nord. Near Ghent we turned west on the Ghent-Ostend Canal, the usual dirty Belgian affair without locks or other relieving features. For a canal that carries a fair amount of traffic it has, however, one peculiarity, a short section considerably narrower than the rest. This may not seem especially strange but as we went through it I noticed there might be a problem if we encountered another barge coming toward us. And so it would later prove, but all thought of future problems vanished on our arrival in Bruges on June 21, the summer solstice. There we found *Thetis*, our boatyard companion, already waiting with friends aboard. We had covered the distance from Mailly to Bruges in just under three weeks, arriving three days ahead of our planned target date.

Boatyard

After such a long hard run, our arrival in Bruges seemed especially sweet, combining a reunion with the crew of *Thetis*, and their welcoming bottle of champagne. The two boats were tied against a grassy bank under trees with two windmills slowly turning nearby, and the town itself only a walk away. The old square with its famous bell tower was still as I remembered from my twenties and my enjoyment of it only mildly impaired by the throngs of young summer tourists. But there seemed less time than needed to do justice to Bruges, and I longed to spend more time exploring it. However, we were occupied with our boats and the impending boatyard visit, the precise date of which still hadn't been fixed. Over the next four days there was much telephoning to the boatyard and both boats shortly left Bruges to moor in the canal near the yard. There was yet more delay but we were at least in close touch with the yard, could look it over and talk to its boss. A day or so later we finally brought the two boats through the narrow opening from the canal and into the boatyard basin.

Lionel had been in boatyards of the same type before but never one as big, and never one capable of taking really large barges out of the water. Such boatyards are usually in three parts: the workshop buildings, a wide shallow slope of land, and a basin of the same width adjacent to it, some of its bottom also sloped. On the sloping parts tracks are laid at frequent intervals and continue into the water. Wheeled cradles run on these, moved by winch-powered cables. To take a boat out of the water several cradles are lowered enough to allow the boat to float above them at right angles to the tracks. Two cradles near the bow and stern of the boat have vertical steel pipes sticking above the water to locate the cradles and provide a temporary mooring for the boat. As the cradles are pulled up the slope the boat will go with them, gradually seating itself on the cradles as they rise. This continues until the boat is high enough for men to work underneath the hull, and the cradles are then wedged in place.

Following this routine Ian and a helper took *Thetis* up on the cradles first, to be followed by Melodie and me aboard *Lionel*, the two boats ending up close together high off the ground, and against a background of giant barges, looking like two rowboats lost amidst a convoy of freighters. The other clients of the yard were five enormous barges, each 240–300 feet long. Surprisingly, *Soraya*, last seen on the Canal du Nord, was also there, but moored in the dark, oily pond of the boatyard having had its hull inspected after damaging it near Antwerp on rocks no chart had bothered to show.

When the boats were out of the water their hulls would be cleaned with high pressure hoses, then allowed to dry. At this point, a very serious

part of the whole business would take place and much depended on the skill, thoroughness and integrity of the men who would carry it out. Nowadays, usually done with a sonic measuring device, hull inspections determine the thickness of the steel plate, where patches are needed, their required dimensions and so on. This is a specialist's job, on whom one must rely to ensure the necessary work is done to make the hull watertight for the next few years.

Once up on the cradles *Lionel*'s deck was about ten feet above the ground. Access to it was only possible by climbing a steeply sloping ladder with narrow steps like a companion way. Life had clearly taken on a new aspect for Melodie, Polly, and me. Some things remained the same. We had water from our own tank replenished as needed with a boatyard hose. Melodie had to shop by taxi but could cook as usual and waste water from dishwashing simply drained from the kitchen sink onto the ground below. But other things were certainly not the same. There was now no usable WC aboard *Lionel* but we had a key to something similar in a workshop building. Getting there and back, however, was anything but easy or pleasant. The ladder to ground level was simple enough providing you didn't miss your footing and pitch off it from one of the higher rungs. But once on the ground your journey had only just begun. Stretched out before you lay a dark and messy landscape littered with a spaghetti of welding cables and wires, large chunks of wood, oddly shaped bits of steel, myriad little pools of tar, a general scattering of miscellaneous detritus, and the formidable obstacles posed by the cradles themselves with their greased wire cable tethers a foot or two above the ground. It was a gloomy terrain set with traps to step over or trip on. But, in addition to what was on or near the ground, the voyager in search of plumbing must navigate under two or three vast barge hulls, their great bellies low enough to demand an uncomfortable stoop and bound, sooner or later, to leave indelible rust or tar marks on whatever was covering one's shoulders. Only in very dire necessity would one ever consider such a trek during the night. And that was why Melodie wisely chose a bucket for nocturnal use, postponing the journey down the ladder and under the barges until the following day.

I suppose Polly, being young and unworldly, took much of this as just the way things were and even a good deal more interesting than her home turf. The ladder, however, was a different matter. For her it became a daunting obstacle which she had to overcome in both directions several times each day. She was so reluctant to climb or descend it that bribery seemed the only solution. With Polly, as with most dogs, an insatiable desire for food dominated her every waking moment; food of any kind, any time, anywhere. It was her constant companion in life and we played on this flaw in her character unmercifully. To persuade her to climb the ladder, biscuits were clearly placed on the deck and she responded as expected, slowly but with great determination, placing each long leg in turn carefully on each tread until she reached her goal. Going down was a little different. With the biscuits now at the bottom her eagerness for them was so great that she had to be restrained with a leash to prevent her sliding most of the way. It never ceased to amaze me that she ever seriously considered going down the steep ladder at all with her nose leading the way for her body in a near vertical position.

For the inspection of the hulls Ian and I, being unfamiliar with the local conditions, were unable to select a known and reliable inspector, and had to rely on the owner of the boatyard. He was not at all the type of person one would expect to find running such a place. In his knowledge of English, manners, level of education and dress, he was a man far more likely to be found in a sophisticated line of work rather than the grubby, noisy world of a boatyard. He was a pleasant man to deal with, and we hoped, honest. In the circumstances it was, therefore, this man who chose the hull inspectors, a father and son team with the latter working on *Lionel*.

Neither Ian nor I were happy with the inspections. They seemed casual, lacked precision, left doubt about the thickness of steel in some areas,

didn't indicate exact size and location of needed patches, and in fact, were quite inadequate in all important respects. Only by persuading the man inspecting *Lionel* to provide the missing information was I reluctantly prepared to accept his work. It was, by any measure, a shoddy job.

With the inspection over, the patch plates were cut, bent as required and welding began. At least there was no problem with the skilled welders who knew their job after doing it hundreds of times before. But when the hull was being welded we had to be very watchful inside the boat since the steel, red hot from welding, could start fires in the abutting cabinet work inside, as happened under Melodie's bunk where an incipient fire had to be doused with water. During this phase one of us was always down below watching for tell-tale smoke. When the welding was done and repairs to rudder post, propeller, keel cooling pipe and instruments were finished, the hull received a coat of two-part epoxy, and apart from paying bills, *Lionel* was ready for the water again.

High and Dry—Again

For anyone who has a barge, boatyards specializing in their repair and construction are fascinating places. For that reason I don't begrudge the week we had to spend in one but they also impose problems, inconvenience and often heavy expense so we were not sorry to be released on July 2 into the freedom of the canals. After arrival in Bruges we hadn't properly explored the old town, so turned west down the canal for another visit. We didn't get far. In that tricky narrow part of the canal noticed before, we encountered the very situation I had hoped to avoid—an oncoming unloaded barge going like a bat out of hell in the middle of the canal. We had to pass and I did the best I could in a bad situation. Not only was there minimal room for passing but the barge was unloaded and going fast, both factors raising the height of its bow and creating a large blind area ahead for its captain. I didn't know whether the *marinier* at the wheel was asserting some sort of priority, didn't see us at all or simply didn't care. To avoid an inevitable collision, *Lionel* was squeezed to within a yard of the canal's stone wall. Just before the moment of passing I slowed the boat to bare steerage way and stopped the propeller turning, expecting *Lionel* to drop the normal few inches as the barge passed. After that, my only hope was that the water would be deep enough alongside the wall. It wasn't. Nor was there gravel or anything soft on the canal bottom. What *was* there announced itself unmistakably with that horrible grinding, gut-wrenching sound of rock chewing at steel as *Lionel*'s newly repaired hull drove hard onto solid, damaging stuff.

As the Belgian barge disappeared down the canal not knowing or caring what trouble its thoughtless handling had caused, we began to investigate our situation. Since the propeller was free I tried first to power *Lionel* off backwards but saw not a sign of movement. Some helpful canal-side residents came out of their houses to help. They rocked the boat back and forth while I tried unsuccessfully with the propeller again. One of them kindly phoned the canal authorities who said nothing could be done until the following day.

We were obviously stuck for the night. No leaks had yet shown themselves but surely would when *Lionel* was off the rocks. All we could do was keep a careful watch on the water in the bilge so Melodie or I monitored it every two hours through the night. I was asleep at three in the morning when she woke me to announce the almost unbelievable news that more water had come into the canal during the night and *Lionel* was afloat at right angles to the canal wall. It almost seemed miraculous but I immediately went to work, mooring the boat parallel to the tow path and far enough out to be clear of the rocks. There is a standard barge method for doing this, using special knots and two long poles always carried on *Lionel* for the purpose.

All thought of another visit to Bruges was displaced by the need for urgent repairs to the hull, which had finally begun to leak. Returning to the boatyard, we found it closed for a holiday, and unable to cope with *Lionel* for five days. We then decided to go down the canal to Ghent, leaky boat or not. Ghent had a double appeal, being another of Belgium's old towns yet to be visited and seeing our friend, Ian, moored there in his barge *Thetis*. Ghent is a very welcoming city to visit in a boat, allowing them to come right into its heart. From the main ring canal around Ghent a narrow winding waterway leads the visitor into the centre of the city where good mooring is provided amongst the old buildings of the town. It was there we found *Thetis* with its captain aboard and spent a pleasant but mildly worrying few days seeing friends, and exploring Ghent in between monitoring the rising water in *Lionel*'s bilge.

Ghent was originally a centre of the drapers' craft, many of their guild houses and the Gothic Cloth Hall still ornamenting the old city centre.

The canals that wind through Ghent were at one time scenes of intense commercial activity with sailing ships moored outside warehouses, some of which still remain. It was an active port with water connections to the sea, and although it was hard to realize from the old surroundings of our mooring, Ghent still provides a major modern port on its outskirts, which in Belgium, is second only to the enormous one at Antwerp. But, our interest was centred on *Lionel*'s immediate neighbourhood where there was much to see and pleasant places to walk, less crowded by the tourists so numerous in Bruges. Ghent is a lovely old city, greatly enhanced by the canals that thread gracefully between the gabled buildings, and rightly called the "City of Flowers" for they were everywhere. But there is nothing like a leaking boat to drag you away from a pleasant stroll, so back to *Lionel* we would go to find water higher in the bilge and to start pumping once more. After those few pleasant days in Ghent it was back down the canal and into the boatyard again.

There were certainly enough problems with the boat but Polly added yet more—a whole set of them—when she tore a toenail to its roots while with me on one of her high energy walks. She had done this with the same toenail so badly a few months before in Canada that a veterinarian had decided to remove it. He did but clearly not well enough for it was a stubborn toenail and grew in again. It was this second-growth toenail that was torn again and bleeding profusely. I took her back to the boat where Melodie, *Lionel*'s resident nurse, bound it up. Then, with great difficulty, I summoned a taxi to the boatyard from the local village. Even without a common language the driver made his concern about blood on the car seats abundantly clear. I don't know how but I reassured him about that and off we went to a local vet. He seemed an unfeeling man and rough with Polly but there was little I could do as he examined her, told me what had to be done, tied a bandage muzzle around her snout and yanked her into the surgery. Feeling badly about leaving her in such hands I arranged to pick her up the next day.

Polly and her messed-about foot greatly complicated our lives in the boatyard where persuading her to go up or down the ladder was now made unbelievably difficult. We reduced these trips to the minimum and even tried, without much success, to get her to overcome training and do on the deck whatever she deemed pressing at the moment. In addition, her dressings had to be changed every three hours, a most unpopular operation with her, and because of that, very difficult for us. The stitches, of course, would have to be removed later by some other vet on our way south.

Finally, *Lionel* went back on the slip again with three robust streams of water running from holes in the hull. Three new plates were welded to the hull which was then, once again, assumed watertight. While standing beside the boat during this process, the boatyard's owner said to me: "You know, the hull of your boat should really have been double plated" (adding a new layer of steel plate to the entire hull below the waterline). I was astonished that he should have chosen this moment to tell me when the whole boatyard was just closing for a three-week holiday. If the inspection had been done properly, I should have been told then, and might very well have agreed to have the work done when the boatyard was in full operation. But when the owner made this remark it was far too late. Having come so far, spent so much and not been properly advised by supposed experts in the trade was outrageous. I was extremely annoyed, complained at the time and wrote a strong follow-up letter, none of which seemed to accomplish anything. At least, for that second visit I wasn't charged the full amount for the little work done. I was grateful for that small bonus, but overall I'm sure the boatyard profited well from *Lionel*'s two visits.

Going South

At last, on July 11 we joyfully left the boatyard for the last time and headed south with a sense of release. The canalized River Lys took us through Kortrijk and beyond to the French border at Menen on July 14, Bastille Day. It had been a dismal trip through boring country and the usual polluted waters. Most of the journey south was very similar and one I would not choose to do again. At Menen *Lionel* tied up near a French barge waiting for the price to rise on its load of grain before going north into Belgium. As is so often done on barges with the children home from school for the summer, the *marinier* had put them all to work sanding and painting the family boat.

The next day on the Canal de la Deule we sailed past the industrial and built-up centre of Lille before joining the Liaison Dunkirk-Valenciennes once again. After the important barge town of Douai we turned south on the canalized Schelde to join the Canal de St Quentin at Cambrai, a canal with thirty-five locks, two tunnels and the first attractive country in several weeks. Once one of the busiest canals in France, it has now lost much of its traffic to the more recent Canal du Nord. But it is the canal of choice in that part of France for the pleasure of the country it traverses, and the charm of its paired, mechanized locks with the brightly painted steel and glass control cabins set between them. Unfortunately, plans to modernize threaten the present appeal of the canal. The paired locks will be reduced to a single automated one that presumably will have little need of the elegant control cabins now used. Even worse, there has been talk of replacing the St Quentin with an entirely new 3,000 tonne capacity canal, even bigger and uglier than the Canal du Nord.

After twenty-six kilometres we faced the entrance to the Souterrain de Bony, one of the two tunnels on the canal, and at 5.67 kilometres, by far the longest we have traversed in *Lionel*. Bony and its much shorter neighbour, the Souterrain de Lesdins were used by the Germans in the First World War as part of the Hindenburg Line defences, providing shelter and protection for stables, hospitals and command centres. But Bony is an unusual tunnel even today. It is not only long but also narrow, so narrow that at some time in its past one of its two towpaths was removed to widen it. And it is still so long and narrow that barges are not allowed to go through under their own power because of excessive exhaust fumes. Instead, long trains of barges are now tied together, and with engines off, are pulled through by an electric tug twice a day.

The barges are assembled into a convoy with loaded barges in front and the lightest boats, such as *Lionel*, at the other end of the line. They all then loosely rope each other together. Being at the end we weren't sure when the whole motley collection was going to take off but threw a rope to the boat ahead just in time and were soon pulled into the tunnel with the rest. It was a weird experience to travel through a long dark tunnel with so many boats and not a sound aside from the gentle swish of water, and the human voices echoing back occasionally from several boats ahead. And, thank God, I didn't have to steer!

Our English friends, Wendy and Ray, bringing their new barge south from Belgium have little reason to remember *their* passage of these tunnels with much pleasure. They arrived at the northern portal in time for the last tow of the day in late November. It was cold, already dark, and pelting with rain. Lacking any kind of spotlight, their sole source of light was a small flashlight with batteries on the decline. Once hitched to the end of the convoy they were dragged through the long tunnel partly sideways, bumping and scraping along the tunnel wall. Finally through the first tunnel and into the night rain again they were thrown their rope and understood they were to wait in the canal for the next tow through the second tunnel at 6:30 the following morning. Even with the questionable help of the feeble little flashlight they could see nothing in the dark and decided to follow the barges just ahead, which at least had lights and presumably knew where to moor. But Wendy and Ray couldn't keep up with the barges, so long suffering Wendy stood in the bow, in the dark and the rain, pointing her faint little light at the canal bank to show the way ahead to Ray, in the comfort of the wheelhouse. Wendy got a few other clues from the momentary glimpses of canal bends and bridges spotlit by barges, but they weren't a lot of help. Still Wendy stayed loyally at her post, thinking longingly of the warm wheelhouse.

This fumbling through the dark seemed to go on for an eternity until they came, at last, to the second tunnel. It was here they understood the next tow would start. But the barges ahead weren't stopping, so Wendy and Ray followed them into a magically different world—a dry and brightly lit one. Wendy immediately left her bow station and rejoined Ray in the wheelhouse. It was a lovely change but a brief one, for the lights soon went out and Wendy dutifully returned to the bow with her dim little light as they rattled through half a mile of tunnel in total darkness. Once out of the tunnel it was still pouring rain, still impenetrably dark with the moribund flashlight her only help. They caught up with the barges at last near a lock, hunted in the gloom for bollards and finally tied to them totally exhausted at 10:30 in the evening. "I'm sure," Wendy recalled, "It wasn't just rain pouring down my face by this time."

While the Canal de St Quentin has its attractions and oddities, the town bearing its name was damaged so badly in the wars it has lost much of whatever it had. We tied up overnight to an old railway track and continued south the next day on the Canal de l'Oise à l'Aisne and its continuation the Canal Latéral à l'Aisne, both with quite heavy barge traffic, going through mainly flat but sometimes rolling country with much growth along their banks. At Berry au Bac, turning south for Reims and the Marne, we discovered the Canal de l'Aisne à la Marne was a canal with a clear and troublesome difference. Although attractive in its southern part where it passes through pleasant rolling terrain, the canal's tendency to leak water poses navigational problems. The banks and bottom of the canal are lined with concrete, intended to solve the leakage problem, but this measure has not really done its job, and mooring on the canal overnight is not permitted so that boats will not become trapped by low water. Over time the concrete bottom lining has cracked and broken, causing another hazard. The prohibition of overnight mooring also meant that all twenty-four locks had to be done in one day's cruising. On hearing this Melodie let out an audible groan.

Due to the canal's heavy traffic, passing barges loaded or unloaded was unavoidable. The canal was also neither wide nor deep, the latter being the normal minimum of 1.8 metres for a commercial Freycinet canal. These facts pointed to the need for caution in passing loaded barges particularly since I had learnt from experience that their large displacement of water causes a passing boat like *Lionel* to drop five to six inches. In a shallow canal with a broken concrete bottom those few inches could be critical and were. Under the circumstances I did everything I should: reduce speed, stop the propeller, stay as close as I could to the middle of the canal and still allow enough room for the barge to pass. In spite of all this, *Lionel* hit the fractured concrete bottom quite hard several times. Yet another leak was born, and arriving in Reims, the bilge was once again slowly filling with water! Monitoring the bilge started once more at Reims but shore power at least made the job of pumping easier and quieter than it had been with the generator.

Reims is the city where French kings were crowned in its great cathedral, but is also well known as one of the two principal towns of the champagne industry. Although constantly nagged by the seemingly endless problem of the leaky hull, we felt it would be inconceivable to hurry on without pausing in this famous town. So, during a rather short patrol we saw what we could, concentrating on the Cathedral, one of the famous ones in that country of great churches. I suppose I must have expected more for I was mildly disappointed, having seen others that have greatly exceeded it in grandeur of concept, architectural harmony and spirit.

Once back to the mundane world of leaky boats I phoned the English mechanic and welder at Mailly la Ville who we have known for a long time, having frequently left our boat in his yard over the winter. Knowing him to be of great help in situations like the one at that moment, I told him of our problems and made arrangements for *Lionel* to go into dry dock later at Joigny on the Yonne.

Once on the river it was only a short run to Epernay, the other famous champagne town which we couldn't visit in a previous year. The hull was still leaking and we were still pumping and recording on long lists the high-water marks reached in the bilge at different times of the day. On the brighter side, our mooring at the Club Nautique d'Epernay was one of the pleasantest I can remember, and we stayed in this idyllic spot for over two weeks, our friend Ian and his *Thetis* joining us there a few days after

our arrival. The Club Nautique was in some way connected with the great champagne house of Moët et Chandon, known throughout the world for their champagne and also for the clever publicity the company has achieved by making sure a big bottle of their product is always front and centre at major sporting events. The Club Nautique didn't seem to do much boating on the river beside it, but they did have a long dock with power and water outlets, beautiful, well maintained grounds with grass and mature trees, tennis courts, a building where members could have cooling drinks and snacks, and John, a pleasant retired British naval officer. John lived on his own boat, kept an eye on everything, and was very helpful to the Canadians while we were moored at the Club dock. Polly also approved of the Club Nautique for she had lots of grass to snuff about in along the river bank.

It wasn't difficult to enjoy life at Epernay, especially with the freedom provided by our car which I brought from Mailly la Ville. We went for drives through the vineyards with John providing guidance, and at a restaurant shaded by trees in the countryside, we lunched with him on a huge platter of marvellous *fruits de mer*: shrimp, oysters, clams, lobster, mussels, monkfish, *écrivisses*, all nesting together on a bed of lettuce and couscous with a heaping bowl of *aïoli*, the garlic mayonnaise and two bottles of chilled white wine within easy reach. We also explored the affordable restaurants of the town, visited a winery where champagne went through its elaborate early youth, and another extraordinary place like a huge aviary, but populated entirely by butterflies in their myriad multicoloured varieties. I also painted *Lionel* by myself from waterline to top of mast, a long labour but with the rewarding finale of a brightly painted boat, looking sharper than I'd ever seen it before.

In the middle of August we sadly left Epernay and set off down the Marne, stopping two days later at Chateau-Thierry where on approaching the quay, *Lionel* unavoidably dislodged an abandoned fishing line and rod that was, alas, lost to the river. It belonged to a boy who was really at fault for leaving it unattended on the quay. He turned up a few minutes later making a quite understandable fuss. I also felt badly but the situation quickly changed with the arrival of the boy's father. I immediately foresaw a typical riverside rumble but Papa didn't support his son's complaint, castigating him instead for his carelessness. On the point of giving the boy some money to help replace the rod, my feeling of guilt quickly evaporated and there the matter ended.

As *Lionel* left the quay on the following morning a casual glance over the engine dials showed the oil pressure at zero. This was worrying, whatever the cause, and I returned to the quay so I could find a mechanic. With the help of the local Syndicat d'Initiative, an office for promoting tourism, I found a marine mechanic who turned up an hour or so later in an enormous American car looking like a vintage stretched Cadillac. He quickly found the trouble in the oil pressure gauge and we arranged to meet at his workshop down river at Nogent-l'Artaud. There we found a mooring on the verge of impossible for anything but a rowboat. Monsieur Huguenin was, however, there to assist us as I poked the bow through shallow water to get within jumping distance of the rocky shore, the rest of *Lionel* sticking out into the Marne. Nice old Monsieur H fixed the faulty instrument in his minute but immaculate workshop and off we went again with water, in its slow sneaky way still trying to fill the bilge. But where, in God's name, was the wretched hole?

Moored farther down the river, in the quietest moments of a very quiet night Melodie heard the extremely faint sound of running water. Alert as always to unusual sounds on *Lionel*, she instantly recognized this tiny invasion of the night's still silence as of fundamental significance and

woke me at 4:00 a.m. to tell me about it. I was a trifle grumpy at first but rapidly snapped wide awake on realizing the import of her discovery. We roughly located the source of the sound that night and the next day, zeroing in on the target, I grabbed a power saw and with almost demented relish attacked the two-inch floor planking. At last as the boards came up, there it was in the shower room, a little fountain, a tiny *jet d'eau* reminiscent of Versailles and charming in its way. But after all the trouble it had caused, I had no regrets at bringing its evil little life to an end. I carved a small piece of wood and jammed it into the hole. The leak was stopped! Then it remained to apply a more reliable patch of *ciment rapide*, or rapid drying cement. A little while later, asking a couple on the towpath where I might buy the magic stuff, the man said he had some and went off, returning shortly with a small plastic bag of it. We thanked him warmly, gave the couple a bottle of wine, and because they had visited Canada, a small Canadian flag as well. Not long after, I built a little mountain of *ciment rapide* over our leak and felt much more confidence in *Lionel*'s creaky old hull than I'd had for several weeks.

Reaching the Seine with a few leak-free days ahead we took a short break in the Arsenal to enjoy Paris. And then it was back up the Seine and the Yonne to Joigny where *Lionel* was to go into a small dry dock for a further inspection and necessary repairs. The Yonne is not a popular river with people in boats largely because of its locks and their keepers. The former are very long, slow to fill or empty and the sloping sides of many create their own unique problems. The characteristics of the keepers vary as widely as humans do but the Yonne has garnered an unusually high proportion of keepers who are lazy, stubborn, rude, inefficient or simply absent. We have experienced all of these or combinations of them. On our way home after several months of travel it was the first lock that caused most trouble. After much tooting of horns and waiting, Melodie went ashore and continued the wake-up effort with shouting and knocking on doors. Soon it was obvious that the lock-keeper was not there and I started calling on the VHF radio. After waiting at the lock for an hour I finally reached the keeper of a lock upstream who came to our aid. He was one of our favourite lock-keepers on the river, a good man and an old acquaintance. Once through the lock, our friend came on board *Lionel* so we could take him back to his own lock, giving him the unexpected pleasure of driving *Lionel* most of the way.

At Joigny it wasn't easy inserting *Lionel* stern first into the small dry dock, barely long enough for the job, and it was even trickier getting the underwater trestles properly placed to carry the boat when the water drained out. Once in residence aboard *Lionel* we found that the dry dock posed its own brands of inconvenience. There was water for drinking and washing until our tank ran dry, and after that, there being no hose or reliable water at the dry dock, it had to be brought in *bidons* from a local campsite. The biggest inconvenience of all, however, was the total absence of a usable WC either on *Lionel* or anywhere else within half a mile. Polly at least was content with her surroundings where she could wander at will exploring the local scenery. But for Melodie and me there was only one solution to this problem, not unlike Polly's—the local bushes and patches of forest. Since we were to be in the dry dock for two or more weeks this lack soon became an aggravating detail of everyday life.

After the hull was cleaned and allowed to dry, it was inspected a good deal more thoroughly than in Belgium, using not only a sonic device but also a hammer and punch. This probing investigation revealed at last the true state of the old hull, a state far removed from the wildly optimistic report tendered by the inspector in the Belgian boatyard, about whom I was then entertaining very dark thoughts. In spite of the long journey to

Belgium and the attentions of the boatyard there, *Lionel*'s hull was in bad shape. A large plate about 2 by 2.5 metres was needed in the front one-third of the hull plus smaller plates elsewhere and some spot welding. The plates took several days to arrive and were eventually welded in place by the dry dock staff with some difficulty due to the poor condition of the sur-rounding steel. Then the job was finished with a coat of tar.

One of the happy results of our stay in this dry dock was the remark-ably low cost of using it, really only nominal, and all the labour free except for two good bottles of Burgundy and one of Armagnac as *pourboires* for the skilled labour force. It was an extraordinary arrangement, explained in part by the fact that the dry dock was operated by the Yonne River author-ities who let it be used occasionally by private boats to make a little money for the pieces of equipment or tools their headquarters wouldn't pay for. This kind of heaven-sent arrangement was, however, out of the question when it came to the hull inspection and the steel plate for which a sub-stantial account was forthcoming and paid.

Lionel then moved out of the dry dock to moor on the river. A day later, on the point of leaving Joigny with some pleasure, I turned the ignition key to start the engine. This resulted not in the deep-voiced pounding of the

six-cylinder diesel but in the horrible, raucous, grinding scream of machinery mashing itself into a painful demise. I swiftly turned the key off, and in the silence that followed I meditated on the incident. My God, I thought, I've done it again! Over the years there has been a fairly noticeable pattern of wounds inflicted on the mechanical and electrical elements of *Lionel* by the boat's very own inept owner. And this noisy event was only the latest in a line going back many years. What had happened was simple enough. The ignition switch has three positions: off, a mid-position involving a red light to do with battery charging, and start. The red light had not been working for some time, so the captain decided to fix it. I made what I thought were the right electrical connections. They weren't. What I'd done had greatly upset the starter motor which bitterly complained, fortunately without damaging results. Someone who knew what they were doing corrected my mistake and we departed up the Yonne.

Return to Base

In the warm, sad, hazy days of autumn *Lionel* travelled towards Auxerre. For the last night on the Yonne, we were aground and atilt at our mooring. There we remained until morning in the company of a large, strange bird perched on a bare branch sticking out of the river's still water. It sat motionless and alone, viewing the river world in silence, and challenging me to find out who it was. There was no bird quite like it in my book but that is not unusual. If I'd been in southern Italy or Turkey, night heron could have been the right call. It wasn't in Burgundy. Just before the light failed, the bird turned its head and showed a slight hook at the end of its beak. With that hook, dark wings, back and head, it had to be a cormorant but I was puzzled by its lighter front. Back to the bird book again and there it was, an immature cormorant revealed at last in a tiny drawing overlooked before. I could go happily to bed.

The end of our voyage followed soon after as we passed through the last lock on the Yonne and entered the port of Auxerre. After several months of travel, it was good to be arriving there again. We had old friends to see and the town to enjoy, a town we had come to know so well since going there first eight years before in the autumn of 1982. Moving slowly through the port in search of a mooring and familiar boats, my mind tumbled with memories of that place and the part it had played in our lives. After buying the boat and bringing it from St-Cloud, *Lionel* acquired a new life and purpose in Auxerre, over several agonizing winter months of work. It was then that I learnt my first important lessons about barges, and it was during the same winter that lasting friendships were made with others also wintering there on their own boats.

In the years that have passed since we first arrived in Auxerre, the outskirts have grown but the attractive old town seems to be much the same. The river is busier with hire-boats, and the quays are largely occupied by private and hotel barges, making moorings harder to find than before. The commercial barges, whose appearance had always been infrequent but welcome in the port are, alas, now relegated to their own new port farther downstream.

Before wrapping *Lionel* up for its long winter rest a few miles south at Mailly la Ville, we lingered for a little while in the port. There was the enjoyment of walking the steep crooked streets to shop in the old town, of coffee in a café, of dinners with friends, of the constant coming and going of boats on the river, and of the people walking their dogs along the towpath. We enjoyed our chats with strollers, and when they saw our flag, were amused at their predictable question about sailing the Atlantic. And there was always the special pleasure of our Argentinian friend, Lobo, with his hilarious accounts of recent excitements in his life, major and minor, personal and technical.

We took day-long drives over back roads in the lovely summer country around Auxerre, past vineyards and cherry orchards, picturesque villages in the hills, visiting the cold, cobweb-covered cellars at St-Bris-le-Vineux, and journeys to Bailly where you can drive a car several hundred yards inside the caves to buy Crémant de Bourgogne, the region's excellent

sparkling wine. The caves, it is said, were originally cut in the twelfth and thirteenth centuries to extract stone for some of the great cathedrals in France, even Notre Dame in Paris. They are so extensive that the Germans used them as a factory in the last war.

Up beyond the caves, in these same hills, we went one fine day for a picnic with friends. It must have been the queen of picnic spots, perched high on a steep hill, with Auxerre holding one end of the sweeping panorama, and at the other, barely visible among the blue hills, the towering pilgrimage church of Vézelay. Below us lay the valley of the Yonne, the river and its companion canal shimmering through the green fields. Beyond them, Burgundy gently rolled away towards a misty horizon.

Then, early one sunny, still morning, hot air balloons began to appear over the port from the south, low down in the sky. At first one by one and then in groups, they rose above the horizon and floated silently down the river. Soon, almost fifty were in the air above us; great elongated balls of colour and pattern, all floating past above their watery mirror images and expelling occasional rasping fiery breaths to regain lost height. Some flew low over the water, one bumping its basket on the railings of the foot-bridge crossing the river, several floating by only yards from the boats, and one bright red balloon showing both bravado and surprising control, remained motionless for several minutes with its basket on the water, before shooting up over the cathedral in an exhilarating exit, to vanish as a dot high in the sky above the town.

The port of Auxerre was, however, at its quiet best one September evening. It was warm, and not the lightest breath of wind ruffled the water of the Yonne. With the old town mounting the hill on the opposite shore the huge orange disc of the autumn sun slid slowly and sedately towards the earth. Its descent was enlivened briefly by puffy, fragmented little clouds moving across its path, the resulting shafts of light causing a momentary opalescent diversion in the pale blue sky. It would be hard to see Auxerre at a better moment than this. The dying sun hovered above the stony jumble of old houses, the spiky top of the town's clock tower poking above the roofs, and the three great churches at the summit of the hill. The sun finally down, and dusk settling on the river, floodlights began to bathe the three churches in a pale glow, picking them out from the surrounding town, first faintly against the twilight sky but brighter and brighter as darkness fell. It was an unforgettable evening for remarkable old Auxerre, putting on its finest show for a brief but precious renewal of a long and treasured friendship.

Epilogue

The journey in the summer of 1990 was anything but the gentle cruise it might have been. For the most part it was an arduous slog through the unattractive terrain of northern France and Belgium's polluted waterways. The scenery, at least, improved as we came south again, but the year as a whole was marred for us by costly sessions in boatyards, running hard onto rocks, a persistently leaking hull, mechanical problems, and in Melodie's case, fatigue on the rushed trip north. For her it was a decisive year.

On *Lionel* Melodie and I shared the work—we were its only crew. I ran the boat, was the pilot, navigator, sometime amateur engineer and incompetent electrician. She went ashore (often up ladders) to tie mooring lines, helped lock-keepers with gates and paddles, cooked meals because of her skill and love of good food, and did countless other chores as part of her day. A lot of it was hard work, some of it hard physically, and by 1990 Melodie was 68, an age nearing the limit for strenuous work on a boat. However, it was not age or one bad voyage that made Melodie feel a growing disenchantment with life on the waterways. She simply decided in 1990 that eight years had been enough. The years on *Lionel* had been enjoyable for both of us, but for Melodie, it had come time to stop and focus on something else. I was not yet as ready to bring our life on the boat to an end but without her there could be no other choice and *Lionel* was put up for sale.

When it comes to selling large things like houses or boats I seem to suffer from an unusual jinx that limits the possible buyers to one, robbing me of the higher price that competition usually ensures. And so it was with *Lionel*, with one important difference. After being on the market for several months, one offer was duly received in accordance with Massey tradition, but surprisingly for a sum higher than expected. After the customary but minimal negotiation, the deal was settled, leaving only one final step in the sale to complete, and I returned to France to see it taken. Since barge hulls rust and eventually leak, the prudent purchaser usually requires a hull inspection, so in October 1991, a friend's son, Simon, and I set off for the dry dock at Joigny on the Yonne River twenty-eight locks to the north.

Once in the dry dock, the trestles were positioned, the water drained out and the inspection began. The new owners, the dry dock workers, and a few casual observers were present as the inspector methodically did his job, moving slowly from stern to bow, crawling along in the wet, cramped space beneath the hull. For an owner this can be a nervous business, since everything hangs on getting a good report. I was understandably fearful that the old hull might reveal yet another dreadful new weakness, so I tried to avoid the tension by escaping for a few minutes on the boat's bicycle.

When it was over, the inspection showed a hull healthier than expected, and needing only minor repairs. These were done and everyone departed, leaving Simon and me with *Lionel* in the water again and the dry dock gates open. We tried to leave, but found that low water in the river prevented the boat from floating off its trestles. It simply wouldn't move even with the propeller at full thrust. It was late afternoon on a Friday and no dockyard workers would return for two days. The only person who might help was the operator of the weir on the river. I asked him to raise it, which he did, but its effect on the water level was minimal. Simon and I had to cope with the crisis ourselves—probably the last crisis of many for *Lionel* under the old management.

Something else had to be done if we were to escape this unusual trap. Simon, with much boat experience, contrived a clever cat's cradle of rope, stringing lines from bollards and trees to the boat's winch whose additional power might make the difference between leaving the dry dock or

spending the weekend there. When the crucial moment arrived, the engine was at full throttle, and the propeller spinning as fast as it could. Simon then turned the wheel of the winch to tighten the ropes into near twanging tension. At last, *Lionel* reluctantly started to drag itself, inch by stubborn inch, off the trestles towards the open gates and the freedom of the river.

The river and canal between Mailly la Ville and Joigny was for us one of the most familiar waterways in France, which Melodie and I had travelled more times than I can count. After several years we knew many of the lock-keepers, the peculiarities of the locks, the changing landscape, and the character of each town and village. Normally a pleasant cruise, I found that last trip affecting me in a way I didn't expect. When Melodie had made her decision I was still not yet ready to sell the boat, feeling there was more pleasure to be found with *Lionel*, but in 1991 going through all those locks, one after the other on the return trip to Mailly la Ville, I finally realized that I too didn't want to do that anymore. I'd also had enough. Although a little later than Melodie, I came at last to the same conclusion, and finally accepted the sale of *Lionel*. It really *was* time to draw those marvellous years to a close and move on to other things.